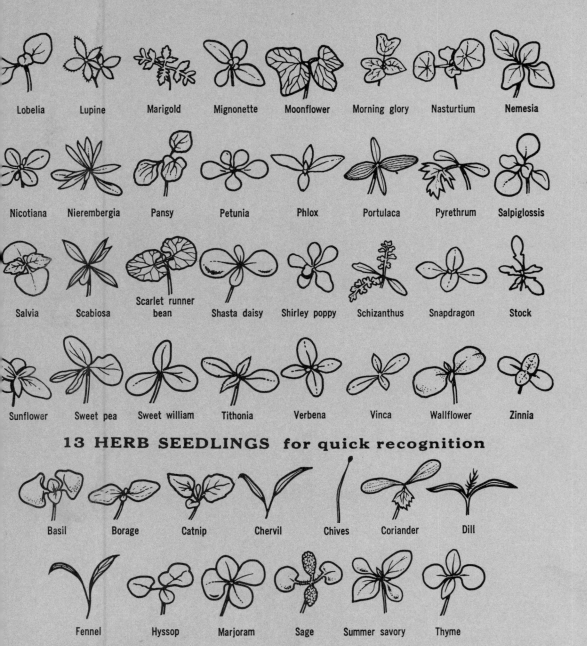

Lobelia Lupine Marigold Mignonette Moonflower Morning glory Nasturtium Nemesia

Nicotiana Nierembergia Pansy Petunia Phlox Portulaca Pyrethrum Salpiglossis

Salvia Scabiosa Scarlet runner bean Shasta daisy Shirley poppy Schizanthus Snapdragon Stock

Sunflower Sweet pea Sweet william Tithonia Verbena Vinca Wallflower Zinnia

13 HERB SEEDLINGS for quick recognition

Basil Borage Catnip Chervil Chives Coriander Dill

Fennel Hyssop Marjoram Sage Summer savory Thyme

THE COMPLETE BOOK OF GROWING PLANTS FROM SEED

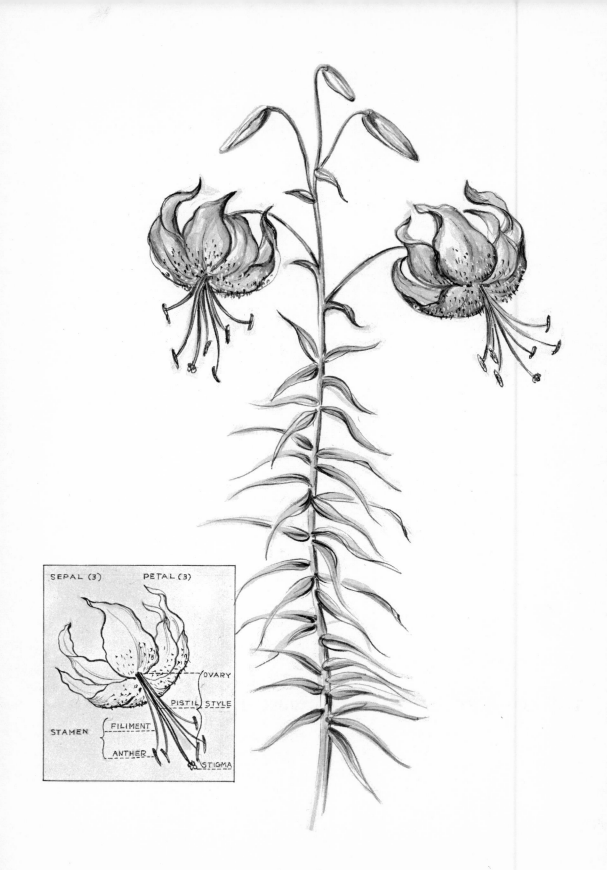

SEPAL (3)   PETAL (3)

OVARY

PISTIL STYLE

STAMEN { FILIMENT

ANTHER

STIGMA

The
Complete
Book
Of
Growing Plants
From
SEED

By Elda Haring

ILLUSTRATIONS BY KATHLEEN BOURKE

PHOTOGRAPHS BY WALTER HARING
(except as noted in credits)

DIVERSITY BOOKS, INC.
GRANDVIEW, MISSOURI

FOR

Walt

Contents

List of Illustrations

First credit for this book must go to Elvin McDonald, author, editor, publisher and fine horticulturist, for it was his idea that not only was such a book as this needed, but that I possessed the necessary ability, qualifications and knowledge to do it. It was he who first saw possibilities in my work as a garden writer and I shall be eternally grateful to him for opening up a new world for me and providing an outlet for my gardening enthusiasm.

This book is dedicated to my husband, Walter, known affectionately as "Walt" to his many friends and relatives, and whose passion for gardening transcends that of mine. We have gardened together happily for more than twenty-five years and enjoy together a love for nature. Particular thanks go to him for his unfailing good humor and patience while enduring my mercurial temperament. Without his encouragement, advice, criticism and especially without his help with my struggles in writing the second chapter this book would never have been finished. Thanks also go to him for writing part of the section on how to construct a coldframe and for the encylopedia of vegetables, as well as many hours of taking photos which graphically explain the how-to text.

I wish also to thank Victor Boswell, Assistant Director of the United States Department of Agriculture, Agricultural Research Service, for permitting me to quote from the U.S.D.A. *Yearbook* for 1961, entitled *Seed,* and to John W. McKay, now of the Tree Nut Investigations, Fruit and Nut Crops Research branch of the U.S.D.A. for permitting me to quote his material from the same book. Howard Bodger, president of Bodger Seeds, Ltd., El Monte, California, graciously gave permission for me to quote from articles he wrote for the same book.

Thanks to Miss Jeanette Lowe, of the customer service department of the W. Atlee Burpee Company for sending me much material in order that I might write intelligently about the progress of the development of F_1 hybrids and to Joseph Harris of the Joseph Harris Company, Inc., of Rochester, New York, for writing at length to describe for me the "why" of treated seeds.

Thanks also to W. Ray Hastings, Executive Secretary-Treasurer of All-America Selections for sending me much material in order that I might explain this very important service. To my friend, Noreen "Pat" Koenig for sharing her horticultural adventures with me and for advice and moral support I needed while writing this book. To my young friends Sherry and Gordon Clark who were willing to share with my readers their experiences with growing plants under lights.

Also thanks to my friend Zelma (Mrs. Cleve) Clark . . . no relation to the young people . . . not only for allowing us to interview her to obtain information as to how she grows her plants under the fluorescent lights but allowed us to photograph her set-up and took extra photos with her own camera for our use.

I also wish to thank Mr. Klaus Neubner, Plant Research Director of the George W. Park Seed Co., Inc., Greenwood, South Carolina, and Prof. James Boodley, Cornell University, for providing me with literature on growing plants under fluorescent lights.

A special accolade to Kathleen ("Katie") Bourke, not only for her delightful artistry, but for capturing so completely the spirit of the text.

And last but certainly not least my heart-felt thanks to Irene Salomon Miller who typed most of the final manuscript and without whose help I should never have made the deadline.

ELDA HARING

Greenwich, Connecticut
January
1967

THE COMPLETE BOOK OF GROWING PLANTS FROM SEED

1. The Seed

How would you define the word "seed?" The botanists tell us that a seed is a ripened embryo which results from fertilization within the flower and which is used for propagation, but this is not the whole story for it does not tell us anything at all about seeds. To me a seed is a wonderful mystery. How can there spring from a tiny little speck of dust a beautiful flower like the African violet or the snapdragon? Seed is the beginning of all life. Without it, there would be no life as we know it. No human beings, no animals, no trees, no grass, no flowers. Seed is the source of food for all life on our planet. Without seeds new life would not have spread from place to place throughout the ages.

Look at a seed of one plant and then examine that of another. Their forms and structures differ, yet they have the same purpose. They are the basis of a new plant. Seeds are things of beauty ranging in size from dust-like particles to huge ones like the coconut. When the seed has fulfilled its final purpose, that of producing a new plant, it has brought about another form of beauty—the plant with its own form, stem, shape, texture and color of the foliage, the beauty of its flower and fruit.

Scientists have studied for years to learn all they possibly can about seeds. The research continues because, while we have learned how seeds are formed and what they do, we still are unable to ascertain why. Thus seeds take on a mystical value to those of us who grow plants from seeds.

The flower of the plant is the receptacle for producing the seed. We think of the flower as being the ultimate purpose of the plant, unless it is one which we have planted for the fruit. In this event we concentrate on the fruit rather than on the flower and its purpose.

Thus we see that there are two organs needed to produce a seed or fruit. The stamen produces pollen grains that later form the male cells. The stamen has a filament at the tip of which is the pollen sac. The pistil which is usually in the center of the flower is the female organ. Usually there are three parts comprising the pistil; the ovary which contains one or more ovules or immature seeds; a tube above the ovary and at the tip the stigma on which the pollen is deposited for fertilization. Generally speaking a seed is a ripened ovule containing an embryo and a fruit is a ripened ovary containing seeds. In some plants the reproductive organs are formed in separate flowers on the same plant while other plants produce flowers in which both stamens and ovaries are present. These are called "perfect" flowers. Some species have flowers on a plant that may have only stamens and flowers of another plant may contain only the pistils. These are dioecious plants. This is why gardeners soon learn that there should be a male and a female holly plant for instance in order to produce fruit. Pollen must be transferred from the male cells to the female ones, hence nature gives plants an assist in the pollination process by providing insects, birds and breezes as means to transport the pollen.

I am not a student of botany, and I do not feel that the reader of this book is especially interested in botany. However, it does seem necessary for gardeners to know a little about the basic processes of development of the seed. Mr. John W. McKay, a horticulturist at the U. S. Department of Agriculture, Plant Industry Station, Beltsville, Maryland, has graciously given me permission to quote from an article entitled, "How Seeds Are Formed," which he wrote for the USDA Yearbook of Agriculture in 1961. It seems to me that this explanation is so clear that even the most inexperienced gardener can well understand it. "The formation of seed in the higher plants depends on processes of sexual reproduction in the flower. One should know the nature of these processes and where they occur.

"Six steps in the development of the reproductive plant structures leading to formation of seed are:

(1) The formation of stamens and pistils in flower buds.

(2) The opening of the flower which signals the sexual maturity of these organs.

(3) Pollination which consists in transfer of the pollen from the stamen to the pistil.

(4) Germination of the pollen and formation of the pollen tube.

(5) Fertilization of the egg and polar nuclei by sperm nuclei from the pollen tube.

(6) Growth of the fertilized egg and its differentiation into an embryo plus a surrounding coat—the seed; and maturing of the seed usually with the accumulation of stored food.

"Pollen grains are carried from the stamens to the stigma of the pistil by insects, wind or gravity. This crucial step may be seriously impeded if conditions are not right. For example, honey bees pollinate clover flowers in fields grown for seed production. If the clover flowers during a long rainy period when the bees do not fly, the seed crop may fall short of the normal because of inadequate pollination. Insects are attracted to flowers by odor, color or nectar. Some of the clovers produce great amounts of nectar. Much of the commercial honey available in markets is made by bees working in clover fields. This is an example of partnership in nature in which the bees, by pollinating the clover blossoms, play a necessary part in seed production and in return receive nectar for their services.

"The pollen grain germinates on the surface of the stigma and produces a long slender tube which grows through tissue of the style to the ovule. Two male nuclei or sperms move down each pollen tube to the ovule. One unites with the egg in the embryo sac of the ovule; the other with two polar nuclei. This is called double fertilization. The fertilized egg develops into a rudimentary plant, the embryo of the seed which is the starting point of the next plant generation. The fertilized polar nuclei develop into a tissue called the endosperm which surrounds and nourishes the growing embryo. The endosperm in most seeds is absorbed completely by the embryo by the time the seed matures. Among the plants whose seeds contain no endosperm are bean, watermelon, garden pea and pumpkin. The edible part of the coconut is the endosperm. In corn, wheat and other cereals the endosperm makes up a large part of the nutriment in the seed.

"After fertilization, the embryo which starts as a single cell, grows rapidly and the ovule expands to accommodate the enlarging structures within. The embryo is a mass of differentiated cells in its early stages. As enlargement continues, three well defined structures are formed: The epicotyl, or young shoot, the hypocotyl or young root and the one or two cotyledons, or seed leaves. Usually the cotyledons of the embryo become thickened to permit storage of food materials, such as starch, sugar, oil or protein. The accumulation of stored food in the embryo or other parts of the seed usually signals maturity. The period of filling' of the embryo or endosperm is one of stress on the mother plant because large amounts of organic food materials must be manufactured by the leaves and transported to the developing seed. Finally, enlargement of the embryo ceases, the parts become dry and the seed becomes a dormant living organism prepared to withstand adverse conditions."

After seeds have ripened on the plant, they are protected by a coating which preserves them until conditions are right for germination. Many seeds need an after ripening period before they are receptive to germination. First nature must disperse the seeds of plants so that they will find a good seed bed. Dispersal depends on the character and form of the seed coat. Nature has been most ingenious in devising dispersal methods. Some have wings to let them fly through the air. Dandelions, thistle, milkweed are some whose seeds are provided with "fluff," each seed having a silky appendage to enable it to literally "take wing." Some seeds have prickly coats like the hooked burrs of the burdock which, attaching themselves to animals, both wild and domestic, are carried far afield from the original home of the plant. The neighbors' dogs, running through our own meadowland, carry upon their backs, up and over the wall and far away in their pursuit of the elusive rabbit, seeds of wild aster, goldenrod and tick-trefoil. The little boys who live nearby pick the milkweed pods, break them open and laugh heartily as the wind picks up the silk, carries the little seeds into the air into the next field where eventually they will fall possibly in some receptive spot on mother earth, have assisted in perpetuating the life of the milkweed. The little first grader who picks the dried "basket" of Queen Anne's lace while walking home from school, dreamily contemplates the shape and form of the basket, but eventually discards it along the road side has unwittingly helped nature disperse her seeds.

Birds and squirrels and other animals too have their uses in this desire of nature to continue the process. The Blue Jay in late fall takes sunflower seed from our bird feeder, and flying to a soft spot in the flower border "plants" the seed and gives nature a further assist by covering the seed with leaves. Undoubtedly the Blue Jay follows the same procedure with nuts and other seeds he finds provided by the plants he encounters. Squirrels and chipmunks have a way of "planting" nuts and hard seeds by burying them. We frequently find hickory nuts "buried" in flowerpots of soil in our greenhouse in late summer when doors and windows are open and the chipmunk goes in

2   HALF OF THE SEEDHEADS ON THIS
DANDELION PLANT HAVE ALREADY PARA-
CHUTED THEIR SEEDS INTO THE WIND.

3   THE "FLYING EQUIPMENT" OF THE
MAPLE SEEDS—TO ASSURE DISPERSION.

and out at will. All of these explain in a small way how plants continue to survive and spring up in places where such plants have never before been seen.

Seeds which have the capability of germinating and starting to grow under proper conditions are said to be "viable," that is, they are capable of living. Many seeds are viable for only a short time and must be carefully harvested and stored in order to retain this viability. Thousands of other seeds will retain viability for many years. Some years ago a Japanese botanist found lotus seeds in a dry lake in Manchuria. Some experts estimate that these seeds had lain there for over a thousand years, others insist that they were from 300 to 400 years old. Germination tests made on these lotus seeds proved them to be still alive, for when planted, most of them germinated. Wild seeds in our soils live for many years and when exposed to the proper conditions will germinate readily. My husband and I have experienced this in our own garden. The section chosen for a combination cutting and vegetable garden was covered with pasture grasses. There were few if any weeds visible. When this section was plowed and readied for gardening, ragweed by the hundreds came up over the entire area. These plants were cut down before they flowered and were turned under. The next year ragweed did not appear, but bindweed became a pest to be eradicated. This would indicate that disturbance of the soil brought these seeds into conditions suitable for their germination. Some authorities believe that seeds of ragweed will remain viable in our soils for more than fifty years. Seeds of the common evening primrose and mullein have been known to remain viable for more than 70 years. The United States Department of Agriculture and the various State Departments of Agriculture are constantly doing research and tests on seeds to determine the length of time they will remain viable.

Germination of flower and vegetable seeds as well as those of shrubs and trees depends upon a proper set of conditions of moisture, warmth, soil and so on. Some seeds not only need an after ripening period to start to germinate but have been provided with hard coats so that they will not, for instance, drop from the mother plant, germinate immediately only to have the small plant killed by the first frost. Nature, in other words, provided this seed with a protective coating so that life would not begin until the proper time in order that the species might be perpetuated. Acorns and nuts of all kinds are in this category as well as seeds of many annuals, perennials and wild flowers. After being exposed to alternate freezing and thawing throughout the winter, dormancy is broken at the proper time and the seed comes to life.

Small reserves of food have also been provided to give the new embryo nourishment. Very small seeds have infinitesimal amounts of food but they are present. Some seeds have been provided by nature with starchy food and some with oil. Some seeds need low temperatures to stir the new life and some have a built-in block which makes it difficult for them to start to grow at high temperatures, and in our efforts to reproduce new plants by means of seeds we need to know and understand their special requirements for germination.

Man has been fascinated by seed since prehistoric times. In the Bible there are many references to seed and seed sowing. The need to save seed in order that there would always be food was pointed up by the story of Joseph and the seven lean years.

The early settlers in our country brought with them precious packets of seed. When they arrived on these shores, colonists from Europe found the Indians growing corn, beans and squash and as the settlers moved westward they found huge plantings covering hundreds of acres on the Plains to the foothills of the Rocky Mountains. On Columbus' second voyage he brought seed of barley, wheat, sugar cane and grapes to the New World. Ships subsequently sent by the Spanish government to the New World (Indies, Peru, Florida, Mexico) brought alfalfa, flax, oats, apricots, lemons, olives, oranges, peaches, pears, walnuts, cabbage, lettuce, peas, spinach, turnips, anise, fennel, mustard, saffron, thyme, bamboo, carnations, daffodils, iris and poppies. The Spanish in turn adopted such crops of the American Indians as corn, white potatoes, tobacco, cotton, avocado, kidney beans and lima beans, cacao, the chili pepper, gourd, guava, cassava, pineapple, pricklypear, pumpkin, quinoa, squash, sweet potato and tomato.

John Bartram of Philadelphia was considered by the great Swedish botanist Carolius Linnaeus to be the greatest natural botanist in the world. In his garden, Bartram specialized in plants of this continent. Benjamin Franklin, Thomas Jefferson and other Americans traveling abroad sent him seeds and plants from all over the world.

George Washington may have been the "Father of his country" and General of the Revolutionary Army but he also was a plantation owner and vitally interested in plants both for food for the stomach and as food for the soul. During the years after the war he carried on extensive correspondence with plantsmen all over the globe and imported many trees, shrubs, edible fruits and flowers for his Mount Vernon estate. He was especially interested in growing plants from seeds. A visit to his restored estate in Mount Vernon is a journey into yesterday. The vegetable gardens are kept very much as they were when the General lived there. The flower gardens are most fascinating, as are all the trees and shrubs used for landscaping. Seeds of flowers, shrubs and trees growing at the plantation are sold in a little shop at the side of the garden. On our last visit there my husband and I purchased a number of packets of flower seeds, and a few of shrubs. We were especially interested in the shrub called amorpha (false indigo) which is not considered hardy north of Washington. Seeds germinated quickly for us and now, five years later, several of these interesting shrubs are growing in our garden and have attained a height of 6 feet and as much in width.

In the early days of the history of our nation crop seeds were indispensible. Most seed was home saved. Seeds for new crops were obtained by trade or purchased from other farmers. Wealthy men and they were few, could afford to obtain seeds from far away places for testing on farm lands. The first seed house was that of David Landreth & Son of Philadelphia which opened for business in 1780. By 1850 there were forty-five thriving seed firms. The need for new crops and superior crop seeds caused the Congress to appropriate money for collecting and distributing seeds in 1838. Some of the seeds were distributed free in many of the States by their Congressmen and this practice continued until 1923.

The United States Department of Agriculture was established in 1862 under the Homestead Act. Its objective was to "collect new and valuable seeds and plants; to test by cultivation the value of such of them as may require tests; to propagate such as may be worthy of propagation and to distribute them among Horticulturists."

Since that time the United States Department of Agriculture has concerned itself with agricultural research and Federal support has encouraged State Agriculture Experimental Stations as well as supplied state colleges with funds for agricultural research. Dedicated scientists, laboratory technicians and agriculturists at the Plant Research Department of the USDA, Beltsville, Maryland, are engaged in testing plants of all kinds, not only food crops but also trees, shrubs, flowers and bulbs. The USDA also has the responsibility for the exploration of seeds and plants, their introduction from other countries and the essential quarantines to safeguard the country from seed and plant insects and pests. The Department also works with commercial seed companies and nurseries in an effort to produce better quality food crops, finer forest trees, as well as shrubs, flowers and vegetables for the home gardener. In 1956 the Agriculture Research Service expanded its research program to cooperate with State Agriculture Experimental Stations to find seed crops more profitable for the farmer to grow not only for food but also crops that may supply strategic raw materials for industrial uses.

When we purchase a few packets of vegetable and flower seeds at the counter in our local stores or when ordering from the catalog of our favorite seed supplier few if any of us give any thought as to how this seed was grown and packaged. We confidently expect these seeds will grow and produce satisfactory flowers or vegetables in our home gardens. To attempt to tell the full story of seed production by commercial growers would be far beyond the ability of this writer. Those of us who have been growing flowers and vegetables from seed in our home gardens for many years are only dimly aware of the tremendous amount of work being done by plant breeders to give us dependable seeds.

Seeds of nearly 5,000 varieties of flowers and vegetables are offered for sale to home gardeners in the United States. The acreage for producing these seeds comprises small plantings of many crops. Each species grown for seed has its own planting time, culture, pollination and harvesting. For good seed production there is one basic requirement; a mild climate with little rain during the growing and harvesting seasons. That is the reason so many flower and vegetable seed crops are produced in California where favorable conditions prevail. Planting there is continuous from November to May and harvesting goes on from June to December. Rain is necessary before flowering but rain during the flowering period encourages fungi in the seed head, prohibits pollination, natural or artificial, and reduces the number of seeds harvested. Other seeds, due to their peculiar growing needs are produced in colder climates. Colorado, Oregon, Washington, Texas, Utah, Indiana, Ohio, New York, Connecticut and New Jersey are among these.

Seed companies necessarily maintain large staffs of highly trained technicians, plant breeders and growers in order to bring to the home gardener the finest of seed to grow hardy plants. These are dedicated men and women who must know the cultural requirements of the vegetables and flowers they are growing throughout the life of the plants. Growers must know whether their crops are self or cross pollinated and if insects or wind carry the pollen. On such facts depend the necessary isolation distance between fields. Many new cultural, chemical and genetic techniques have been found by these highly skilled workers whose lively interests and craftsmanship are widely respected. Growers of seed for the home gardener expend at least 5 per cent of their income in seeking ways to bring us the very best strains and work constantly to improve these strains each year.

Plant breeders are always alert to discover and create more attractive and easily grown types of flowers and vegetables for the gardening public. One of the most valuable tools for the plant breeder is the drug colchicine, extracted from the corm of the fall crocus, *Colchicum autumnale.* About 25 years ago this drug was proved to be very effective in doubling the chromosome number of the plants. The chromosomes, tiny darkly-staining particles found in all living tissues are the carriers of hereditary characteristics. Frequently, when the chromosome number of a plant is doubled, desirable changes occur, such as stronger stems, darker green foliage and larger flowers. In 1940 through the work and cooperation of Drs. B. R. and F. R. Nebel at the New York Agriculture Experiment Station, the W. Atlee Burpee Seed Company presented to the public the Tetra marigold, the first introduction of a colchicine-created new type of flower. Zinnias, phlox and snapdragons are other flowers which have been improved by this treatment.

Hybrid seed is produced by hand crossing. This is done by removing the anthers of all flowers to be crossed before the pollen has been shed and keeping them protected from insects or windblown pollen. Crosses combine carefully chosen parent plants. Resulting seeds need to be planted the next season and carefully observed for performance. Plants which do not measure up have to be removed and discarded. Seed of those which show promise must be again grown before the seed of these hybrids can be offered to the public. Cross pollinating two different plants of the same variety with some especially desirable characteristics is often the beginning of a slow but expensive route to new selections. Each year, for from ten to fifteen years, the most desirable progeny of the original cross combining all the good features are selected and re-selected until the seed is ready to be produced for the gardener.

During such a flower building program, millions of plants are grown, studied and evaluated with only about 5 per cent of them chosen. It took 16 years, for instance, to produce the 'Bonanza' zinnia. Imagine, if you will, the skill, perserverance and patience which must have been necessary to produce this flower, to say nothing of the expense. The nature of the production of the F_1 hybrid seed is the development of the unique parent strains for use in a specific and controlled cross. The research work is such that only the well organized major seed companies are in a position to initiate or contract for seed production. The crop requires a supervisor with the equivalent technical education of the flower and vegetable breeder.

Petunias, according to Mr. Howard Bodger, president of Bodger Seeds, Ltd., (a leading growing firm in California) are the most important greenhouse crop of flower seeds in dollar value. The reason is that some colors (scarlet and coral) and forms (doubles and 100 per cent large-flowered singles) can be had only as hybrids grown in the greenhouse. The essence of the production of F_1 hybrid seed is the development of unique parent strains for use in a specific and controlled cross. The research work involved is such that production must be conducted under a glass or plastic cover. Plastic is used in summer or the whole year in California. Usually even the ventilators are screened to keep out insects that might bear contaminating pollen. The sanitary precautions to prevent disease are formidable. The seed parent (female) is pot or bench grown. The anthers and stamens of each flower are removed before it opens. This procedure is called emasculation. The pollen parent is grown elsewhere and its pollen is gathered when ripe. The pistil of the seed parent is receptive about a week after emasculation, and pollen from the male parent is applied to fertilize the flower. In six weeks the seed capsule has matured, at which time it is harvested by hand.

Production is measured in ounces per thousand plants. Only a few of the dozens of varieties on the market reach a production rate of 100 ounces a year or more, but the value of that amount exceeds 10 thousand dollars at wholesale prices.

Visitors to flower farms are amazed that much flower seed is harvested and threshed by machinery similar to that used for grain. Even the fine seed of petunia is so handled. Hand picking or cutting saves more seed but high labor costs and the need for speed dictate mechanical methods whenever possible. Crops are harvested occasionally with a combine but much more commonly the plants are cut and windrowed until they can dry to a moisture content suitable for machine threshing. Methods of threshing vary. Seed of nasturtium may be windrowed on the ground. Species with seed heads that shatter at a touch must go onto large canvas sheets. Stems of petunia plants are so sticky that even though the seed shatters, a significant amount of it adheres to the stem and can be saved only if the whole plant is put on sheets to dry. The cutting operation is carried out when morning dew is on the plants to avoid loss of seed. The drying period is usually 10 to 20 days. Rain at this time would be catastrophic. With perennials, such as delphinium, several handpickings precede the final cutting because the plants have a long flowering period and seed production is continuous. Zinnias are commonly handpicked and the flower heads must be flat rolled preparatory to threshing as the seeds stick tenaciously to the central cone.

After harvesting, seeds must be cleaned to remove all chaff and extraneous particles so that when packaged only fine, clean, viable seed will go out to the home gardener. Essential to this process are screens, sieves and disks to handle all shapes and sizes of seed.

Packages for seeds used to be nothing more than mere containers, but since seeds will retain good viability only if they are kept dry, moisture proof packaging is most important. Paper products are used extensively for packaging seed. Small packets are made of laminates of paper, polyethylene and aluminum foil. All are designed to contain a measured amount of seed properly protected against moisture. A number of methods are used for filling packages. Some seeds are packaged by filling machines automatically controlled and other machines are controlled by hand. Seeds need to be handled with great care as their physical qualities can be damaged by improper handling. Usually in packaging flower and vegetable seed for the home gardener there is measured into the package enough seed to sow one row. Picture packets are produced by a few printers who maintain large lists of color pictures for the use by all seedsmen. These picture packets are usually intended for display in neighborhood shops. Mail-order packets are printed with type as the home gardener has made the purchase on the basis of pictures and descriptions in the catalog. Many flower and vegetable seed producers for the home garden add valuable information as to growing the specific seed enclosed in the packet. Some packets show zone maps which give time of planting. Others show small plantlets to enable the home gardener to distinguish plant from weed. Tapes and mats impregnated with seed are also offered for the convenience of the home gardener as well as pre-seeded flats for indoor starting of seeds. Coated seeds are also available to facilitate planting of seeds.

4   A SAMPLING OF TODAY'S SEED PACKETS
—SOME COLORFUL AND FANCY, OTHERS
PLAIN AND PRACTICAL.

Flowers and vegetables can be grown from home saved seed of course, and many gardeners do just that. In my own garden there are many perennial plants, shrubs and trees which we have propagated from home saved seed, but I do not save seeds of annual flowers or vegetables for the very good reason that most of the plants are hybrids and those produced in the home garden are not likely to be exactly like the parent plant either in size or quality. Neither in the case of vegetables nor in the case of flowers will the resultant plant have the same characteristic of the parent but is most likely to "revert" to some unsatisfactory aspect of one of the parent plants used in developing the hybrids. The home gardener has no facilities for preventing cross pollination so that in a small planting of melons and squash for instance, seed saved from these may have been pollinated by nearby plants. This resultant seed then will not produce squash or melon like the parents and the crop would likely be useless.

Experienced gardeners know that home saved seed of petunias will rarely produce the lovely clear colors of the parent but will usually revert to muddy or faded colors. The perennial phlox rarely ever grows true from seed. The majority of phlox seedlings grown from home saved seed will be of an undesirable magenta hue. Seeds saved from zinnias and marigolds will form good flowers of course but they cannot begin to compare in size and texture to the gorgeous hybrids which are available for only a few cents per package. If the gardener goes to a great deal of time and trouble to prepare a seed bed, why should he not plant the very best of seed from reputable seed companies, thereby ensuring a beautiful garden worthy of his efforts and which will be the joy of the neighborhood? As has been noted, the plant seedsman has spent much money and many years to produce superior plants and flowers for the home gardener, who simply cannot produce superior seed in his own back yard.

A few years ago a friend of my husband's visited our garden in mid-summer. He was amazed at the quality and size of our annuals indicating that it was a revelation to him that annuals could be had in separate colors. This gentlemen had only recently acquired his own home and the only flowers he had grown were those given him by a kind neighbor who has for years been growing flowers from seed saved from his own garden. When our friend looked over our rows of hybrid zinnias and marigolds, double petunias, snapdragons and asters he began to realize how truly superior plants grown from hybrid seed can be. Suffice to say last year this gentlemen's garden contained beautiful flowers grown from seed obtained from a leading seed firm. If you are a "hold out" for home saved seed, I hope you will try some of the newer varieties of flowers and vegetables available and prove to your own satisfaction that the finest plants are grown from seed purchased at a small cost from the seedsmen who has spent a life time producing seeds for the home gardener.

Perhaps nothing in this country has stimulated competition among plant breeders in their search for new and hardy varieties of flowers and vegetables than has the All-America Selections. AAS is incorporated as a non-profit educational institution for the testing and rating of proposed new varieties before introduction to the public, having nothing to do with the *sales* of the seeds. It is sponsored by the seed industry of the United States and Canada and

5   THE HARVEST CREW AT BURPEE'S FLOR-   CROP. STATICE GROWS IN THE FOREGROUND.
ADALE FARMS BRINGS IN THE COSMOS SEED   *Burpee Seeds*

6 BRIGHT BUTTERFLIES SNAPDRAGONS WON A COVETED ALL-AMERICA SELECTIONS HONOR IN 1966. *Goldsmith Seeds, Inc.*

7 AMETHYST VERBENA ALSO WON AN ALL-AMERICA SELECTIONS MEDAL IN 1966.

8 GOLD NUGGET SQUASH WAS AWARDED THE ALL-AMERICA SELECTIONS SILVER MEDAL IN 1966.

'9 SAMSON CANTALOUPE WON THE ALL-AMERICA SELECTIONS SILVER MEDAL IN 1965.

provides that award varieties may be available to all seed firms for cooperative introduction and help in promotion of these worthy varieties. According to Mr. W. Ray Hastings who is Executive Secretary-Treasurer, All-America Selections originated at Atlanta, Georgia, in 1932 with the Southern Seedsmen's Association. In 1933 the American Seed Trade Association joined sponsorship. The Pacific, Western, New England (now Atlantic), Canadian and Northern Associations likewise endorsed and co-sponsored it.

All known plant breeders from around the world were invited to enter their proposed new varieties or discoveries in these All-America trials. For the protection of both breeder and the public there is an AAS gentlemen's agreement whereby all seeds of award winners must be grown from breeders' stocks by their original growers for the first three years from introduction. Other seed growers go by this agreement and will offer no seeds *of their own growing* of these varieties for these first three years and all seed firms agree to purchase these seeds only from the original growers for these first three years. Proposed new varieties from all known seed plant breeders including some amateurs, commercial firms and public institutions in North America and abroad are regularly solicited.

There are now twenty-six flower and twenty-six vegetable AAS trial locations throughout the country, located from Montreal, Quebec, to Vancouver, B.C., across southern Canada and Massachusetts to Florida in the East and to Washington and California in the West. There are three vegetable trials in Mexico. Trial locations represent chief gardening and growing areas of North America. An award variety must be widely adapted and may be depended upon to perform satisfactorily wherever that kind of flower or vegetable may be successfully grown. Judges are well known plant breeders and horticulturists.

Before the advent of AAS it frequently took at least five years to establish a new variety. A breeder used to keep his new selections or lines very secret, not allowing other seedsmen to see them until he or his firm introduced them. Many good varieties were lost because the owners could not afford to promote them. Promotion costs were more than a firm could get for the seeds. Rival seed growers could buy a few seeds and have them to sell the next year without breeding costs. On the most worthy new varieties AAS has remedied much of that. An award winner is assured of successful introduction. All seed firms have equal opportunity of getting seeds from the original grower to offer their customers in this cooperative introduction and promotion. Whenever you see the words "All-America Selection" marked opposite a flower or vegetable variety in your favorite seed catalog, rest assured that these have been tested and approved by the finest and most qualified of judges.

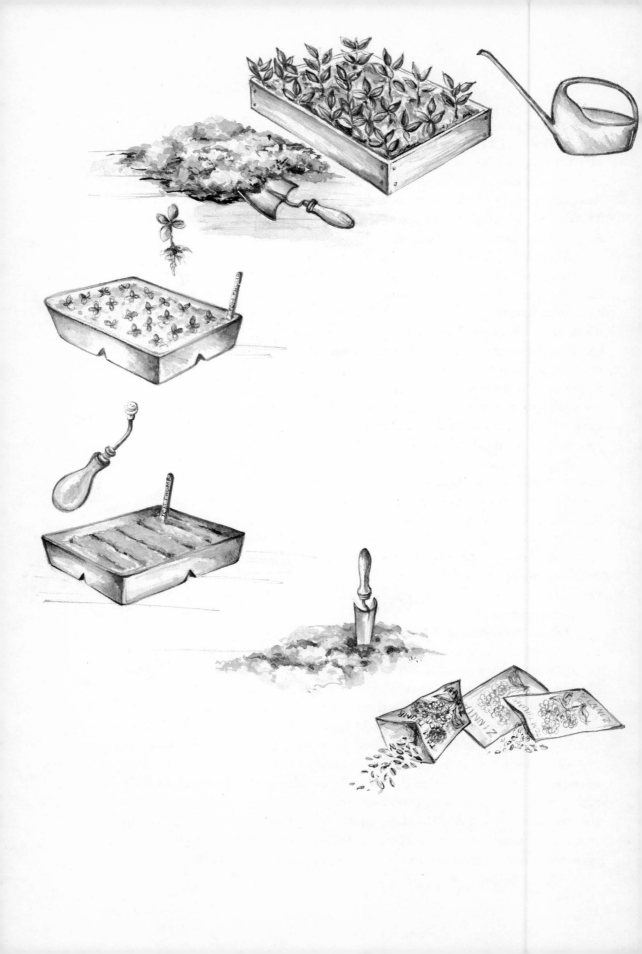

2. From Seed Packet to the Garden

Most seed catalogs are available for the asking; a few ask a modest charge to defray mailing costs. Advertisements for them are found in the garden sections of newspapers and in all home and garden magazines. The true dyed-in-the-wool gardener looks forward each year to spending hours poring over the newest seed catalogs. Here, both experienced and inexperienced gardeners can find valuable gardening information. As you look through the catalog, give a thought to the splendid work which made it possible. First the growing of the seed, harvesting, cleaning and packaging. The seedsman must know in advance of printing, amounts of seed from each variety he has available to sell to the public. Pictures must go along with the descriptions. Think of the hours of work someone spent on such a project! Think of all the wealth of material on gardening contained within the pages of these catalogs at no cost at all to the home gardener! The gardeners of America owe these companies a huge vote of thanks for their dedication and tireless efforts on our behalf.

Each year some one of my gardening friends will ask me where we obtain our seeds and will go on to tell me not to purchase seed from this one or that one because the seed was "no good;" it germinated poorly; or not at all. Before you blame the seedsman, take stock of your own methods. Did you plant the seed according to directions? Was it kept moist so as to encourage germination or did it start to grow then wither under too hot a sun? The seedsmen have spent so much time, effort and money to give the gardening public the finest of seed that rarely ever is the seed at fault. One year I planted two seed pans of sweet alyssum using seed from the same packet. One pan germinated almost one hundred per cent, the other not at all. Since the seed came from the same packet, I can only explain the failure in the one seed pan to something I did or failed to do when sowing the seed.

I decided that I had covered the seed too deeply with seedling medium as both pans were kept in the same location and cared for in the same way. One of the reasons for writing this book is to encourage the home gardener to learn for himself what a thrilling experience it is to grow his own plants from seed. For twenty-five years this method of propagation has thrilled and excited me and I find it a never-ending fascination to watch a little plant unfold and grow to its ultimate beauty. In this book I shall share with other home gardeners my own successes and failures and those of my friends in the hope that you will gain greater pleasure and satisfaction from your garden.

THE COLDFRAME

Most "casual" gardeners, which excludes the devotees and specialists, but who represent the bulk of the seedsmen's customers, cannot justify, in their limited endeavors, the operation of a greenhouse. However, no plot is too small to accommodate a 3 x 6 foot coldframe, which, in its diversified uses, I consider to be the most essential equipment available to any gardener. The busy housewife with a small dooryard garden will find a coldframe as worthy in her gardening activity as is the dishwasher in her kitchen chores— and considerably less costly to operate!

A coldframe will hasten the spring and delay the fall; serve as a refrigerator for forcing bulbs; protect doubtfully hardy plant treasures through the winter storms and more pertinent to the subject of this book, permit you the gardener to grow under ideal protected conditions, the specific varieties of plants that are desired and which might not be available at the local nursery and at a fraction of their cost.

Since seeds of many plants need a period of alternate freezing and thawing to break dormancy, a coldframe is an excellent place to start them in late fall or early winter.

If you have no facilities for starting seeds indoors, they may be started in the frame during the early weeks of spring before the weather is suitable for outdoor seed sowing. Perennials and biennials may be started by the middle of March in the frame and seeds of more tender annuals and vegetables can be started by the second week in April in the northern section of the country.

Although coldframes can be of any size suitable to work around or reach into, many years of experience have resulted in the standard 3' x 6' frame and sash or multiples thereof as the most convenient and acceptable. Many garden supply centers and lumber millwork suppliers carry the 3' x 6' sash, glazed or unglazed in stock. In recent years, half-sash (3' x 3') have become available, no doubt as a sales appeal to women who consider the standard glazed sash a bit awkward to handle. As might be expected these small sash are more expensive (on a square-foot basis) than the popular standard size and severely limit usable space. However, there are no restrictions as to the size nor the type of material that may be used. Our first coldframe, constructed of some discarded shelving, was sized to accommodate some glazed kitchen cupboard doors given us by a contractor who was modernizing a kitchen with the "new look" flush panel cupboards. They were not made of the long lived cedar or redwood and the many coats of paint applied over the years continued to peel under the exposure conditions for several seasons but we found this make-shift frame as adequate as the most sophisticated "store bought" variety. The enterprising gardener can find local sources of used or discarded window sash and storm doors, which in many cases can be had for the asking, or if not, you may construct your own sash.

In the simplest terms, a coldframe is nothing more than a bottomless box set on, or in, the ground with a suitable protective cover to provide the required conditions of light, shade, ventilation and temperature to accommodate plant needs.

Although I shall confine this text to the 3' x 6' frame, it will apply to any size to suit your use or convenience.

Most basic and essential, the frame should be located in full sun and the long axis of the frame set on an approximate north-south line. In our garden we have several groups—one group, set fully exposed near our garden area and the others located against the south foundation of our greenhouse.

The frames pictured in the photographs are ten years old and were made of sheets of half-inch thick Transite, a dense cement-asbestos board, bolted to 2-inch angle irons at each corner. This material is as durable as reinforced

10   A GROUP OF THREE OF THE AUTHOR'S COLDFRAMES, ONE UNCOVERED, ONE WITH A LATH SHADING PANEL AND ONE WITH A PLASTIC-SCREEN-GLAZED SASH.

11   A GROUP OF COLDFRAMES ON THE SOUTH SIDE OF THE GREENHOUSE. NOTICE THE PITCH FROM BACK TO FRONT TO PROVIDE DRAINAGE.

12   A MULIPLE COLDFRAME, STURDILY BUILT OF REDWOOD PLANKS. HERE AT WHITE FLOWER FARMS, LITCHFIELD, CONNECTICUT, SOME OF THESE FRAMES ARE EQUIPPED WITH HEATING FACILITIES.

13   ANOTHER UNIT AT WHITE FLOWER FARMS WITH LATH STRIP SHADING.

14   COMMERCIAL GROWERS ARE INGENIUS LIKE HOME GARDENERS! HERE WHITE FLOWER FARMS PROTECT FIELD-GROWN AZALEAS UNDER SCREEN SHADING SUPPORTED BY PACKING CASES—BY-PRODUCTS OF HOLLAND BULB SHIPMENTS.

concrete, but expensive, extremely heavy and most difficult to work. I fell heir to the material, and its assembly by my husband was a labor of love.

The commercial growers who use frames build, at the outset, permanent facilities to minimize maintenance costs. In many of these installations the frames are built of reinforced concrete or concrete block with footings below frost line. I have seen many, all 6 feet wide (to take the standard frames set side by side) 150 to 200 feet long. Some could more realistically be called pit greenhouses since they are equipped with circulating hot water piping to maintain appropriate growing temperatures. However, this is sophistication

15 A GLASS-GLAZED FRAME, BADLY IN NEED OF PUTTY—BUT STILL DOING DUTY. NOTICE THE OVERLAPPING GLASS, LIKE SHINGLES, PROVIDING FAST DRAINAGE.

16 A SASH SHOWING THE USE OF PLASTIC SCREENING INSTEAD OF GLASS.

to the ultimate and hardly realistic or desirable for the inexperienced or the small home gardener.

Consideration should be given in constructing the frame, to pitch the top from back to front, so that the sash may shed water. Our frames are 6-inches lower in the front, providing fast drainage. However, a minimum pitch of 3 inches would suffice.

The standard sash (see photo 15) is designed to facilitate drainage. You will note there are no exposed horizontal members which interrupt the water flow. The vertical sides of the intermediate members (mullions) are grooved (rabbited) to receive the glass panes which overlap each other as do roofing shingles. In lieu of using glass—and I personally have found fully glass-glazed sash difficult to handle and subject to breakage, some of the new plastic media are most applicable. We have used a heavy (6 or 8 mil) polyethylene or polyvinyl clear plastic or, preferably, a clear plastic coated screening either one adding no weight to the unglazed sash. The clear plastic is inexpensive, has little structural strength and will require renewal about every two years. The plastic screening is highly durable—surprisingly punctureproof—and we have this material on sash which are still in good condition after six years of use. Compared to clear glass, the plastic screening does reduce somewhat the available light in the frame. We have found this condition to be an attribute rather than a fault for growing plants from seed. There never has been observed, as would be indicated by leggy seedlings, that there is a deterimental lack of light, and we can delay and sometimes eliminate shading on these frames when we find it necessary to shade the frames under clear glass.

If polyethylene plastic or plastic-covered screening is used, it is applied reasonably taut to the sash frame in one full 3- x 6-foot piece and is held in place by strips of wood. We like to use half round moulding for this, nailed with brads to the sash frame members. One word of caution—if the location is exposed to high winds, use a hook and eye on two diagonally opposite corners. Once, after a gusty windstorm preceeding a summer thundershower, we found one of our sash out in the open garden, a hundred feet from the frames. It must have literally "sailed through the air with the greatest of ease," landed on a corner and completely shattered! All of our frames and sash are now provided with hooks and eyes on all *four* corners.

The making of the frame should be within the ability of the "unhandiest" handyman who has had any experience with hammer and saw. If either time or ability is limited the local lumber yard will cut square and true to sketch all the required materials ready to assemble. All that is required are two sides, two ends and four corner post nailers. The corner posts could be omitted but they add much to the stability and secure corner fastening.

The sides and ends should be of minimum 1-inch thick (nominal) lumber or ¾-inch exterior plywood or hard board (for example, tempered Masonite or Novaply). If the sides and ends are to be made up of pieces rather than full sheets, they should be tightly butted to each other (a difficult job) to the point of perfection to assure that the joints are *airtight*. The use of tongue and grooved or ship-lap material is preferable if one-piece panels are not available. Corners posts should be minimum 2″ x 2″ (half of a 2″ x 4″) or preferably of 2″ x 3 ″lumber.

The frame, using the materials described, can be made in a convenient work area—garage, terrace or cellar—and upon completion carried to the permanent location.

If the frame is made of new or unpainted lumber give all surfaces a saturating coat of a copper naphthanate preservative sealer such as Cuprinol, Creoseal, or their equivalents. These materials, containing copper, contribute greatly in deterring the decomposition processes which prevail when wood is in contact with damp soils by providing resistance to mildew and fungus.

The frame, when complete, may be set *on* the ground and banked 6 inches high on all four sides with soil, compost, leaves, grass, salt hay or sawdust. The lighter materials should be wetted and tramped in and if in a very windy situation covered with a layer of sand, soil or a few boards.

We prefer to bury our frames about 6 inches below ground level and carry the soil level inside the frame at the bottom edge of the frame approximately 6 inches below the ground level outside the frame. This provides the same headroom inside the frame as if it were set on the ground—less frequent watering is required and level ground conditions around the frame afford more comfortable working conditions.

The soil can be prepared for planting prior to placing the frame or with the frame in place. We prefer to place the frame before preparing the soil. If the soil at the desired location is completely unsuitable it should be removed to a depth of 12 inches and replaced. If, however, as in our case, the basic soil is acceptable as a component of the planting mix it may be removed to a depth of 12 inches and screened through ¼-inch mesh hardware cloth to remove sod and stones and reused in the soil mix.

Since our soil is a well-textured clay loam we use as a growing medium two parts soil, one part sand, one part peat moss or well-rotted screened compost and add to each bushel a 3-inch pot of steamed bone meal. Soil media for growing seed is discussed in further detail in this chapter to guide those who may be blessed and/or cursed with extremely heavy or very light soils.

The growing medium when thoroughly mixed, is placed into the frame, lightly tamped—we use the back of a rake—and watered thoroughly to prevent puddling, with the hose nozzle set to a fine spray. The following day with the soil damp and well textured, seed may be planted. If seed planting is delayed for several days or longer and especially if dry weather prevails, a light watering several hours before planting may be necessary. The sash is not put into place until planting has been accomplished.

When ready to plant seeds, assemble your seed packets and identifying labels—plastic or wood—and a waterproof marking pencil, both of the latter available at your local garden supply store. We have found the thin inexpensive plastic labels excellent for greenhouse and houseplant use, but they become brittle during a season of outside exposure so that we prefer the 6-inch painted wood labels. We note on each label the generic name, i.e. "Petunia," the variety or cultivar name, i.e. "Sugar Plum," and on the reverse side of the label the date planted and the seedsman.

A spacing of about 3 to 4 inches between rows provides ideal light and

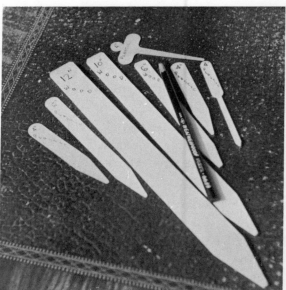

17   A FEW OF THE LABELS USED BY THE AUTHOR.

ventilation for seedling plants. As a spacer guide, we use a piece of 1- x 3-inch lumber about 34 inches long and starting at one end of the frame, this guide serves as a straight edge to mark the rows and as a spacer between rows, eliminating any need to guess or to measure for proper spacing.

A small mason's pointing trowel, which we prefer, or the pointed end of a wooden label guided along the edge of the wooden spacer is used to create a *shallow* furrow. The identifying label is placed at the end of the row and the seeds tapped gently from the packet or hand and thinly sown in the furrow. Very fine seeds such as petunia and foxglove are not covered but slightly pressed with the finger to assure good contact with the soil. Medium size seeds such as aquilegia and delphinium are *lightly* covered and *barely* pressed. Large

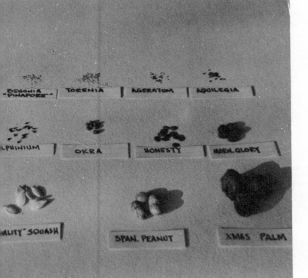

18   THE AUTHOR'S FAVORITE GARDENING TOOL IS A MASON'S POINTING TROWEL. ALSO NEEDED: A WATERPROOF MARKING PENCIL AND BASIC INFORMATION TO INCLUDE ON A PLANT TAG (TWO LABELS USED TO SHOW WHAT WOULD APPEAR ON EACH SIDE OF ONE ACTUAL LABEL).

19   MARKING OFF ROWS PRIOR TO PLANT- ING SEEDS.

20   NOTE THE VARIATIONS IN SEED SIZE FROM THE "DUST" OF BEGONIAS TO THE WALNUT-SIZE OF CHRISTMAS PALM.

21   USING A VERY FINE SPRAY TO AVOID WASHING OUT OR BURYING NEWLY SOWN SEEDS.

22   A LATH-STRIP SHADING PANEL FOR A THREE- BY SIX-FOOT COLDFRAME SASH. LATHS ARE SPACED THEIR OWN WIDTH AND NAILED ON FURRING STRIPS.

23   SEEDS PLANTED IN FALL, WINTERING OVER IN FRAME WITH A LIGHT COVERING OF SALT HAY.

24   THE SAME FRAME IN MIDWINTER. THE COVERING SASH WAS PUT ON AFTER THE GROUND FROZE.

seeds, such as canna, morning glory and sweet pea are covered with soil to a depth equivalent to their diameter and the soil lightly firmed.

After planting, the frame is well watered using a *fine spray* to assure that the soil covering the seeds is not disturbed nor the very fine uncovered seeds floated out of their furrows or buried.

And now the *most important requirement* for successful growing from seed: *NEVER EVER* let the seed bed dry out. The hairlike seed sprouts or the tiny tender seedlings will die within hours on a sunny day if they lack moisture. With a tight frame and sash, evaporation loss is at a minimum. However, the soil should be watched carefully and watered if necessary, using a fine spray.

To minimize the mid-day ventilating chore, so vital, particularly during the seed germination and small seedling stage, a shading "device" may be used. As previously mentioned a sash covered with plastic coated screening provides light shading. However, even here under bright sun and warm temperatures, some ventilation is required. For sash covered with clear plastic or with glass-glazed sash, *shading* is most desirable and at times absolutely essential. Tiny seedlings with their fine hair-like limited root systems will wilt and be fatally injured under bright sun conditions. Although the seed bed is moist, the yet undeveloped root system is not capable of supplying enough water to the leaves (even though miniature) to keep up with the rapid transpiration (loss of moisture) from the leaves.

The most popular shading device is a wood lath panel the size of the sash with the spaces between the lath strips equal to the width of the strip. As the sun moves the shadows cast by the lath strips move providing alternate sun and shade on the seed bed. Some gardeners paint the glass with a shading paint, others use cheese cloth tacked to a 3-inch wood strip on each end, to hold it in place and to serve as a roller when shading is not required. The materials and methods used to shade a frame are as varied as the ingenuity and imagination of the individual.

In chilly weather the frame may be left undisturbed. On bright sunny days with temperatures above 60 degrees it is advisable during the mid-day to provide some ventilation to prevent the seed bed from becoming too hot. Seed bed temperatures over 80 degrees could prove disastrous to seeds in the germinating stage. The sash may be blocked up so that an inch of space is left all around between frame and sash, or the sash may be pulled slightly aside to allow air to enter the frame. In late afternoon before the air becomes chilly the frame should be closed for the night.

When seeds are planted in the frame in late fall or early winter, planting procedures are the same as already outlined. However, the sash is left off the frame until such time as the ground has frozen hard. At this time mulch the seed bed with salt hay and replace the sash, hooking it into place so that winter winds will not displace it. This sash may be left on the frame until the end of March when it may be removed and the lath frame substituted. A careful watch must be kept at all times to see that the seed bed does not dry out.

INDOOR SEED SOWING

As a general rule the main purpose for starting seed indoors is to get a headstart on the gardening season. There are many plants which need a long growing season in order to come into flower or fruit before frost and these definitely need early sowing. Even in the southern section of the country where spring comes early enough to give a long growing season it is wise to start indoors or in frames seeds of the all-double petunias for instance, or other fine dust-like seeds which, if weather-exposed, heavy rains might bury or float away. Seeds of "fussy" plants and rare or unusual ones for which the gardener pays a premium price should also be started in this manner. Seeds of house plants should be started indoors in order that they may be watched and cared for. The earlier we start our biennials and perennials for the garden the more mature and well established they will be by the time the winter season begins and bloom will come earlier the following year. Most of our garden encyclopedias suggest starting biennials and perennials in August. While this might be good advice for areas where there is a long lingering fall and winter comes late, as in North Carolina for instance, in the northern sections plants started from seed in August are not usually of adequate size by fall and will not be mature enough to give typical bloom until a second growing season has gone by.

There are also several benefits which should not be discounted. Frequently the variety of vegetable or color of flower that is especially desired for your garden will not be available at your local garden center. Even average success will provide plants in quantity for pennies. As an example, recently from a double packet of 'Midget Blue' ageratum at a cost of just 60¢ we grew 750 plants and still had seed left over. Several years ago when Big Boy tomato was being introduced and potted plants sold for 75¢ at our local garden nursery, we grew 38 plants from a 50¢ packet of seed which stated it held 30 seeds. We assume that Mr. Burpee was overly generous with his count!

Many methods have been used to start seed indoors and I shall attempt to describe in a general fashion as many as I can. Through years of trial and error, my husband and I have evolved methods which we feel are superior, although many of our gardening friends use other methods and are just as happy with the results. If the gardener is satisfied with the methods he uses, he should continue to use them; as they say "nothing succeeds like success!" If however, you are searching for a better way than you have been using, you may find some methods herein which you would like to try.

At this point I assume you have seed packets in hand ready to get started with the gardening season. The gardening season, as dictated by the last killing frost, varies by latitude as does the coming of spring. Spring arrives in the Gulf Coast late in March and walks leisurely northward to arrive in Michigan and Wisconsin in May, two months later. Someone has said that spring and the robins travel northward at the rate of 30 miles per day, a reasonably close estimate.

No matter whether it be in Alabama or Wisconsin the enterprising and enthusiastic gardener wants to get a running start. Whether his incentive is to lengthen the growing season for its pure pleasure or to get the first ripe tomato in the neighborhood, it does not matter.

Appropriately, then, I feel the first consideration should be given to these "early birds" to the extent of exploring the methods whereby, under protective conditions, we can get that "jump" on spring.

SEEDLING MEDIA

The same growing medium is used for pan or tray seed sowing in the greenhouse, under fluorescent lights, in the cellar window or on the upstairs window sills. Soil preparation methods in the open garden or in the cold-frame will be discussed later in this chapter.

Because there is a soil borne fungus known as "damp-off" it is better to use one of the sterile mixes available today. Damp-off is evidenced by the little seedlings seemingly rotting at the soil line and falling over. With the relatively inexpensive sterile media available it is foolhardy to attempt to use anything else. You can mix your own materials or purchase mixes already prepared for your use. Some of these prepared mixes are variously known as "Jiffy Mix" or "Peat-Lite" and are offered by some of the leading seedsmen whose catalogs are available to all gardeners everywhere. Many garden supply centers stock some of these materials to meet the growing demands of gardeners. If it is desired to start only a few plants from seed these would probably be the best bet especially for the inexperienced seed sower.

VERMICULITE This is a form of expanded mica with a tremendous capacity for holding moisture. It can be used with excellent results. The agricultural grade used for seed starting is the one known as "Terralite" the granules are relatively small and the product relatively dust free. Some gardeners find that it is inclined to hold too much moisture and I agree that it can be tricky to control.

MILLED SPHAGNUM Finely milled sphagnum moss has been used for starting seedlings for a good many years. Used alone, in most cases, it gives excellent results. Many of our gardening friends use this medium alone for starting plants and find it most highly suitable. However, in our experience we find it has a tendency to "cake" or "crust," especially when used for seed which need a long period for germination. We have had some of the more vigorous seedlings come up with a crust on the seedling leaves, appearing as though they were wearing straw mandarin hats!

PERLITE Perlite, a volcanic ash, when used alone has one or two qualities which we personally do not like. It stays quite cool or even chilly, which might possibly be good for those seeds which need to be kept cool for germination but not so for those which need warmth. It does not absorb moisture but rather holds the moisture around each little granule and it has a tendency to float and disturb the seed bed, which we find objectionable.

EQUAL PARTS OF VERMICULITE, MILLED SPHAGNUM AND PERLITE
Our personal preference for starting seeds is a mixture of all three of these in
which the composite mix seems to result in the blending of the advantages of
all three, without their faults. We feel this is the perfect mix. It is light, clean
and easy to handle. It holds moisture but readily drains. For those gardeners
who have not been absolutely satisfied with the seedling medium they have
been using I can recommend this mixture whole-heartedly. Since we have
been using vermiculite and/or this mix, hard seeds like those of lupine and
morning glory which authorities assert must be soaked or nicked prior to
sowing have for us germinated readily in three to four days. Seedlings in this
mix, may, if necessary, be fed with a liquid fertilizer to keep them healthy and
strong. For this purpose we use either Rapid-Gro, Miracle-Gro, Hyponex or
Plant Marvel, diluted to one-fourth strength when the seedlings are very small,
increasing the strength to one-half that recommended on the package and
feeding weekly until they are either transplanted to flats or placed directly
from seed pan to the garden.

25   NOTE THE GRANULAR CONSISTENCY OF
THE VERMICULITE AND PERLITE. THE FINE
MILLED SPHAGNUM SERVES AS A FILLER TO
GIVE THE THREE-PART MIX A HIGHLY SUIT-
ABLE TEXTURE.

26   THE INGREDIENTS FOR THE AUTHOR'S
FAVORITE STARTING MEDIUM. "LARGE ECON-
OMY SIZES" ARE SHOWN, BUT ALL ARE AVAIL-
ABLE IN A VARIETY OF SMALLER SIZES.

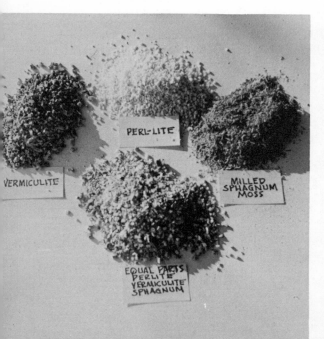

PEAT MOSS MIXED WITH EQUAL PARTS OF BUILDERS SAND   This is recommended for growing cacti and other succulents and is excellent for fine seeds. I have found that it does not hold moisture as well as the vermiculite-milled sphagnum-perlite mix that I like to use. In growing cacti and other succulents, however, I have had equal success with both media.

NORTH PLATTE MIX   This mix is recommended by a number of authorities and is used with excellent results by some of my friends. In this mix one part of milled sphagnum is used to two parts each of vermiculite and perlite. Feeding is necessary the same as that recommended in the paragraph under equal parts of vermiculite-milled sphagnum and perlite.

PACKAGED SOIL MIXES   These are good if nothing else is available. However, when purchasing, make sure that the printing on the bag states definitely that it is a sterile mix as some packaged mixes have not been sterilized.

SOIL MIXES   Garden soil whether wholly of loam or loam mixed with peat and sand I do not recommend. However, soil can be used but should be baked a small quantity at a time at 350 degrees to destroy the damp-off fungi and other soil-borne diseases as well as weed seed. Bury a small potato in the middle of the mix. When the potato is cooked, the mix should be sterile. Spread out to dry and cool. Then place in a clean container, sprinkle a little water over it and cover with a piece of plastic to restore soil moisture which is most necessary as all moisture is lost during the baking process. When I use this method, I usually open the container and stir the soil and sprinkle the surface with water for several days prior to using for seed sowing, so that the soil will be uniformly moist, but not wet.

UNSTERILIZED SOIL WITH SPHAGNUM TOPPING   Some gardeners like to use a soil mix in the bottom of a seed pan, flat or container with an inch of sterile milled sphagnum on the top for sowing seeds and find that this gives good results; the sphagnum protecting the little seedlings from fungi present in the bottom layer of soil and the soil below providing a food source for the root system of vigorous seedlings.

The various seed medium mixes are legion and many experienced gardeners have developed their own "secret formulas" for what they consider to be the ideal medium with a pinch of this and that. As I noted before, "nothing succeeds like success." My husband and I have experimented with many mixes during our thirty years of gardening and feel our basic recommended mix is most satisfactory—particularly for the inexperienced or beginning gardener for whom this text is intended.

I would be remiss to leave this section without mentioning the various products on the market which can be used to control the damp-off disease. I personally have not found it necessary to use them since sowing my seeds in the sterile mixes. Semesan is the best known of these disinfectants. Captan is used with everything *except* petunias and tomatoes. Spergon and Rootone are also suggested. They should be used exactly as directed on can or package. A pinch of powder or a few drops of liquid are all that is necessary. *Too much can be damaging.*

SEED-STARTING CONTAINERS

The pan which you select to start seeds may be as professional or as amateurish as you wish. Plantsmen and garden supply shops carry complete starting kits, including starting trays, transplanting pots (usually peat), plant labels and the planting medium and they hope to sell you, also, the required seeds. There are also appearing in greater variety each succeeding year what my husband jokingly calls the "effortless kit"—a prepared plastic wrapped tray, about market pack size, with six or twelve compartments each containing a seed, ready to place on the shelf or sill, water and wait for results. My husband considers this expedient to be almost as unchallenging as buying the grown plants from the local nurseryman. However, it is my personal opinion that the inexperienced gardener might become interested enough to try growing his own plants, if he is successful with the started kit. It could become inspiring enough for the home gardener to branch out and try some of the methods suggested in this book.

We mostly use as shown in the photos the by-products of supplies that we require in our own household. We favor coffee cans, plastic or fibrous market packs, aluminum-foil loaf pans and cheese containers and squat clay

27 SAMPLING OF CONTAINERS THE AU-THOR USES FOR SEED SOWING.

28 THESE FIVE-INCH POTS, FROM LEFT TO RIGHT, ARE KNOWN AS STANDARD, AZALEA AND BULB PAN. THE SQUAT BULB PAN IS MOST SUITABLE FOR STARTING SEEDS.

29 A TYPICAL 12- X 18-INCH FLAT, ABOUT 2¾THS INCHES DEEP. THIS FLAT WITH DRAINAGE SPACING BETWEEN THE BOTTOM BOARDS WILL NEED A SINGLE THICKNESS OF NEWSPAPER ON THE BOTTOM TO RETAIN THE GROWING MEDIUM.

or plastic flowerpots. The enterprising "string saver" could, I am sure extend this list ad infinitum.

All of the containers whether from the garden center or your own "salvage" have one essential and basic requirement—they should be 2½ to 3 inches deep. They can be deeper but it is not necessary and only results in the additional effort to prepare and handle the excess material. Photographs shown in the section on transplanting seedlings will indicate the extensive root systems of these small seedlings, disclosing the need for a sufficiently deep growing medium.

30 GERMINATING SEED PANS, PLASTIC-
COVERED, ON A SOUTH WINDOW SILL.

31 PLASTIC-COVERED SEED PANS ON SHELF
AT CELLAR WINDOW, WAITING GERMINATION.
THE SEEDS HAVE GERMINATED IN THE UN-
COVERED TRAY.

You will find if you attempt to use shallow containers, such as the aluminum-foil roll or pie trays, the planting mix, designed to be light and porous, dries out quickly. More frequent watering is needed and considerably more attention and care are required.

Since we start seeds in the greenhouse, under lights or on trays on shelves in the cellar windows we are not concerned with a bit of excess water that might result from drainage or overly exhuberant watering. As we find bottom watering so satisfactory in seed starting we perforate the bottoms of our containers with a number of small holes, conveniently done with an ice pick, small chisel or screw driver. The holes should be small enough so that the dry mix will not seep out before watering, or will not drip out after watering.

If, however, your containers must be assigned to a window sill or a table at a well-lighted window where water spillage would cause damage, then your container needs to be watertight.

The same inexpensive containers can be used, with a little different treatment—a clay pot, but with a saucer under; or a perforated aluminum-foil loaf pan set in one that is not perforated which contains a little gravel or small stones to create a drainage system. Both of these methods will permit bottom watering.

Drainless containers can be used by placing a half-inch of gravel in the bottom but covering the gravel layer with one thickness of paper towel before you put in the growing mix, in order to create a drainage reservoir.

If space permits, as in a greenhouse or under lights, the typical flat lends itself well to starting seedlings. The same mix as described in this chapter is used, but owing to the size of the flat, usually about 12 x 18 inches, the seeds are sown in rows, 2 to 3 inches apart.

All the rules of pre-watering, covering of seeds and after-care as described in the next section under seed-sowing apply. Although a surprising number of seedlings can be grown in a single flat, I feel the beginner should not attempt this method as a "first try." Some knowledge of variety habit is required. For instance, if a slow-growing perennial is planted in a row next to a fast-germinating annual, the annual could be ready for transplanting before the perennial even germinates which, of course, would result in disturbing the seed beds of the slow varieties.

SEED SOWING

With your starting containers selected and the planting mix prepared and ready, fill all the containers which you will need for your sowing. Fill the pans level within a quarter-inch of the top. We have found over the years

32 SOAKING SEED TRAYS (WITH PERFO-RATED BOTTOMS) TO THOROUGHLY DAMPEN MEDIUM BEFORE PLANTING.

33 SOAKING SEED TRAYS AFTER PLANTING SEEDS.

that healthier seedlings result with the level of the planting medium near the top of the pan than if kept lower. It is our opinion that better ventilation is provided with the seedlings set high with less susceptibility to the fungus diseases which flourish in a humid, stagnant air environment.

It is very important that all of these mixes, whichever you use, be thoroughly moistened before sowing the seeds. Get in the habit of watering thoroughly and letting them drain for at least two hours *before* sowing seed. We like to water ours by placing in a 6-inch-deep tray which my husband made especially for this purpose and use the watering can to pour water over the top of the mix to settle it. Containers may be left in the pan without watering the top surface and when moisture is seen on the top layer of the mix you will know that the entire medium has been watered thoroughly. Our recommended mix is so light weight when dry that it is inclined to rise in the seed pan if watered from the bottom too rapidly; for example if you permit the container to float while soaking. The container may be submerged slowly, or top-watered to partially wet the medium.

While the containers are draining, assemble the seed packets and prepare the plant labels with a waterproof pencil. Note on each label the generic name, i.e. "Petunia;" the variety or cultivar name, i.e. "Sugar Plum," and on the reverse side of the label the date planted and the seedsman. We use an inexpensive white lightweight 4-inch plastic tag, perfect for short-term use, but neither large enough nor sufficiently durable for the open garden or flower beds.

Discussion of seed sowing in this section pertains to the seeds of many varieties of annuals, perennials and vegetables, which as they come from the packet are properly ripened and conditioned to germinate. A very few of these seeds with thick protective coats need to be pre-soaked to hasten germination. These few cases are indicated under the specific variety growing hints in a later chapter.

Many shrub and tree seeds must go through a cycle of freezing and thawing simulating nature's winter to break dormancy prior to germination. Special treatment of such seeds is covered in a later chapter.

With the containers ready for sowing and the plant label in place, open packet at one end and spread top to make a spout. My husband holds the package over the seed container and *taps* lightly with forefinger. A great many authorities recommend this method. Being a very impatient person myself and sort of "slap dash" I am not very good at achieving good results with this "tapping method." I prefer to empty a few seeds from the packet into the palm of my hand, and, taking a pinch or two at a time, go back and forth over the container in an effort to cover the whole surface. If the packet should

34   SOWING BY TAPPING SEEDS OUT OF THE
PACKET.

35   SOWING FROM THE HANDS, A PINCH
OF SEEDS AT A TIME.

36   STATICE, TWO WEEKS AFTER PLANTING.
HERE, A GARDEN LABEL DIVIDER (BARELY
VISIBLE) SEPARATES THE WHITE 'ICEBERG'
FROM THE MIXED. THIS SMALL MARKET-PAK
PLANTING PRODUCED OVER SEVENTY-FIVE
PLANTS.

contain only a few dustlike seeds they will undoubtedly be found in a little
glassine envelope placed inside the outer package. In this case, I slit one side
and end of the little envelope, hold it over the container and let the little
seeds roll out one by one, moving it a little each time so as to get as even
sowing as possible.

Another good method for sowing small seeds is to crease a piece of
bond paper in the middle, empty the seeds onto the crease in the paper and
use it for letting the fine seeds roll out into the seed pan. If some of the
seed packets contain relatively few seeds, as with some of the new expensive
hybrids, several varieties can be planted in the same tray. A plastic label (see
photo 36) may be used as a divider between the different varieties.

Beginners and sometimes we too, are inclined to sow too thickly which
because of the crowded condition in the pan encourages damping off and
leggy seedling growth. Seedlings, as do the mature plants, require for *optimum*
growth, adequate moisture, light and air. Well-spaced seedlings will develop
stocky top growth and comparable vigorous root systems. You will also find
transplanting of the sturdy seedlings considerably easier and less likely to
be damaged in the process than the weak, leggy ones.

Fine seeds, such as those of snapdragon, petunia, ageratum, foxglove, canterbury bells and others of like size are never covered but pressed very *lightly* into the seedling medium. Large seeds such as morning glory are covered only just enough so that they will not be seen. Press lightly to firm the covering medium but be careful not to use a heavy hand. Water by placing the seed pan in a container of water until the moisture is seen coming to the top of the medium. We use a copper trough that formerly lined a planter box. Any container large enough to take several of your planting pans at one time would suffice. A dishpan or large roasting pan, or, if you must . . . use the wash tub or the kitchen sink! May I caution you to have the water in the "soaking tub" only about three-fourths the depth of the seed tray that is being watered. If too deep, the seeds that you have just carefully sown, will along with the mix, likely be afloat! You may also water by using an extremely fine spray from a rubber bulb spray available at your garden supply store— also handy for sprinkling clothes. Never use the fine spray from the hose unless you have had considerable experience. Personally, I prefer to water from the bottom because in that way I can be sure that the seeds have not been buried too deeply or disturbed in any way and that the entire medium from top to bottom has been thoroughly watered.

If instructions for sowing the seed indicate that it should be sown in warmth, place near a radiator for window-sill growing; 6 inches below

37   PANS WITH SEEDS THAT REQUIRE AL-
TERNATE FREEZING AND THAWING TO BREAK
DORMANCY ARE PLACED IN A COLDFRAME IN
LATE FEBRUARY FOR TWO OR THREE WEEKS,
AND COVERED WITH A SASH TO RETAIN
MOISTURE AND FOR PROTECTION.

38   ALUMINUM LOAF PAN, WATERED, AND
IN A PLASTIC BAG READY TO GO TO GREEN-
HOUSE, UNDER THE FLUORESCENT LIGHTS,
OR ON A BRIGHT WINDOW SILL.

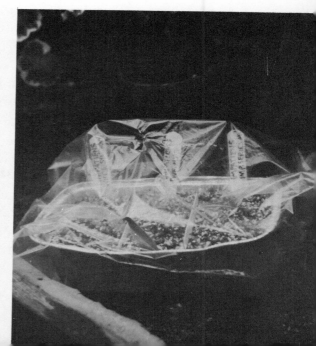

fluorescent lights if you are using such for starting your seeds, or in the greenhouse near the source of heat to provide the warmth desired. In our greenhouse we place our seed trays needing warmth at the south end of our bench with a canopy so that the sun slants in on the east, south and west but when overhead the seed pan is shaded. Warmth from the heater located at the south end of the greenhouse is trapped under the canopy and also helps to hasten germination. Conversely if coolness is indicated for germination, the seed pan is placed at the extreme north end of the bench away from the heat and where cold air enters around the door located at this end of the house. If alternate freezing and thawing is indicated the seed pan is placed in a covered coldframe at the end of February or early March for several weeks prior to bringing into the warmth of the greenhouse, sunny window, or under fluorescent lights which aids in germination with such stubborn seeds. Wherever possible in the text of this book, needs of individual plants are discussed under the proper title headings such as annuals, perennials or trees.

After the seed has been planted and you are sure it is *thoroughly* moistened, cover with a piece of plastic. It does not matter too much if the plastic is clear or translucent, but it is necessary to make sure that the plastic *does not rest* on the seedling medium. If the plastic is lightweight an extra plant tag in the seed pan will hold up the plastic. Plastic bags are excellent if you are only doing a few seed pans. This covering helps keep the medium uniformly moist which in my opinion is the *most important* factor for germination. The container should be placed in *strong* light and as soon as most of the seeds have germinated the plastic is removed and the container should be placed into sunlight to develop strong, sturdy seedlings.

I do not recommend placing the seed pans in a dark area, *ever.* Nor covering them with cardboard, black plastic or newspaper. Seed pans should be placed in *full light* and as soon as germination has taken place should then be given all possible sunlight. Even close to the window they will have a tendency to lean toward the light, and therefore in such location containers should be turned every day or two.

It used to be the opinion of most authorities that darkness is essential for germination. However in the many years that my husband and I have been growing plants from seed, we have not found this to be the case. We contend that the moment the little seedling leaves emerge they need strong light. Insufficient light will make them move upward. Seedlings which should be stocky will become "leggy," long and spindly in the search for light. The distance between the seedling leaf and the "true" leaf will be elongated and the plant will never be compact.

With the seed pans placed in a well-lighted location and covered with the plastic, you will note condensation forming inside the plastic cover. Be aware that the presence of condensate on the plastic does not necessarily mean that the seed medium is moist enough. If you have selected a location near a radiator or other source of heat you will find the porous starting mix dries out quickly. If seed pans are over or near a radiator or air register they should be checked *twice a day* to be sure that they do not dry out. Test the medium with your finger or lift the container and if it is comparatively light, water at once and thoroughly. You will quickly discern the difference in weight between a dry seed pan and one that is amply moist. That period when the little roots are forming and the small seedling leaves are pushing up and emerging from the surface of the seedling medium is the most critical time in the life of the plant.

FEEDING

Most annuals germinate quickly and the seedlings grow rapidly to transplanting size so that they are in the sterile medium a relatively short time. However, a few annuals and many of the perennials, shrubs and trees grow slowly after germination and must remain in the sterile mix for substantial periods to attain sufficient size to accept transplanting. When the small amount of "food" stored within the seed to support the initial germination is used up, the small newly developed root system becomes the provider. Since the sterile mix has no nutrient it becomes necessary to artificially supply the required plant food by the application of liquid fertilizers. Rapid-Gro, Hyponex, Miracle Gro and Plant Marvel are all suitable for this use. Be very careful with these highly concentrated soluble fertilizers and use according to directions. If in doubt, use more water for a weaker dilution. For small seedlings, at this stage, I use one-half the recommended strength. For instance if directions indicate one teaspoon per quart of water, I use one-half teaspoon. I have found that such feedings at ten-day intervals keep the small plants "fat and sassy" and growing steadily until such time as they can be transplanted to flats, plant bands or peat pots.

Feeding is best accomplished by mixing the plant food with water and filling dish pan or trough with the mix to the desired height and allowing the seedling mix to take up the nutrient from the bottom. Feeding can be done overhead by using the rubber spray bulb, but I feel this can be a bad practice for on dull days the little plants do not become dry and "damp-off" may be the result of the moisture clinging to the small leaves. This is especially true if the seeds were sown too thickly in the seed pan.

WINDOW SILL AND LIGHTS

Although the basic seed sowing is the same, a few comments are in order concerning the special conditions that prevail when starting seedlings in the sunny upstairs window or under fluorescent lights.

The sunny window whether in the living quarters or on a porch should be at a location where in late February or March (in the northern states) daytime temperatures do not exceed 75 degrees nor do night temperatures go lower than 55 degrees.

We have discussed under *Containers* the need to have window-sill seed pans watertight, and that clay pots or perforated bottom trays could be used with suitable protection. Such containers can be bottom watered by the usual pan-soaking procedure, or if more convenient, just put them in an inch of water in the kitchen sink till the surface is damp; let drain and return to the window sill.

Even drain-less containers can be used by placing a half-inch of gravel in the bottom (cover gravel with a piece of paper towel before you add the growing medium) to provide a reservoir for excess water. Here however caution must be used not to overwater but if you do you can *carefully,* so as not to disturb the mix, turn the pan on its side to drain the excess. Completely saturated and water logged growing media will, by excluding air, very quickly drown the seedlings.

Watering the drain-less container should be done slowly and carefully so as not to disturb the seeds—but *thoroughly.* A rubber bulb spray can be used. The mist spray will not disturb even the smallest seeds if gently used. Do not spray forcibly or allow the water to puddle on the surface and again— in the fond hope of being repetitious—do *more* than dampen the surface and be certain the medium is wetted to its full depth.

At the window-sill locations the need to water will be greatly reduced, if the seed trays are covered with a piece of clear plastic or enclosed in a plastic bag. Keep the plastic from resting directly on the surface and do not assume watering is not needed because there are water droplets on the plastic. Resort to the tried and true test with a finger tip. You will find also that you will quickly be able to judge the need for water by the weight of the container. This latter method has become my standard practice.

Until the seeds germinate place the pans in *strong* light, not directly in the sun. A thin curtain at a sunny window will be adequate protection from the rays of the sun. When the seeds germinate remove the plastic cover. Now watering will be more frequent, and at this point bring them into full sunshine.

At any sill location the seedlings (also mature plants for that matter) will tend to incline towards the light resulting in leggy and lopsided growth. Turning the pan or tray every day or two will assure sturdy and compact seedlings.

If in your window-sill seed starting venture there is no room for transplanting to other pots or containers, sow your seed pans very thinly, and after good germination, thin plants so that there will be at least 1 inch between seedlings. Feed weekly until such time as they can be hardened off before placing into the open garden.

FLUORESCENT LIGHT

Recently a new growing environment, fluorescent lighting, has come into its own and has attained spectacular universal acceptance and appeal. Fluorescent lamps became available about 1938. The many lighting advantages of fluorescent lamps immediately became apparent and supplanted much of the incandescent lighting in industrial and commercial properties during World War II.

Research and development, spearheaded by the lamp manufacturers, United States Department of Agriculture and colleges and universities, promptly realized the potential of this cool, relatively high intensity source of light in the horticultural field.

Much has been written on all phases of "growing under the lights." Informative material is available from the United States Department of Agriculture Experiment Stations and from the manufacturers of fluorescent lamps as well as the various State Colleges of Agriculture. A number of books with specific how-to instructions written by experienced and knowledgeable authors are available at local bookstores and libraries.

Being fortunate enough to own a small greenhouse where warmer temperatures can be maintained than in our basement, most of our seed growing activities are done under glass. We have, however, for the past ten years operated a fluorescent light set-up in our basement which has provided many hours of pleasure and most satisfactory results. Our installation, completely assembled by my husband with rough lumber, consists of four shelves, each 2 feet wide and 4 feet long with four 4-foot, 40-watt tubes over each shelf. This all adds up to a respectable total of 32 square feet of growing area; just a little less than the space covered by a 5- x 7-foot rug. We used secondhand salvaged industrial type fixtures and have experimented with cool white, warm white and the more recent specialized horticultural lamps such as Gro-Lux by Sylvania. We have had good results with all types but feel the warm white or the horticultural type preferable and at present intermix them, using two of each above each shelf.

Because of the popularity of this growing atmosphere there are available on the market at most garden centers various fluorescent light set-ups. There are single-tube industrial units that can be mounted over your own shelves; lamps on legs to straddle table plants or boxes, prefabricated multiple-shelved carts with lighting above each shelf and many others. Regardless of the means to mount the lamp either decoratively or in the rough, your horticultural efforts can be satisfactorily rewarding.

Under these conditions the seed pans or trays are prepared as previously discussed for greenhouse or window sill, seeded, thoroughly watered, covered with plastic and placed from 6 to 8 inches from the lights. Again keep the growing medium thoroughly moist at all times. If you are using our recommended medium or a similar one which is completely sterile it will be necessary after germination to supply nutrients to keep the seedlings growing vigorously. When the "true" leaves begin to form (these come a little after the seedling leaves) we give the seedlings weekly feedings of a soluble plant food.

When seedlings have developed the second set of "true" leaves, they may be transplanted to individual pots (clay or peat) or to flats and returned to their places under the lights keeping the tops of plants at least 8 inches away from the lights so as to continue their growth until the time when weather permits the hardening off process before setting them to their permanent places in the garden. If a good soil mix is used in the flats or pots used for transplanting, no further feeding should be necessary. If a sterile potting mix is used, the diluted weekly feeding may be continued until the hardening-off period. It is very important not to let these little plantlets in pots or flats dry out at any time. Do not keep them wet, but it is most essential that they *be kept moist.* Make sure before transplanting that soil in flats or pots is thoroughly moist. Test with finger or plant label to the bottom of the flat to make sure that the medium is moist to the bottom, especially if the soil mix you are using was bone dry before starting to fill flats. Sometimes I have watered prior to transplanting only to discover that the top half-inch or so of the flat was good and moist but below that level the soil was still dry. Making sure that the flats or pots of soil are completely moist *before* transplanting will save many a disappointment.

Much experimentation has been done by scientists and plant research groups both at the state level and the United States Department of Agriculture plant research departments. Studies show that certain plants require short-day periods and others a longer light period to germinate and grow well under lights. Feeling that the average home gardener who wishes to start a few plants indoors would become discouraged if there had to be two sets of lights for starting different kinds of plants I talked with several friends who had been starting outdoor plants under fluorescent light, who were willing and eager to share their experiences.

One young couple who lived in a converted barn set up a stand similar to ours in the furnace room. As this was a hot-air furnace the temperature in the room stayed about 55 degrees during March when the bulk of their seed sowing was attempted. They used milled sphagnum for the seedling medium. Seed pans were set 8 inches from the lights and the lights were kept on for 24 hours a day. The only difficulty they encountered was a mold which formed on top of the moss. Using Panodrench at exactly the strength recommended disposed of this problem. Seedlings were transplanted to flats or peat pots and kept growing under the lights until time for hardening off which was accomplished by placing them in a semishaded spot in the shelter of an angle between garage and house for a week or so before placing in the garden. They were watched carefully to prevent drying out and were brought in for overnight if frost threatened. These young people had had no previous gardening experience, but their first attempt at starting plants from seed was so successful that not only did they have a lovely garden, but won seven blue ribbons at the local flower show in the fall of that year. This should certainly convince inexperienced gardeners that growing plants from seed can be an exciting and most satisfactory venture.

The other friend whom I interviewed is a lady quite knowledgeable in horticulture. This busy lady commutes to the city to her position as secretary to a United States District Court Judge and has only a few weeks vacation each summer. She was kind enough to allow my husband to photograph her set-up and to answer my questions. Her methods of sowing seeds are essentially the same as advocated earlier in this chapter. She keeps her lights on for ten hours a day and does not attempt to differentiate between short-day and long-day plants. She feels that burning the lamps ten to twelve hours a day is satisfactory and her results confirm this practice. Her seeds are sown in the North Platte mix described earlier in this chapter. Perennials and those annuals which need a long growing season are sown in March. Quick growing annuals are started in mid-April. When seedlings reach a suitable size they are transplanted to flats or Jiffy pots and continue to grow under the lights until time for hardening off. This lady uses packaged potting mixes in her flats but adds a portion of vermiculite or peat moss or both to make the material a little more "spongy." About a quart of either of the latter to an average bag of potting mix is recommended. Her plants are hardened off by being placed on a protected terrace facing east covered at first by a tent of tobacco cloth to protect them until they have become accustomed to being out of doors. If

39   SHELVES ARE ARRANGED SO THAT THEY CAN BE MOVED TO ACCOMMODATE VARIOUS HEIGHT PLANTS.

40   HERE THE PLANT TRAYS ARE ON A SHELF WHICH IS ABOUT TWELVE INCHES BELOW THE FLUORESCENT TUBE.

41   LIGHT FROM ABOVE, COMBINED WITH WARMTH FROM A HEATING CABLE BELOW, ASSURES IDEAL GROWING CONDITIONS. NOTE THE STOCKY 'NITTANY LION' GERANIUM SEEDLINGS.

42   TYPICAL OF THE STURDY SEEDLINGS THAT CAN BE GROWN UNDER FLUORESCENT LIGHTS.

43   A SAMPLING OF HOW MANY QUALITY SEEDLINGS CAN BE PRODUCED ON TWO, FORTY-EIGHT-INCH, LIGHTED SHELVES.

frost threatens, heavier tarpaulins are placed over them or flats are brought indoors.

All of this work is done long before the lady's vacation begins in late June. Her garden is a delight; walks lined with petunias, stocks, snapdragons, verbena and coleus to add color to the garden. Besides a cutting and vegetable garden there is an interesting perennial bed in the making containing delphinium, digitalis and others which my friend grows from seeds sown under her lights. Beneath a large old tree growing in dappled sunshine a large bed of geraniums gives color and pleasure near the patio all summer. At the time the accompanying photos were taken in late March plants of snapdragon, petunia, peppers, tomatoes, parsley, verbena, coleus, delphinium, stock, pansies and 'Nittany Lion' geraniums were flourishing under the lights.

As my own experience with sowing seeds under lights, with the exception of a few house plants, had been most limited, recently I tried some experiments of my own with starting seeds of outdoor plants under our own light set-up, which we burn for 12 hours each day. Seed pans were prepared and placed 6 inches from the lights. A thermometer placed on the stand with them showed a temperature of 80 degrees while the lights were on. At this season

44   SEED PANS, SIX INCHES FROM LIGHTS, AWAITING GERMINATION. THIS BENCH, NORMALLY USED FOR HOUSE PLANTS, HAS BEEN ADAPTED, IN A MAKESHIFT FASHION, BY THE USE OF FLOWERPOTS AND FLATS, TO START SEEDS.

45   THE SEEDLINGS DON'T NEED A FANCY CONTAINER—AS LONG AS IT IS DEEP ENOUGH. THE COFFEE CAN, WITH BOTTOM PERFORATED, HAS BEEN A FAVORITE OF THE AUTHOR'S FOR YEARS. UNFORTUNATELY, IN THIS SIZE THEY ARE NO LONGER AVAILABLE.

46   DELPHINIUM SEEDLINGS, SHOWING A FEW TRUE LEAVES, FOUR WEEKS AFTER PLANTING. THESE ARE ALMOST READY TO TRANSPLANT.

47   DAHLIA SEEDLINGS IN AN ALUMINUM LOAF-PAN. SEED GERMINATION IN THREE DAYS. THESE SEEDLINGS ARE FOURTEEN DAYS OLD AND READY TO BE TRANSPLANTED.

of the year in March, the cellar where our lights are located maintains a temperature of 65 to 70 degrees. Since this was merely an experiment I sowed small rows of seeds in the pans placing in the same pan seeds of plants such as larkspur and rosemary which customarily need to be kept quite cool for good germination as well as seeds of scarlet sage and sweet alyssum which need warmth for good germination. Larkspur and rosemary which had had a pre-cooling period in the coldframe before bringing into the greenhouse germinated in seventeen days, but under the lights with no pre-chilling at all they germinated in less than two weeks. Scarlet sage took two weeks and sweet alyssum six days under the lights. I also tried seeds of trees such as oxydendron, Norway spruce, Mugho pine, *Ilex crenata* and exochorda, all of which germinated within three weeks under the lights with no pre-chilling conditions.

I inquired of a leading professor of floriculture if he could explain this phenomenon and he indicated that he had not done any experiments of this kind. He did explain, however, that many of the seeds which for years had been believed to need a pre-chilling condition for good germination have been found to germinate quite well under other conditions. Starting seeds under lights and the growing of all kinds of plants under the lights is still in the experimental stage. The many leaflets and pamphlets on the subject prove to be helpful but most of this experimental and research work has naturally been done with the florist or commercial greenhouse grower in mind. Much development is being done on this fascinating subject and I have no doubt that sooner or later the answers to these puzzling questions will be forthcoming to the satisfaction of the home gardener.

TRANSPLANTING SEEDLINGS

Some gardeners do not transplant seedlings to flats, pots or other containers before planting out of doors. We have rather reluctantly on occasion resorted to this practice only because of expediency when lack of time prevented this intermediate transplanting or when we were unable to get a variety started early enough.

The seedling plants, unless very thinly sown (or if germination is sparse) will, because of crowded conditions, grow tall and leggy in their quest for light. Weak stems result and crowded conditions in the growing medium limit development of a substantial root system. Such seedlings are frail, difficult to handle and highly susceptible to damage from sun, wind, rain and disease. I have found that a prompt and timely intermediate transplant from the seed pan to flats or pots before setting out into the garden results in strong, compact and sturdy plants. Such transplants can take the exposed conditions in the open garden, suffer no set-back and continue in active growth.

A few gardeners like to transplant the seedlings to a flat and then transplant again to peat or clay pots. They feel that the plant develops better this way than to be planted at once into a pot too large for the root system. This additional transplanting is a matter of preference by the individual gardener. We have never had the time for this intermediate transplanting nor have we felt it necessary. My husband and I like to do our transplanting when the first set of "true" leaves develop.

The first leaves which develop from the emerging seedlings are called "seedling" leaves and are not typical of the size and shape of the "true" leaf of the plant. After the first pair of "true" leaves are showing, the little plants are ready for transplanting. In transplanting take out a few seedlings at a time with a plant label, or fingers if you prefer, without disturbing any more seedlings than necessary. My husband likes to use a label. I like to use the handle of a small teaspoon for doing this job. Handle the young plants carefully so as to limit the disturbance to the roots.

Although seedlings may be transplanted to pots or other suitable or convenient containers we transplant our seedlings to flats containing an all-

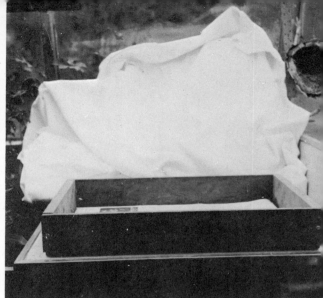

48 TYPICAL FLATS: THE ONE ON THE RIGHT, WITH OPENINGS BETWEEN BOTTOM BOARDS WILL NEED A SINGLE THICKNESS OF NEWSPAPER ON THE BOTTOM BEFORE FILLING WITH SOIL. MOST FLATS ARE ABOUT TWELVE BY EIGHTEEN INCHES AND 2¾THS INCHES DEEP.

49 STANDARD FLAT, WITH ONE THICKNESS OF NEWSPAPER ON BOTTOM (TO COVER CRACKS), READY FOR SOIL.

50 FLAT FILLED, LIGHTLY PRESSED, READY TO BE MOISTENED AND PLANTED.

51 STANDARD FLAT SET UP WITH 2 X 2 X 2½-INCH PLANT BANDS, READY FOR SOIL. THE AUTHOR USES THESE FOR THE CHOICEST (MOST EXPENSIVE) SEEDLINGS, OR FOR THE TAP-ROOTED KINDS WHICH RESENT TRANSPLANTING.

52 PLANT-BANDED FLAT, READY TO RECEIVE THE ELUSIVE AND THE "FUSSY" ONES.

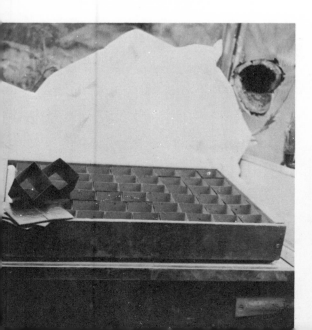

53   TO CONSERVE SPACE, USE A DIVIDER AND PLANT SEVERAL VARIETIES IN ONE CONTAINER. HERE TWO KINDS OF LUPINES ARE PLANTED IN A MARKET-PAK.

54   LUPINE SEEDLINGS TWO WEEKS AFTER PLANTING.

55   LUPINE SEEDLING READY TO TRANSPLANT TO FLAT OR POT. NOTE THE STARTING MEDIUM PARTICLES CLINGING TO THE GENEROUS ROOT SYSTEM.

56   MARKING OFF ROWS, SPACED TWO INCHES APART, USING A STRAIGHT EDGE AND AN OLD KITCHEN KNIFE.

57   "TUCKING" THE TRANSPLANTS IN THE FLAT USING A SIX-INCH WOODEN GARDEN LABEL AS A PIECE OF FINE EQUIPMENT.

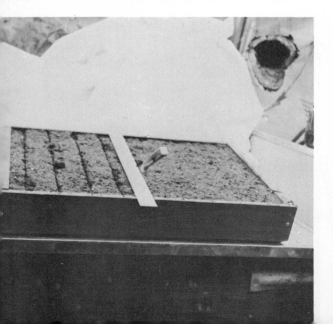

58　RUSSELL LUPINES, READY TO TRANS-PLANT, FOUR WEEKS AFTER PLANTING SEEDS.

59　"EASING-OUT" LUPINE SEEDLINGS FROM STARTING MEDIUM, USING A SIX-INCH WOODEN LABEL.

60　THE PLANTS, AS WELL AS THE ROWS, ARE SPACED ABOUT TWO INCHES APART TO PROVIDE ADEQUATE GROWING ROOM.

61　THE FULLY PLANTED FLAT, WITH THREE KINDS OF RUSSELL LUPINES, NOW TO BE ASSIGNED TO THE GREENHOUSE BENCH FOR GROWING ON.

purpose soil mix that we use as a potting mix for most plants. This mix is comprised of two parts garden soil, one part builders sand, and one part peat moss or well-rotted, screened compost with a 3-inch pot of steamed bone meal per bushel.

The flat is filled to the top with soil only lightly compacted by tapping the flat. The soil mix should then be lightly but thoroughly watered. We do not plant the flat at once but prefer to let it set a few hours to drain off the pre-watering. Do not attempt to set the little seedlings in muddy, sloppy soil. Such an attempt is not only exasperating but could prove disastrous for the seedlings. After the pre-watering, test the soil *to the bottom* of the flat with finger or plant label to be sure the flat is deeply watered and there is no dry soil on the bottom.

My husband made most of our flats of redwood. They are 12 x 18 inches, although we do have various other sizes which we have come by. A flat about 12 x 18 inches is not too heavy to handle when filled with soil and is large enough to sustain a good number of plants. We set the plants in rows starting 1 inch from the end of the flat with 2 inches between each plant. The plants in each row are also set 1 inch in from each side of the flat also with 2 inches between each plant. A 12 x 18-inch flat so planted will contain 54 plants. Sounds complicated doesn't it, but the accompanying illustrations disclose how simply it is done. The plants do not have to be set with mechanical precision but scored row guidelines are a big help.

With the flat ready for planting, the rows are marked off in the moist soil using a straight edge (we find a 15-inch metal rule ideal) and marking the rows with a knife blade. We have a small saw-cut at 2-inch intervals on the sides of the flats but a pencil mark will suffice as a guide for the rows.

Although I continue to talk of transplanting seedlings to *flats* the same methods apply if you are transplanting to peat pots, flowerpots, loaf pans or any other suitable container that will afford ample spacing for the seedlings to develop without being crowded. Each spring we grow for our garden in excess of 3000 plants so that the "flat method" is most essential in our operation.

Lift up the seedlings in the seed pan with a wood label or spoon handle so that the seedling may be lifted with all roots intact. Using the same label or spoon, open the soil in the marked off row in the flat to accommodate the seedlings roots and "tuck-in." Set the little plants *deep*—right up to the first pair of leaves (the seedling leaves). Gently press the soil around the plants to put the roots in good contact with the soil.

Water flat or container immediately after transplanting and keep in strong light but *out of the sun* for two or three days to give the little plants

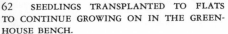

62   SEEDLINGS TRANSPLANTED TO FLATS
TO CONTINUE GROWING ON IN THE GREEN-
HOUSE BENCH.

a chance to recover from the move and then give all possible sunlight. If immediately after transplanting there should be a period of two or three days of cloudy weather, pans or flats may go right into the window where they are to grow. Should there be no place to keep them except in the sun, then protect them with a tent of brown paper, newspaper or cheesecloth as the hot sun at this point will cause severe wilting and may set back or injure them to a point where they will not recover.

CARE IN FLATS

Now that the seedlings have been assigned to a new growing medium to wait for their ultimate move to the outdoors, the gardener has only one objective—*to keep them growing!*

Do not attempt to set yourself a routine schedule of watering every other day or twice weekly. Water loss is slow on cloudy days and rapid when sunny and dry, so the need for water varies. Feel the soil with your finger and if not moist, water deeply and thoroughly.

The seedlings from this stage, with the proper conditions of temperature, light and water, should show healthy growth. Possibly there will be some casualties—a few losses from damp-off, from rough treatment in transplanting, or the house cat walking along the window sill—but the extremely critical seedling stages are behind you.

63 STARTING TO PINCH A FLAT OF 'RED PILLAR' SALVIA TO INDUCE STOCKY, BRANCHING GROWTH. THUMB NAIL AND FOREFINGER IS THE PREFERRED "TOOL."

64 THE PINCHING DEED IS DONE!

Do not neglect to "turn" the window sill containers occasionally to keep the seedlings growing upright.

PINCHING

Many seedlings benefit by one or two "pinchings" before they are ready for the garden to encourage them to branch and become compact and stocky. As you will note in the photos, pinching is nothing more than nipping out the top growth of the stem with thumb and forefinger. This practice is most beneficial for plants with a single stem, such as snapdragon, bedding dahlias and *Salvia farinacea,* but even petunias will be improved as the crown of the plant will be forced to send out horizontal side branches so necessary to keep the plant low growing. In the case of stem-branching plants, new side stems will be forced to grow near the bottom of the plant, resulting in sturdy, bushy growth.

HARDENING OFF

When the transplanted seedlings have become large enough to be placed in their permanent outdoor location *and* outside temperatures are suitable, it is essential that they be "acclimated" to their new environment.

Plants grown indoors are tender and exposure to outside sun, wind and temperatures without first hardening them off can cause the plant to wilt. Subjecting to chilly temperatures as in the case of some annuals and vegetables can cause the plants to become stunted. Therefore they should be placed in a protected area out of doors for a few days and nights before being planted to places in the garden. Should a night be unusually chilly, return the flats or pots to window or sun porch and place out of doors again the next day. When we speak of "protected areas," this means on a porch, in coldframes, under a shrub or at the foundation of the house, but it is very important they be placed where no wind or breezes will blow on them and they must be *partially shaded* with protection from full sun.

After several days in this position they may be given stronger sun but still must be protected from strong breezes. After exposing to the sun for several days to a week the plants should be ready for transplanting to the garden. During this period when water loss can be rapid, every care should be taken to see that the soil in flats or containers is kept moist *at all times.* Drying out at this stage can be fatal to the plants. If the gardener owns a coldframe, or will take the time to prepare a makeshift frame, there is no more ideal place for hardening off seedlings. The cover of the frame can be left on if the weather becomes unseasonably cold and removed when necessary. Excellent wind protection is afforded by the coldframe yet full light is available

65 DAHLIA SEEDLINGS TRANSPLANTED TO PLANTEX BANDS IN A FLAT. THESE SEEDLINGS DEVELOP SMALL TUBERS BY THE TIME THEY ARE READY TO BE SET OUT IN THE OPEN SO THAT THE LIMITED FIBROUS ROOT SYSTEM IS RELATIVELY UNDISTURBED BY THE USE OF INDIVIDUAL PLANT BANDS.

66 DAHLIAS, ALREADY PINCHED AND LARGE ENOUGH TO GO TO THE OPEN GARDEN OR FLOWERBED.

67   FLATS IN COLDFRAME, BROUGHT FROM
GREENHOUSE TO START THE HARDENING-OFF
PERIOD. THESE WILL BE COVERED WITH A
SASH FOR A WHILE.

68   FLATS UNDER PROTECTION FORM SUN
AND WIND, HARDENING OFF BEFORE TRANS-
PLANTING TO OPEN BEDS.

to the flats. Flats or containers are more easily watered and cared for in a frame. Should it not be possible to place plants in the garden at the proper time because of more urgent garden chores, or adverse weather conditions, it is an easy matter to feed the plants with a water-soluble fertilizer and keep them in good condition, growing vigorously, until such time as they are planted to permanent places in the garden.

While the plants are becoming accustomed to outdoor temperatures, the weather and the soil in all likelihood will also be warming up so that when the plants are set to the garden they will be ready for the change and active growth will continue.

At this point please let me add this one word of warning, and this is *most important.* These plants even though "hardened off" are still tender. Although they may be in the perennial family, which, when mature, start to grow while the weather is still cold and chilly and frost occurs often, they have been sown indoors, grown indoors and cared for indoors and are still not impervious to frost damage, although well hardened off to withstand outdoor conditions.

None of these plants which have been started indoors including those started in April in glass-covered coldframes can be exposed to *freezing* temperatures. Therefore, they should *never* be placed into the open garden *until all danger of frost has past.* One of my friends lost a whole flat of lovely delphinium seedlings because after hardening them off properly, she placed them in her garden a little too soon and the last frost killed them. Do not be too impatient. It is better to be safe than sorry. Care for your young plants until you can be sure it is safe to place them in the open garden.

PREPARATION OF SOIL FOR TRANSPLANTS

With the flatted or potted transplants hardened off and ready to be set out of doors, it seems timely to discuss the preparation of the soil at the permanent location in the garden or flower bed.

If you are one of those well organized individuals, and want to prepare the soil well in advance of the time when plants can be set out, so much the better. Just be sure that the soil is dry enough to be tilled or forked over. We always put in an early spring vegetable garden and we use the following tried and true test of whether the soil can be worked: Turn over a forkful and squeeze a handful of soil into a ball. Drop the ball from waist high and if it crumbles, it is ready to be worked. If the soil stays intact it is still too wet. Do not attempt to work wet soil. Soil moist, but with a crumbly consistency is a pleasure to work and an ideal growing medium. Working the earth while it is still wet and sticky destroys the good texture of the soil causing it to become lumpy and makes it extremely difficult to handle.

The soil should be dug and pulverized to a depth of at least 8 inches; 12 to 18 inches is better. For small areas a spade or a spading fork (our preference) can be used; for larger areas, in deference to an aching back, a small garden tiller can be rented on an hourly basis.

Even though the soil is fertile, it should be enriched with compost, leaf mold and/or peat moss and dried cow manure. Such organic matter contains only a small amount of fertilizer but it acts as a soil conditioner; it increases the bacterial growth which, as it decomposes, makes available to the plants nutrients in the soil. The reason for applying fertilizers is to prevent plant food deficiencies in the soil. Therefore soil testing is important so that you may have an accurate idea of what the deficiencies, if any, might be and the required type and quantity of any supplemental materials.

Most garden plants thrive on a soil which tests at a pH of 6.0 to 6.9 which is a shade under neutral. On the pH scale, 7.0 is considered neutral or in other words soil is neither acid nor alkaline but the two conditions are in exact balance. Too high or too low a pH can lock up certain needed elements in the soil to the detriment of the plants you are growing. Some plants such as azaleas and rhododendron, thrive only at 4.5 pH, a considerably acid

69   LOOKING SOUTH AT THE HARING'S
FIRST BACKYARD GARDEN, MAY 1940.

condition, but by and large the flowers and vegetables we grow do well in the range of pH 6.0 to 6.9.

A small soil test kit is most helpful to determine what essential ingredients the soil may lack and whether or not it is on the acid or alkaline side. While it is admitted that results of using soil test kits are not absolutely accurate, they do give the neophyte an indication of what the soil needs in the way of lime, nitrogen, phosphorous and potash. The kits are very easy to use if the simple directions are carefully followed. It is to be hoped that all gardeners whether experienced or inexperienced are in the habit of reading the labels and directions of all materials or equipment before embarking on any task of this kind.

The soil in our first garden was subsoil, the topsoil having been removed years before we bought the lot. Our soil test kit did not register any phosphorous at all. Being absolutely ignorant about soils and their make-up we decided there was something wrong with the chemical used in the test. It simply did not occur to us that it could be possible that our soil contained so little phosphorous that it would not register. It was several years before we discovered the truth. However, as we had as yet no compost, leafmold or other organic matter, and our budget was quite limited, we settled for a bag of commercial 5-10-5 fertilizer which supplied enough phosphorus to make our efforts satisfactory. A look at snapshots of our first garden discloses what success was had. Looking back on it now, we wonder how we achieved such excellent results with so little knowledge, so you see, even though you might be the rankest kind of amateur there is hope for you!

Let me digress for the benefit of inexperienced gardeners. When I say "compost," I am speaking of the practice of piling grass clippings, weeds, preferably before they go to seed, from flower beds and raked leaves into a pile in an out-of-the-way spot on the grounds, behind the garage or back of shrubs where these materials can be allowed to decompose to the point where they can be rubbed through a screen of quarter-inch mesh hardware cloth. The resulting materials can be added to your garden to improve and enrich the soil. "Leafmold" is that humus found under the outer covering of undecayed leaves in wooded areas. Very few of us live near wooded areas any more. Some of us are fortunate to have such spots on our own home grounds but the average homeowner does not have access to such material. If your home has been built in a development, you may discover, as we did with our first garden, that the topsoil has been removed and you are going to have to work with subsoil or "hard-pan."

Compost or peatmoss, or both, and sand (not beach sand but the coarser kind used by builders, a sort of light brown-sugar variety of sand) should be added in large quantities to loosen the soil and make it spongy and moisture retentive. Vermiculite, a variety of mica which has been "blown-up" or ex-

70 LOOKING EAST AT THE SAME BACK-YARD GARDEN AREA, TWO YEARS LATER, MAY, 1942.

panded is inexpensive and while it contains no plant food is excellent for improving the soil texture and its ability to hold moisture. Lime is also excellent to use in conditioning the soil in readying it for the garden. Lime has the capability of actually breaking up the hard lumps of subsoil, causing it to break down into smaller particles.

It seems timely to discuss at this point the basic necessity to maintain a proper soil pH for successful gardening. In simple terms the pH scale is an indication, much like a thermometer, of an acid or alkaline condition. The scale starts at 0.0, the most acid, and is graduated in tenths up to 14.0, the most alkaline. At the scale's midpoint, 7.0, is the neutral point, both acid and alkaline conditions are in balance. Since living plants will not endure acid soil conditions below 4.0, nor alkaline conditions above 9.0, the gardener's interest lies in the mid-scale area. In fact, except for the true acid-lovers, such as the rhododendrons and heaths, the great majority of garden plants, both flowers and vegetables, perform at best with soil pH between 6.0 to 6.9.

Here in the Northeast our soils are inclined to be on the acid side so that lime is important to our gardening. Calcium and magnesium, the active elements in lime, are needed by plants. To keep the pH of our garden between 6 and 6.9 we lime every other year. Lime moves very slowly through the soil. We try to apply lime in early winter before we have snow. For home gardeners we recommend ground limestone or an agricultural lime. These are slow acting and do not burn. In sections of the country where the pH is over 7 or near 8, home gardeners should use soil test kits and the materials recommended for reducing the alkalinity of the soil should be used. I recommend strongly that home gardeners apply to local County Agricultural Agents or State Agricultural Experimental stations for leaflets on these important matters.

Now that we have the seedbed pulverized with the required materials added, it is necessary to rake it smooth and free of large stones or lumps. In our area of the Northeast, the rocks seem to "grow." Each year several barrow loads are removed from our garden but there are always many more each time our soil is tilled or turned over. In our first garden, we not only had the back-breaking job of removing the rocks, but had to cart them by wheelbarrow to a spot several blocks away for disposal. We used to find it most amusing and ironic when cousins from south New Jersey visited us to find they actually envied our rocks. We begged them to take home as many as they could and they did! Their soils do not "grow" rocks!

TRANSPLANTING

With the garden or planting bed soil prepared, move the flats, pots or containers to the location where they are to be planted. These transplants should be *thoroughly* watered at least several hours before they are to be set out—and if possible the day before, to fully satisfy thirst needs so they will be plump and turgid with moisture.

Plants in clay or plastic pots can be easily removed with root ball intact by inverting and tapping the rim of the pot on any hard object.

Peat potted seedlings can be planted containers and all. For those in plant bands we prefer to carefully remove the paper bands before planting as we have found in many cases the paper does not disintegrate quickly and inhibits tiny feeder roots of a number of plants. Removing the band precludes this danger to plant roots.

71   CUTTING OUT SEEDLINGS OF AGERATUM WITH MASON'S TROWEL, PRIOR TO PLANTING IN PERMANENT LOCATIONS.

72   A SNAPDRAGON SEEDLING CUT OUT OF A FLAT WITH A MASON'S TROWEL FOR TRANS- PLANTING TO THE OPEN GARDEN.

Plants in flats we find most easy to extract by cutting the soil into cubes, as you would a pan of brownies, with a plant in the center of each cube.

We use a mason's small pointing trowel (our favorite garden tool) although an old kitchen knife will also do. With only a few exceptions as is the case with long tap-rooted plants the little plants come out of the flat as though they had been cast in a mold.

Most single-stem plants such as snapdragon, cosmos and tomatoes may be planted deeper than they were in flat or pot. Those with definite crowns such as delphinium and petunias should be planted exactly, as they grew, at ground level.

TRANSPLANTS IN FLOWER BEDS

In the flower borders or beds the soil should be opened up with a trowel (we use our mason's trowel for this too) creating a hole large enough and deep enough to accomodate the root ball. Work the soil firmly with the fingers or the handle of the trowel into good contact with the roots. Do not pack it in as though you were setting a fence post, but firm enough to be sure no voids or air pockets prevail. Leave a slight depression around the plant to assure that it gets its quota of water until such time as it becomes established. These minor depressions get leveled off the first time the soil is cultivated.

The spacing of the plants in the beds depends upon the variety of the plants. The low-growing bedding plants such as ageratum (dwarf) and 'Signet' marigold are set 6 to 8 inches apart. The tall-growing varieties of marigolds, zinnias and dahlias are set 16 to 20 inches apart. If you are in doubt as to spacing check your seed packet. Most seedsmen suggest on the individual packet the proper spacing between plants and between rows for each variety.

And now, most important, *water*. Do not wait for several hours while you set out several hundred plants. Water a dozen or so thoroughly as they are planted and when you have planted all of them, *water again.* Hopefully, you have been fortunate in selecting a cloudy day, or if not, planted in the late afternoon. If the following few days are sunny and breezy and your planting is not too extensive, some shading such as a berry basket, or a flower-pot over each newly set transplant is desirable. You will find some kinds such as celosia, *Alyssum saxatile* and asters, to mention a few, which resent transplanting and will show displeasure by wilting for three or four days. If possible, protect these "wilters" by shading.

Water all transplants every two or three days unless rains intervene, until they show full recovery and an indication that they *are growing* or as some say, so aptly, until they "take hold."

TRANSPLANTS TO THE OPEN GARDEN

We have discussed specifically the setting of seedling plants in flower beds. However, there will be some gardeners who will be setting out transplants in the open garden in rows rather than in beds. In this category fall the annual "cutting garden," the perennial "replacement" and cutting garden and last but by no means least, the vegetable garden. We, in our overly ambitious enthusiasm, include all of these groups in our garden. We enjoy having cut flowers in season throughout our home and take pleasure in providing visitors with ample bouquets. Our perennial flower beds are each spring refurbished where needed with new plants from the open garden inventory. Naturally we must have garden fresh vegetables, from asparagus in early spring to the frost-bitten rutabagas and Brussel's-sprouts in fall, and peas, beans, tomatoes, squash, peppers, eggplants and others during the summer.

The open garden, large or small is considerably easier to maintain than plantings in beds.

After the soil has been prepared as previously described, a stout stake is driven at each end of the row and a mason's line (a heavy cotton twine) is stretched taut between the stakes with the line 4 to 6 inches above the soil. Using a rake or hoe handle or a trowel, mark a furrow say one-half to 1 inch deep using the taut line as a guide. This procedure is pictured in the section on vegetables. Some folks can set the transplants using the line as a guide, but I find myself often wavering "off course," so I use the furrow to assure that my rows are reasonably straight.

The transplants are set the proper distance apart, depending on the ultimate size, tucked in, watered and shaded, if necessary, like those set in beds.

You will find that plants in rows are easy to cultivate whether by mechanical tiller, hoe or tine cultivator. We set our rows 30 inches apart to accommodate our tiller. With a limited garden area, spacing between rows can be reduced; here again depending on the ultimate size of the plant. Here also refer to the seedsman's packet which will in most cases advise the recommended spacing between plants and between rows.

Water as frequently as the weather requires until the plants are past the wilting stage and give evidence of continuing growth.

From this point, cultivate the soil lightly when seedling weeds appear (at this stage it is a simple, easy and quick chore) with a tine cultivator, rake, hoe or scuffle hoe whichever implement best suits your preference. Water deeply once a week if no rains occur. The home gardener might prefer to use a mulch, if available, at this time to keep down weeds and retain soil moisture.

OPEN GARDEN SEED SOWING

Many seeds of annuals, vegetables and perennials lend themselves to being planted directly to the open garden.

73   WINTER RYE GRASS, GREEN COVER CROP ON VEGETABLE AND CUTTING GARDEN, IN MID-MARCH, FROM OCTOBER SOWING THE PREVIOUS YEAR.

74   TILLING UNDER RYE. AREA WAS LIMED IN LATE FALL AND 5-10-5 AND SUPERPHOS-PHATE APPLIED BEFORE TURNING UNDER.

75   CUTTING GARDEN, TILLED, RAKED AND ROWS MARKED, READY FOR SEEDS.

76   PRE-WATERING FURROWS PRIOR TO PLACING SEEDS, TO ASSURE PROMPT GERM-INATION.

77   SOWING SEEDS, PROPERLY SPACED, DE-PENDING ON VARIETY, AND THEN LIGHTLY PRESSED OR LIGHTLY COVERED, ACCORDING TO THE SIZE OF THE SEED.

There are the "cool" varieties, notably in the vegetable family such as peas, carrots, beets, the cabbage and lettuce "families" and others which germinate well in the cold moist soil of early spring. Most of them also require for best growth and performance, the cool spring and early summer temperatures. Direct planting in the outdoor garden as soon as the soil can be worked in the very early spring is so suitable for these very early "starters" that it seems unnecessary to provide for them the special conditions which would be required to start them prematurely indoors or under glass.

78 THE ROWS HAVE BEEN SEEDED AND THE ENTIRE AREA WATERED WITH A FINE MIST SPRAY USING THE SUPPLEX HOSE. DO NOT PERMIT SOIL TO DRY OR FORM CRUST UNTIL SEEDS ARE WELL STARTED. SEEDLINGS CANNOT PENETRATE A DRY CRUST, NOR WILL THEY SURVIVE IF SOIL MOISTURE IS NOT CONSTANTLY AVAILABLE.

79 THREE MONTHS LATER, IN MID-AUGUST, THE ZINNIA BED IN REAR IS A RIOT OF COLOR AND THE ASTER GARDEN IN THE FOREGROUND IS IN FULL BUD, SETTING THE STAGE FOR A SPECTACULAR SHOW ALL THE WEEKS OF EARLY AUTUMN.

There are also those varieties which respond well to warm soil and pleasant temperatures—those tender things that absolutely refuse to germinate or to grow under chilly conditions, such as the squashes and melons, tomatoes and beans, zinnias, marigolds and many others. It is really not too surprising, for many of these plants have come to us from native haunts in the tropics and subtropics. Most of these lovers of warmth will, with warm soil and balmy night temperatures, germinate in a few days and grow rapidly. They can become a real problem to the inexperienced gardener who attempts to start them too early indoors and finds himself with too many, too large plants with inadequate growing space, particularly if hardening off must await proper weather conditions. This group, sown under proper outdoor conditions will virtually "jump." By judicious thinning the seedlings will continue to grow undisturbed by transplanting, to perform their complete life cycle well before the first killing frosts.

May I refer you to the detailed description in this chapter covering the preparation of the soil under the section "Preparation of Soil for Transplants." I have debated, in view of its importance to successful gardening, whether I should fully repeat those instructions at this point, but have refrained in the interest of brevity.

It has been my intent and fond hope that the inexperienced gardener for whom this book is primarily written will by the time this section has been read have been indelibly impressed with the basic requirements for a properly prepared planting medium.

When we plant seeds directly to the outdoor seedbeds we usually plant them in rows. I do not consider broadcasting seeds over a seedbed to be sensible for the reason that it is difficult to differentiate between flower seedlings and weed seedlings. Even the least experienced gardener can look down a row and from their similarity recognize the seedlings. First a stake is placed at either end of the row with stout twine stretched between stakes. The row is then marked with the end of a rake, or a trowel if preferred.

Distance between rows must be pre-determined by the size of the plant when mature, when seeds are sown to grow and bloom in place. You will find it easy to lay out your rows if you use two sets of stakes. Before you pull up the stakes from your first row, merely measure off the desired spacing from each stake and drive the end stakes for the second row. Progress similarly with each new row and you will be assured of straight and parallel rows, resulting in a better looking garden and one easy to maintain.

Before sowing the seed the rows should be well watered. If you live in a section of the country where the sun is hot and dry you might want to experiment with using vermiculite or milled sphagnum through the length of the row. Although personally we have never had to resort to this method, these materials will hold moisture longer than soil. For watering the row before planting seed, I like to use a watering can. The rose (screw-top spray head) can be removed for this purpose. However, I find that if water is poured slowly from the watering can it can be easily controlled with the rose in place. The shallow furrow serves beautifully as a guiding trench for this pre-watering step.

80   THE AUTHOR'S PREFERRED OPEN GARDEN LABEL, A TWELVE-INCH STURDY WOODEN TAG, HIGHLY LEGIBLE AND NOT DISTURBED BY CULTIVATING.

81   PREPARING TO THIN OUT A ROW OF 'ENVY' ZINNIAS WHICH WERE SEEDED DIRECTLY IN THE OPEN GARDEN.

82   THE THINNINGS ARE PUT INTO A PAN OF WATER TO WHICH A TEASPOON OF RAPID-GRO HAS BEEN ADDED.

83   THINNINGS HAVE BEEN REPLANTED ABOUT TWELVE INCHES APART TO PROVIDE ADDITIONAL PLANTS FOR THE CUTTING GARDEN.

84   A GOOD, DEEP WATERING WITH A SOAKER HOSE IMMEDIATELY AFTER TRANSPLANTING MINIMIZES WILTING. TRANSPLANTS OF THIS SIZE CAN BE EXPECTED TO WILT FOR SEVERAL DAYS.

A good *wooden* label is a "must" for the outdoor seedbed. We prefer 6 inches or larger and it may be painted or unpainted. A waterproof pencil is also a must since an ordinary pencil or pen will soon be obliterated by the weather. These greasetype waterproof marking pencils are available at stationery or garden supply stores. I like to mark the name of the plant, date planted and the name of the seedsman as well. This gives me information on how long it takes for that specific plant to germinate, how good the germination was and from whom seed was ordered to serve as a guide for future seed orders. These labels are most helpful to visitors as well, particularly those who are interested in some specific variety.

Fine dustlike seeds and a little larger such as those of ageratum or snapdragon should *not* be covered but pressed lightly into the soil. Seeds a little larger need only the lightest dusting. Large seeds need to be barely covered. Heavy soils will crust and make it difficult for seedlings to break through, particularly if the weather should be hot and dry after planting. In my present garden the soil is very light yet I follow the same practice for covering seeds, with excellent results, as I used to do when gardening on heavy clay soil. I realize this procedure does not conform with that usually recommended, as many instructions suggest planting seeds with a covering four times the thickness of the seeds. This is difficult for the inexperienced gardener to determine. In the past I have experienced many failures using this method, on both light and heavy soils and I do not personally endorse this procedure.

Weeds must be removed while seedlings are still very small. For this, I like the mason's small pointing trowel which can be bought in any hardware store. I simply sweep away small weed seedlings from along the row. Of necessity, when seedlings are this small, weeds coming up between seedlings must be hand pulled but I find this a most enjoyable chore on a fine spring day with the sun warm on by back; with bird song all about and enjoying the perfume of freshly mown grass. Sitting back on my haunches, I look up at the blue sky and white clouds scudding by and give thanks for just being alive and able to spend time in my garden.

When seedlings have grown to about 3 inches they are thinned to stand in the row according to directions on packet or in catalog. Thinning should ideally be done just after a rain or shower. We put our thinnings to good use also—either by using them as "fill ins" in our own flower beds or giving them to friends who do not have the facilities or the time to grow their own.

As the thinnings are pulled we place them in a bucket with about 4 inches of water to which has been added a tablespoon of soluble fertilizer such as Rapid-Gro or Miracle Gro. In this solution they will stay fresh and turgid for a day or two.

Removal of excess plants usually disturbs roots of wanted plants and if the day should be sunny and hot these plants will likely wilt and be set back sometimes beyond recovery. I prefer to do this chore on a "drizzly" day if possible. However, if the weather is hot and dry and thinning must be done, we use our Supplex hose, a triple-tube, pin-perforated flat hose 50 feet long and water rows well, both before and immediately after thinning.

If mulches are available, such as peat moss, buckwheat hulls, salt hay or grass clippings, fine. These will keep down the weeds and retain soil moisture. However, if using peat moss, make sure the soil is thoroughly wet before applying mulch as the moss is usually so dry it will "steal" moisture from the soil to the detriment of the plants. If sawdust is used as a mulch be sure to apply a good dusting of a complete fertilizer such as 5-10-5 (or sulphate of ammonia) and water in thoroughly as sawdust robs the soil of nitrogen when it starts "breaking down" or decomposing as it were. If you cannot afford to purchase material for mulching do not worry about it. Cultivating the garden after each rain maintains a "dust" mulch, a practice which has been used by gardeners for centuries and is still effective. Of course this must be done often and timely, thus making the work of the gardener more laborious. Such cultivation should be only light enough to break the crust of the soil to permit the rain to penetrate the soil particles more readily and to keep the soil in good tilth. This surface aeration also serves as an insulating layer to minimize loss of soil moisture which accounts for the term "dust mulch."

3. Annual Flowers
from Seed

WHAT are known to gardeners as "annuals" are plants that bloom in the open garden the same year the seeds are sown and that do not live over the following winter. Botanically, annuals are plants that normally complete the entire life cycle within one growing season; roots and crowns die. Many so-called annuals which we grow in the North are actually perennials in warmer climes. Pinks (dianthus), snapdragons, cynoglossum and *Salvia farinacea* are examples of such. In protected gardens these will sometimes live over in the North when winters are mild.

Annuals are often spoken of as hardy, half-hardy and tender. This, I think is very confusing and often misleading. I often see ageratum on lists of hardy annuals, yet this is one which needs warmth for germination and in my garden turns brown at the slightest hint of frost. It is apparently included in the list of hardy annuals because its seed will live over the winter in the garden, but in my experience it does not germinate until long after the last killing frost in spring when both weather and soil have become quite warm. Some annuals are more impervious to frost than others. Larkspur, cornflower and Shirley poppies if permitted to drop their seed will germinate in late fall and the little plants will survive the winter. That is why it is often recommended that they be planted in the fall. They are likely to be very sturdy and produce larger and more perfect blooms than those from spring sowing. All of these resent transplanting although they can be moved in earliest spring if extra care is exercised and will grow quite well in spite of being disturbed.

Some annuals which need a long growing season cannot complete their life cycle in the northern section of the country and so must be sown early either indoors or in coldframes. In our area, April 15 is a good date to sow these if the coldframe method is used. In the greenhouse or in the house some of them need to be started as early as late February. Among these are petunias (especially the doubles and frilled), snapdragon, lobelia, salvia and ageratum.

Other annuals which grow fairly quickly are best sown directly in the garden out of doors, about the first week in May in southern Connecticut. In a protected garden on the south side of a building or wall or near rivers or lakes they can sometimes be safely planted toward the end of April. Some of these are candytuft, zinnias, marigolds, asters, celosia (cockscomb) and others. In the latitude of Philadelphia a week or so earlier; Virginia and North Carolina two to three weeks earlier.

Some annuals germinate very quickly; others take several weeks. Gardeners must learn to be patient and give them every chance to grow. In my garden, bells of Ireland (molucella) for instance, depending upon weather conditions will take as long as three weeks to germinate. Often those slow to germinate also are sporadic in germination. They sometimes will lag around through June and then grow by leaps and bounds and by mid-July will almost have reached full growth.

Annuals are the mainstay of the summer garden. They give us color long after the early perennials have finished for the year and before the colorful display of the chrysanthemums and hardy asters in the late fall. The versatile annuals can be used in many ways. They can be used as ground covers; to overplant tulips and other spring blooming bulbs; to fill vacant spots in perennial beds and borders; to edge walks and paths; to fill in gaps when foundation plantings are young; to hide unsightly spots such as the neighbor's garbage can or clothes dryer!

Annuals are wonderful for renters who do not feel they should spend money to landscape property belonging to someone else, but do want to have colorful flowers during the summer. They can be planted in beds as small as 3 x 6 feet or 2 x 10 feet, provided they get at least six hours of sun daily. A 6- x 6-foot bed of annuals provides a generous supply of flowers for a whole summertime of bouquets.

When I began to work with small horticultural groups, I learned that many beginning gardeners were not aware that they could very easily grow annuals from seed. Because so many flats of annuals are offered for sale in the neighborhood garden supply center, they were of the opinion that it would not be possible for the home gardener to start them for himself. I think it is fine that the garden supply shops sell flats of plants and in dozen quantities for the home garden or window box. These are fine plants grown from seed especially produced by wholesale seedsmen for the purpose and are perfect for those who do not have the time or the facilities for growing plants from seed. Certainly they are the answer if you want an instant effect on the home grounds. However, not all varieties can be bought in this manner and frequently the home gardener cannot find plants which will suit the color scheme in his or her garden. The garden club worker, always on the lookout for flowers which will win blue ribbons in flower shows, can rarely find an unusual or new variety in the local garden supply center, so it behooves this gardener to start from seed.

The leading seedsmen advertise catalogs in newspapers and garden magazines and every gardener should subscribe to at least one garden magazine to keep up with the wondrous things which are going on in the garden world. Send for the catalogs early, most of which are available in early January. Study them. Read what the seedsman has to say about each variety, its habits and needs. Choose the seed carefully for the needs of your garden and send orders for seed early. The supply of really unusual ones may be depleted if you delay too long. Pick up in your local shop any seeds that strike your fancy also. They are there for your convenience and it is fun and a challenge to try something new.

While annuals will grow and bloom in ordinary soil, they will give much more satisfactory results if the beds where they are to be sown are prepared as discussed under open garden seed sowing in chapter two. As suggested also in that chapter, and I feel this needs to be reiterated over and over again for the benefit of the inexperienced, *very fine* seeds should *never* be covered but sprinkled thinly along the row and patted *very* gently into the soil. Seeds a little larger like those of China aster may be *very lightly* covered. For seeds large enough to be covered a light sifting over them so that they may not

85 THE AUTHOR PAUSES FOR A MOMENT TO
APPRECIATE THE GLORIOUS BOUNTY OF
FLOWERS IN HER CUTTING GARDEN.

be seen is sufficient. Covering seed too deeply very frequently accounts for
the failure of annuals to germinate.

The best time to plant seeds of annuals varies over the United States.
The growth and vigor of annuals depend on many factors—soil, fertility,
moisture and general climate in the area. The cultural directions given in this
book are general enough so that anyone, anywhere, can follow them. However,
if you live in the deep South or in areas warmer than the Northeast where I
have had all of my gardening experience, write to your State Agricultural
Experiment Station (see Appendix) for pamphlets on growing annuals and

perennials. The best dates for sowing seed in your area are usually given in these leaflets. Most knowledgeable gardeners are happy to share experiences with others and if you ask, their advice will guide you as to what annuals to plant and when, in your locality. Except for those which need a long growing season to mature, or rare or expensive seeds which need to be protected from heavy rains and other adverse conditions most annuals can be planted directly to the garden. In the Northeast if the gardener is not sure of the safe date to plant seeds to the open garden, it would be wise to delay sowing until the oak leaves are "the size of a squirrel's ears." For those who have never had an opportunity to measure a squirrel's ears, that means about an inch long.

Annuals on the whole are sun lovers. There are only a few which do well in partial shade. Deep shade is almost impossible. However, in our first garden the flower beds received only six to eight hours of sun a day because of the presence of several large trees which we resolutely refused to allow our builder to remove. Our annuals were satisfactory although they did not compare to those which we are able to grow in our present garden where they receive sun for most of the day. Do not think of depriving yourself the pleasures of growing annuals if you cannot give them all the conditions they prefer. They are wonderfully amenable to all but the most impossible conditions. We have a grassy path in our garden approximately 250 feet long lined with flowering crab apples. This walk is edged each year with ageratum backed up by scarlet sage (red salvia). The path receives alternate light and shade and dappled sunlight throughout the summer yet both of these sun-lovers grow and bloom most satisfactorily.

In the encyclopedia of annuals which follows I have endeavored to give as much as possible of my own experiences in growing each kind from seed as well as other helpful hints I have been able to research for this book.

ANNUALS TO GROW FROM SEED

AGATHEA (FELICIA) BLUE DAISY OR KINGFISHER DAISY ☐ Daisy-like flower 1 inch across. Sow indoors March with germination in 10 days; outdoors in late spring, 14 to 20. Needs warmth (65 to 70 degrees) for good germination. May be started in cold-frame in April. Likes sunshine and heat. Very good in the South, where it is usually planted in the early spring. Grows to 1 foot; set plants 4 inches apart.

AGERATUM (FLOSS FLOWER) ☐ Sow indoors February to March with germination in 3 to 5 days; outdoors late spring, 7 to 10 days. Needs warmth for germination. Spring sowing in lower South. May be started in coldframe in April in North. Self-sows readily. Pretty fluffy heads of lavender-blue flowers; blooms all summer. Dwarf sorts good for edging, taller kinds for beds and borders. Sometimes will wilt for a day or two after transplanting but quickly recovers. In very hot weather wilting of leaves indicates need for water. Set dwarfs 4 to 6 inches apart and tall sorts 10 to 12 inches.

ACROCLINIUM ☐ An everlasting also called "strawflower." Sow outdoors when soil has become quite warm with 10 to 12 days for germination. Grows 2½ feet tall; space 15 inches apart. Likes heat and sunshine. May be sown in autumn in lower South for winter bloom.

ARCTOTIS (AFRICAN DAISY OR BLUE-EYED DAISY) ☐ Sow indoors April with germination in 5 days. Needs warmth for germination. Personally I prefer to plant seeds directly to garden outdoors in May with germination in 8 to 10 days. Transplants well if watered thoroughly before and after moving. Plant in early spring in lower South. Does not mind drought conditions once established. Grows 1 to 1½ feet tall; set 12 to 15 inches apart. The new arctotis hybrids come in deep colors of yellow, orange and red. They are lower growing with rosettes hugging the ground and flower stems 8 to 10 inches high. Space 12 inches apart for good bedding effect.

ALYSSUM (SWEET ALYSSUM OR LOBULARIA) ☐ Tiny clusters of fragrant white flowers. Sow indoors April with germination in 3 to 6 days; outdoors late spring, 7 to 10. Needs warmth for germination. We prefer to start in April indoors, then transplant to flats. They grow quickly once germination is had. Shear in July to keep blossoms coming. Good edging plant which blooms all summer. May be had in white, pink lavender or rose. Grows 4 inches high; set 4 to 6 inches apart. Varieties 'Rosie O'Day,' with rose flowers and 'Royal Carpet' with purple are very good.

AMARANTHUS ☐ These plants are grown mostly for colorful foliage. Varieties include 'Aurora,' 'Joseph's Coat,' 'Fountain Plant' (A. salicifolius) and 'Green Tassel.' Best planted outdoors where they are to grow, with germination in warmth in 8 to 15 days. May be started indoors toward end of April in North. Space 18 to 20 inches between plants. Most varieties grow from 3 to 4 feet tall. Some dwarf sorts available. Variety 'Green Tassel' is especially interesting for its clusters of rope like flowers of an unusual shade of pale green.

ANTIRRHINUM (SNAPDRAGON) ☐ Sow indoors in February or March with germination in 7 days; outdoors coldframe in April, 10 to 20 days. Needs warmth for good germination. Self-sows freely. Pinching plant when 3 to 4 inches high helps make a well branched plant with many spikes. We set ours in garden in mid-May giving 15 inches between plants. When fully grown we "hill-up" plants, that is, hoe soil up around bottom of stems for about 4 inches to keep high winds from blowing them over. They may also be staked if preferred. Bloom late June to frost. Spikey flowers in entrancing shades of white, yellow, red, rose, lavender and others. Grow 2½ to 3 feet tall. In the lower South often grown as perennials and in protected spots in the North will often live over a second year. Varieties I can highly recommend are 'Rocket,' 'Ginger Snaps,' 'Trumpet,' 'Supreme,' 'White Rufles,' 'Tetra Snaps' and the dwarf 'Floral Carpet' which grows to 8 inches and is best spaced 6 inches apart. The newer varieties called 'Bright Butterflies' and 'Bellflowers' performed well in my garden the first year although they suffered from drought.

ANCHUSA CAPENSIS (FORGET-ME-NOT) ☐ We prefer to sow this directly to the garden in mid-May. Germinates in 10 to 14 days. Flowers are indigo blue. Variety 'Blue Bird' is my favorite and will often live over to bloom a second year. Self-sows readily. Likes full sun. Shear after the first bloom in order to encourage the plant to continue to send up spikes. Blooms mid-summer to frost in my garden. May be planted in autumn in the lower South. Grows to 15 inches high; space 10 inches apart.

ARGEMONE (PRICKLY POPPY) ☐ Flowers in white or pale yellow with prickly gray and white foliage. Sow indoors in April with germination in 6 days or outdoors in May with germination in 14 to 21 days. Needs warmth for germination. Likes sun and heat. Considered a weed in many places in the lower South. In my garden I find it best sown where it is to bloom but it can be started indoors and transplanted from flats with care. Does well on poor soils. Grows 2 to 3 feet tall. Allow 15 to 20 inches between plants.

ASTER, CHINA ☐ Everyone knows the China aster which comes in shades of white, blue, pink, lavender, wine, yellow and rose. May be sown indoors in April with germination in 7 days; outdoors late spring 10 to 14 days. As asters resent transplanting I prefer to plant mine directly to the garden in May, using early, mid-season and late varieties. They start to bloom in late July and bloom until frost. Allow 15 inches between plants. In my cutting garden I grow them only 8 inches apart with excellent success. Heights vary from 12 to 24 inches. Varieties which have always done well in my garden include 'Fluffy Ruffles,' 'Giant Crego,' 'American Beauty,' 'Giant Fluffy,' 'Early Bird,' 'Curlilocks,' 'Duchess,' 'Powderpuffs,' 'Blue, Rose and Pink Waves' and 'Green Eyes.'

BABY'S-BREATH, SEE GYPSOPHILA

BABY BLUE EYES, SEE NEMOPHILA

BACHELOR'S-BUTTON, SEE CENTAUREA

BALSALM (LADY SLIPPER) ☐ Sow outdoors where they are to grow with germination in 7 to 10 days. Attractive, disease-free foliage with single or double blossoms on main spike. They resent transplanting and wilt badly for a day or two after being moved. Come into bloom very quickly. They have bloomed until frost in my garden in spite of unprecedented drought. Grows to 18 inches. I prefer to space mine fairly close, about 10 inches apart although 15 inches is recommended by most authorities.

BELLS OF IRELAND (MOLUCELLA) ☐ Unusual plant with whorls of bell-shaped green "flowers" (actually these are bracts which surround small white flowers) on long spikes. Sow indoors in March with germination in 8 days or sow where they are to grow in the garden with germination in 14 to 25 days. *This plant needs warmth for good germination.* Seeds germinate best when soil temperature has reached 70 degrees. Germination is slow but sure if the gardener will be patient and give it enough time. Starts to bloom by the end of July in my garden and continues until frost. Self-sows readily but will not germinate until the weather is warm and settled. I do not plant my seeds until May 23 and germination is nearly always 100 per cent. Resents transplanting. Grows 2½ to 3 feet; allow 15 inches between plants.

BRACHYCOME (SWAN RIVER DAISY) ☐ Flowers are daisy-like in a lovely shade of blue, but only about 1 inch across. Sow indoors in April with germination in 6 days; outdoors late spring, 9 to 14. Needs warmth for germination. Does not do well in areas of very hot summers. Grows 12 to 15 inches high. Give but 6 inches between plants for good bedding effect.

BROWALLIA ☐ Semi-trailing plants with white or blue flowers somewhat like campanula. Sow indoors in March with germination in 12 days. Needs 70 to 75 degrees for good germination. Very good for hanging baskets. Pinch plants when 6 inches tall for shaplier, bushier plants. Needs protection from late afternoon sun. Will self-sow under good conditions. 12 to 18 inches in height; allow 10 to 15 inches between plants. Good varieties are 'Blue Bells,' 'Silver Bells' and 'Sapphire.' These plants are very easy to grow.

CACALIA (EMILIA) ☐ Also called tassel flower or Flora's paint brush. I prefer to sow this outdoors where it is to bloom. Germination takes place in 12 to 15 days. Blooms from mid-July to frost in my garden. For good effect space plants 8 inches although spacing them 6 inches apart is satisfactory. Flower is small of unusual shades of orange and scarlet.

CALENDULA ☐ Start indoors in March for early bloom with germination in 7 days. Needs 60 to 65 degrees for good germination. I prefer to sow mine directly where they are to bloom in mid-May. Best blooms are had where summers are cool. In the lower South sow in late fall for winter bloom. Earliest spring sowing is recommended for the upper South for bloom while weather is still cool. Grows 15 inches tall; space about 12 inches between plants. Good varieties are 'Jewel,' 'Sunset' and 'Pacific Beauty.'

CALIFORNIA POPPY (SEE ESCHSCHOLTZIA)

CALLIOPSIS ☐ Sow indoors late March with 5 days for germination. Outdoors May, 8-14 days. Tall or dwarf varieties. Daisy like flowers of gold; some mahogany-tipped. Best planted where they are to grow. For the South do best when sown in the fall. Dwarf sorts grow 8 to 12 inches; space 6 inches apart. Taller varieties to 2 feet; allow 10 to 15 inches between plants. Self-sows freely. Has short blooming season.

CANDYTUFT, SEE IBERIS

CASTOR BEAN, SEE RICINUS

86   ANNUAL ASTERS PROVIDE A SOLID BLANKET OF PASTEL COLOR AT THIS ENTRY ALL DURING AUGUST AND SEPTEMBER.
Bodger Seeds, Ltd.

CELOSIA (CALLED COCKSCOMB) ☐ Sow indoors in late April. Germination 7 days. Outdoors, May, 10 to 20 days. Needs warmth for good germination. Likes sun and heat. Resents transplanting. Variety *cristata* is the crested variety and comes in a variety of gorgeous shades of rose, pink, coral, salmon, pumpkin and yellow. Interesting texture and shapes. Variety *plumosa* is the plumed variety and is spectacular with large fluffy heads of flowers in shades of red and orange as well as yellow and gold. In our garden the largest heads are obtained by sowing seeds directly where they are to grow. Transplanting seems to cause the heads to split although we find the smaller heads better for flower arranging. This is one of the finest flowers for drying for winter bouquets as the colors do not fade. Dwarf sorts: thin to 12 inches apart. Tall ones: 18 to 20 inches apart.

CENTAUREA (BACHELOR'S-BUTTON) ☐ Sow indoors April, germinates 7 days. Outdoors early spring, 10 to 15. Variety *cyanus* or cornflower is best known; flowers are blue, pink, white, maroon or rose. Likes full sun and rich soil. Resents transplanting. We prefer to sow where they are to grow. In the South sow in late fall or early winter for spring bloom. In the North the largest flowers are had by sowing in the fall. The small plantlets will usually live over the winter to start into growth fairly early. Blooming period is only about 6 to 8 weeks in our locality; grows 2-2½ feet tall; space 12 inches apart.

CENTAUREA GYMNOCARPA (DUSTY MILLER) ☐ Grown mostly for the lovely gray foliage. May be started in heat indoors in April and transplanted to flat for garden planting in mid-May in North. Can stand much frost and sometimes in mild winter will live over in my garden. Grows 15-18 inches tall; space 15 inches apart.

CENTAUREA SWEET SULTAN ☐ Fall planting is recommended in the South. I prefer to sow directly to garden in early May where they are to bloom. Flowers are lavender fluffy heads. I like to keep mine fairly close for best effect—about 12 inches apart. Grows 2½ to 3 feet tall.

CENTRANTHERUM MANAOS BEAUTY ☐ Needs warmth for germination. Best started indoors in March. Germinates in 4 days; outdoors late spring in May, 7-14 days. Leaves are crinkled of blue-green with 1-inch flowers of lavender. Loves heat and sun. Grows to 18 inches high. Allow 12 to 18 inches between plants. Withstands drought. Good for bedding and very good as a border along garage or walk. Self-sows freely.

CINERARIA DIAMOND ☐ Another plant known as "Dusty Miller." Start indoors in March with germination in 8 days. Needs warmth for germination. Outdoors late spring in May, 10-15 days. Needs long growing season. Transplants fairly well. Grown mostly for foliage for contrast in beds or borders. Height 12 to 15 inches. Allow 10 inches between plants.

CINERARIA SILVER QUEEN ☐ Lower growing than Diamond and a fine variety. Allow 8 inches between plants for bedding. Will sometimes live over in my garden and produce yellow flowers. Foliage is lovely. I prefer to start this one very early indoors to be of good size when planting season begins.

CHRYSANTHEMUM (ANNUAL) ☐ Start in February or March indoors. Germination 8 days. Outdoors late spring, 15 to 20. These do not like hot, dry summers. Fine in cooler regions and a well grown plant is gorgeous. Frankly it does not do well in my garden as it needs a cooler and moister climate than I can give it. Grows 18 inches, needs 15 inches between plants.

CLARKIA ELEGANS ☐ Indoors 5-7 days for germination; outdoors early spring, 15 to 20. Needs to be cool for germination. Grows best in cool, moist areas like Denver, Seattle and the upper North. Spikey flowers in rose, cream, salmon and white. Sow in autumn in lower South for winter bloom. May be started in coldframe in March in New England. Grows 12 to 15 inches high. Allow 12 inches between plants. The new F_1 hybrids withstand drought and heat quite well in my garden.

CLEOME (SPIDER FLOWER) ☐ I prefer to plant this outdoors where it is to flower. Germination in 10 to 20 days in my garden planted the 10th of May. Prefers warmth for good germination. Loves heat and sun. Grows well in all parts of the country. Flowers are showy heads of pink or white. Seed is very small. Do not cover but pat into soil. Grows 3-6 feet tall, space 24 inches apart. Self-sows freely. Varieties 'Pink Queen' and the white-flowered 'Helen Campbell' are very good.

COLEUS ☐ Grown for its gorgeous foliage; one of the best annuals for shade. Best started indoors any time from February to April with germination in 7 to 10 days. Seeds need warmth. Do not set outdoors until weather has become very warm. Pinch tops when 6 inches high for good bushy plants. Grows 12 to 15 inches high; space 10 to 15 inches apart.

COSMOS ☐ May be started indoors in April. Germination in 5 days. I prefer to sow outdoors in late spring where they are to grow; germination in 5-10 days. One of the easiest annuals to grow. Early blooming varieties are to be had. I particularly like the 'Sensation' varieties which come in pinks, rose and white. The new lower growing variety 'Sunset' which was an All-America Selections winner for 1966 germinates quickly outdoors in my garden. Starts to bloom the first of July. This variety is more dwarf than the others, growing to 2½ feet; space 12 inches apart for bedding. Flowers are bright gold. 'Sensation' varieties grow to 4 feet and should be spaced 15 inches apart.

COCKSCOMB (SEE CELOSIA)

CUPHEA (FIRECRACKER PLANT) ☐ Best started indoors in March in heat as it needs a long growing season to come into bloom in the North. Germination in 7 to 14 days. Loves sun and heat. Will grow most anywhere. 10 to 18 inches tall; allow 8 to 12 inches between plants. Pretty foliage with bright red tubular flowers.

CYNOGLOSSUM AMABILE (CHINESE FORGET-ME-NOT) ☐ Excellent blue flowers although the white ones are pretty too. Very good along north and east walls. Resents hot late afternoon sun. In my garden I prefer to sow in May where they are to grow. These self-sow freely. Blooming season is short, about 8 weeks here in Connecticut.

DAHLBORG DAISY (WAHLENBERGIA OR THYMOPHYLLA) ☐ Needs warmth for germination. Best sown indoors in April in heat, 7 days to germination. Outdoors late spring in May 15 to 20 days. Seeds are very fine; do not cover. Flat out carefully as little plants are very fragile. These are miniature plants with fern-like foliage and pretty half-inch orange or yellow flowers. Darling in rock gardens. Grows 6 inches high; space 3 inches between plants for best effect.

DAHLIA ☐ Although dahlia may belong in the chapter under bulbs, tubers and corms I am including it in this section because the small bedding types are so easily grown from seed that I use them like annuals. Planted indoors in March they germinate in 3-6 days. As I like to use the 'Fall Festival' variety throughout my perennial border for color of flower and foliage after the spring bulb foliage of tulips and daffodils has disappeared I grow these early in my green house and place them in plant bands in flats. They start to bloom in Early July and continue to hard frost, being at their best when days and nights are cool. I have also started these out of doors in my cutting garden where they are to grow and they start to bloom by early August. Gardeners in the upper South in areas where annuals are started in mid-April should try these bedding dahlias planted from seed out of doors. I have also been just as successful with other varieties of dahlias—the cactus-flowered, the giant-flowered and pom-poms from out-of-doors seed sowing. The bedding varieties grow about 15 to 18 inches tall and should be spaced about 12 inches apart.

DATURA (ANGEL'S TRUMPET, ALSO CALLED MOONFLOWER IN THE SOUTH) ☐ Needs warmth for germination; 7 days sown indoors in late March; 15 to 20 days outdoors sown in May in the North. Needs warmth for germination. They come into bloom in July in my garden. Sometimes lives over for several years although a particularly bad winter will kill them. The plant, however, if the crown has lived through the winter, does not show above ground until June in my garden. Self-sows freely. Foliage is lovely gray with gorgeous trumpet-shaped blossoms. Blooms until frost. Variety *meteloides* is the most dependable for my area although I also like the variety *fastuosa* because it has double pale lavender blooms. Variety *suaveolens* is shrub-like, grows to 5 feet and is wonderful in frost-free sections. Plants of *meteloides* and *fastuosa* grow 15 to 20 inches tall and need 18 inches between plants. Wonderful to fill in sparse foundation plantings if they are in sun. Like sun and heat.

DELPHINIUM (ANNUAL LARKSPUR) ☐ This perennial favorite coming in blue or pink shades is lovely when well grown. Seed needs to be kept cool about 60 degrees for germination indoors in March. Germinates under fluorescent lights in 14 days. Although authorities claim this should be planted out of doors as early as soil can be worked in the North, I have found these plants to be superior to the ones started early and placed in plant bands so that there is no shock to transplanting. Those plants which germinate in late fall will live over the winter in our garden and these are the best ones we grow. However, they will bloom for only about a 6-week period. Self-sown plants bloom a little later but are superior to early spring-sown plants. Grow 2½ to 3 feet tall. Space 12 inches apart for good effect. I let some of these self-sow in my perennial border each year where they are really lovely for weeks.

DIANTHUS (PINKS) ☐ These old-fashioned pinks are easily grown from seed; sown indoors in February or March they take 7 days to germinate. Planted in May out of doors they take 10 to 15 days. Bloom early and continue for the summer until frost. These are fine for winter bloom in the deep South. Varieties that I find excellent are Wivelsfield, *chinensis* (which sometimes lives a second year) and the lovely dark red 'Bravo.' Unfortunately the rabbits which abound in our area are particularly fond of pinks so that we cannot grow these charming little flowers except in our fenced-in garden. Dwarf varieties grow 8 to 10 inches; space 6 inches apart. Taller ones grow 12 inches; space 8 inches apart.

DIDISCUS (BLUE LACE FLOWER) ☐ This is one of my favorite flowers. The flower heads resemble Queen Anne's lace but are of a heavenly shade of blue. May be started indoors in April with germination in 7 days. Outdoors in May, 14 to 20 days. Resents transplanting. Likes full sun. Does not do too well in hot, dry areas. Grows to 2 feet; allow 10 inches between plants. Lovely cut flower.

DIMORPHOTHECA (CAPE MARIGOLD) ☐ In the North they should be sown where they are to be grown in late spring; germination 10 to 15 days. They come into bloom very quickly. In sections of the country where temperatures do not go below 25 degrees in winter they are very good for late winter and early spring blooms. Likes sun but prefers cool weather. Grows 12 to 18 inches high; allow 12 inches between plants.

ECHIUM (BUGLOSS) ☐ Flowers are blue forget-me-not-like. Thrives in heat and on poor soil. I prefer to plant mine outdoors in May where they are to bloom. Germination in 8 to 14 days. Two feet tall; allow 12 to 15 inches between plants.

EMILIA (SEE CACALIA)

ESCHSCHOLTZIA (CALIFORNIA POPPY) ☐ Prefers coolness for germination. In the North sow in early May out of doors where they are to grow. May be started early indoors if transplanted with care. Flowers are pretty shades of cream, gold, yellow and rosy red. Lovely blue-green, lacy foliage. Fall sowing gives good results for many gardeners. Self-sows freely. Does well on hot and dry banks. Grows 10 to 15 inches high; allow 8 inches between plants.

EUPHORBIA (SNOW ON THE MOUNTAIN) ☐ Variegated leaves. Grown mostly for its foliage. Needs warmth for germination in 15 days. Best sown where they are to grow but not too difficult to transplant while still small. Grows almost anywhere and prefers full sun. Good in borders for contrast. Self-sows freely. Will withstand hot, dry summers. 3 feet tall; allow 18 inches between plants.

87   BRACHYCOME IBERIDIFOLIA, THE SWAN RIVER DAISY.   *George W. Park Seed Co., Inc.*

88   GLORIOSA DAISY 'PINWHEEL.'   *Burpee Seeds*

89   AMARANTHUS 'EARLY SPLENDOR.'   *T. Sakata & Company*

90   CLARKIA   ELEGANS   WITH   DOUBLE FLOWERS.   *Geo. W. Park Seed Co., Inc.*

EUPHORBIA, PAINTED SPURGE OR MEXICAN FIRE PLANT ☐ Sow outdoors in mid-May in North. Needs heat for germination in 15-18 days. Loves full sun and does well on poor soil. Where winters are frost-free this is a perennial.

EUTOCA (CALIFORNIA BLUE BELL OR BEE'S FRIEND) ☐ Needs heat for germination. Start indoors late March for germination in 6 days. I prefer to plant this where it is to grow outdoors in May. Germination in 15 to 25 days. Does well in full sun and does not mind drought. Pretty little blue flowers on attractive foliage. Grows 12 inches high; allow 8 inches between plants for best effect.

FELICIA (SEE AGATHEA)

FEVERFEW (SEE MATRICARIA)

FOUR O'CLOCK (SEE MIRABILIS)

FLOWERING TOBACCO (SEE NICOTIANA)

GAILLARDIA (ANNUAL VARIETIES) ☐ As easily grown from seed sown directly to the garden as zinnia and marigold. Needs warmth for germination and germinates in 10 to 20 days from May-sown seed in the North. Comes into bloom quickly, flowers are usually orange or yellow and orange- or mahogany-tipped. Blooms all summer up to frost. Fine for northern and southern gardens alike. Autumn sowing best for lower South. Wonderful cut flower. Grows 2 to 2½ feet tall; space 15 inches between plants. The new 'Lollipop' series are excellent varieties for bedding.

GAZANIA ☐ Needs warmth for good germination. Sow indoors in late March or early April; germinates 7 days; outdoors in May, 10 to 15 days. Fairly low-growing plants literally covered all summer with red, gold and orange flowers. They defy heat and drought. Bloom from July until hard freezes in the North. They are wonderful in sections where summers are hot and dry and very good as ground covers in California and Arizona. Grow 10 to 12 inches high; place 8 inches apart for best effect.

GERBERA (AFRICAN DAISY) ☐ These are gorgeous plants but need an early start for successful bloom in the North. Start indoors in January. Germination in 5 to 9 days. Some authorities say the seed should be sown on end and some say the tip should show. I have tried both ways and with seed barely covered and been successful with each method. This is a perennial where winters are frost free although it will stand frost to 30 degrees. Flowers large daisy-like in gorgeous shades of reds, rose, salmon. Blooms over many months in Florida. Crowns of plants grow to 12 inches, flowers to 18 inches or taller. Place plants 12 to 15 inches apart.

GILIA CAPITATA ☐ Needs warmth for germination. Best planted where it is to grow in late spring. Pretty blue flowers shaped like thimbles. Has short blooming season. 2 feet tall; space 10 to 15 inches apart.

GLORIOSA DAISY (SEE RUDBECKIA)

GODETIA (SATIN FLOWER) ☐ Sow indoors March; 7 days to germination. Outdoors in late spring 15 to 20. Plant in the autumn in lower South. Likes cool weather; good in New England and upper central states and mountain areas. Prefers full sun except in exceedingly hot areas. Flowers pink, white or rose; petunia-shaped. Will bloom fairly well in semishade. 10 to 15 inches high; place 10 inches apart.

GOMPHRENA (GLOBE AMARANTH) ☐ Sow indoors in March; 7 days germination. Needs warmth for good germination. Outdoors late spring 10 to 15 days. Thimble-shaped flowers in purple or white. Likes hot sunny spots. Easily grown from seed planted to garden in May in North. Grows almost anywhere in the United States. Excellent for southern gardens. Is used for drying for winter bouquets. 15 inches tall; space 12 inches apart. (Sometimes known as bachelor's-button.)

GYPSOPHILA (BABY'S-BREATH) ☐ Needs warmth for germination. Annual kinds best planted direct to garden in May in the North. Delicate gray branches covered with tiny white flowers. Has short blooming season. May be sown six weeks after first planting for continuous bloom. Does well in hot, dry weather. Dwarf sorts grow 15 to 18 inches tall; space 12 inches apart. Taller ones should be thinned to 24 inches apart.

HELIANTHUS (SUNFLOWER) ☐ Needs warmth for germination which occurs in 5 to 10 days outdoors planted in early May in North. Cover seed with ¼-inch soil. No need to start indoors as it grows quickly if weather is moderate. Comes into bloom early. Most sorts do well in hot, dry weather. Tall varieties used for seed for feeding birds will grow to 8 feet and flowers will attain size of 14 inches across. There are a number of good varieties for the garden where bold foliage and flowers are needed. Two recent varieties I grew, 'Teddy Bear,' bright yellow flowers on 3-foot plants and 'Italian White,' both start to bloom six weeks after planting. These make excellent background or hedging plants. Should be spaced 18-20 inches apart.

HELIOTROPE ☐ This old-fashioned fragrant flower is most attractive with lovely lavender spikes of flowers. Start indoors in March with 6 days to germination or outdoors where they are to grow where it usually takes 20 to 30 days to germination. Does not mind hot weather. 18 to 24 inches tall; space 15 inches apart. Resents transplanting except when quite small.

HELICHRYSUM (STRAWFLOWER) ☐ This is an everlasting. Dwarf plants good for bedding in hot places. Blooms all summer. Needs to be started indoors in North as it needs a long growing season in order to be at its best. Germination in March in 7 days. Grows 2-3 feet tall; space 15 inches apart.

HOLLYHOCK (ANNUAL) ☐ Sow indoors in March; germinates 7 days. Outdoors where to grow in late spring 10 to 15 days. Comes in many varieties, colors from yellow, scarlet, white, rose to red shades. Singles and doubles. Self-sows readily. Tall—4 to 6 feet—excellent background plants. Space 10 to 20 inches apart.

IBERIS (CANDYTUFT) ☐ The annual sorts of candytuft come into bloom quickly so need to be replanted every six weeks to keep a good supply of blooms. Pretty little plants with umbels of flowers in pink, white, lilac, rose or white. Resents transplanting. Indoors germinates in 7 days. Outdoors in late spring, 8 to 20 days. Grows 12 to 15 inches tall; space 8 to 10 inches apart.

IMPATIENS ☐ These well-known plants although often grown as house plants are among the finest for growing in shady spots under trees where they will bloom until hard frost. Best started indoors in February or March. Germination will be had in about 14 to 17 days. Newer dwarf sorts which I grow, 'Snowflake,' a pure white, and the new 'Imp' and Dwarf Mixtures started in February are ready for 1½-inch pots by April. Planted out under the trees near my terrace with buds already showing about the 15th of May, provide by the first week in July a huge area of bright color. Mixtures come in scarlet, orange, fuchsia and pink shades. The white one adds just the right touch of contrast. To make a solid bed, place rather close together, no more than 8 inches apart. Cuttings taken in late August will give excellent plants for winter. Do not wait until the nights are getting cold before taking cuttings as the tissues in the plant seem to undergo a change with the cooler weather and frequently rot before rooting.

KOCHIA (SUMMER CYPRESS) ☐ This is an unusual plant grown for its feathery foliage which turns red in the fall. Enjoys hot dry weather. Sow outdoors in late spring. Germination in 15 to 20 days. Very good to fill in foundation plantings when they are sparse. 30 inches tall; space 20 inches apart for good effect.

LIMONIUM (STATICE OR SEA LAVENDER) ☐ Needs warmth for germination. As it needs a long growing season to produce at its best should be planted indoors in February or March. Germination indoors 5 days; outdoors late spring 15 to 20 days. Statice is wonderful for use as a dried flower in winter bouquets. Comes in beautiful shades of blue, lavender, pink, white and yellow. Needs full sun and does not mind drought conditions. Transplants best when small. Flat rosettes of leaves with stems about 2 feet tall. Space about 15 inches apart. Variety 'Bonduelli' is a fine yellow sort.

LOBELIA ERINUS ☐ This is the annual lobelia used so much for bedding or edging. Seeds are very fine and they do best when planted early indoors in February or March. Germination in 5 to 8 days in warmth. May take longer, up to 14 days on cool window sill. Seedlings are tiny and difficult to transplant. Take up in small bunches for flatting out. These may be taken apart later when ready to set into the garden. Needs a long growing season for good blooming. Will bloom until hard frosts. Most sorts grow 4 to 6 inches and should be spaced 3 to 4 inches apart for best effect. Good for edging beds of petunias or begonias or along walks or fronts of borders. In sections of the country where there is a long growing season seed may be sown out of doors. Seed is so fine it should never be covered but patted gently into the soil. Varieties 'Crystal Palace,' 'Bright Eyes,' 'Blue Stone,' 'Mrs. Clibran' and 'Heavenly' are all very good.

LOVE-IN-A-MIST (SEE NIGELLA)

LUPINE (ANNUAL) ☐ These need to be cool for germination—60 to 70 degrees. Germinates indoors in 2 to 4 days. Outdoors late spring, 14 to 20 days. I prefer to start mine indoors in early March. Can be easily transplanted when quite small. Large plants resent transplanting. Fine for winter bloom in the South where there are frost-free winters. Variety 'Texas Blue Bonnet' has spikes of sky-blue sweet-pea-like flowers. 'Hartwegii' and 'King' types come in a mixture of colors. Suffers in drought.

MANAOS BEAUTY (SEE CENTRANTHERUM)

MARIGOLDS ☐ Even the most inexperienced gardener knows and recognizes marigolds (*Tagetes* species). They are sun lovers and do well most anywhere although they are at best on good rich soil. Prefer full sun but will bloom moderately well with six hours of sunshine, although they will grow taller than usual in part shade. Marigold germinates indoors in April in 5 days, and outdoors in May, 7 to 10 days. If blooms are wanted early start indoors. I usually start dwarfs for edging and taller ones for filling in my perennial border in late April in the greenhouse. All others are planted to the soil in my cutting garden in May. Marigolds transplant easily, wilting only slightly, but recovering quickly if watered immediately upon transplanting. Transplantone takes away some of the shock of moving. I have, actually, to my husband's horror, on occasion pulled up mature plants in bud and planted them in empty spaces in my border in mid-summer. Kept watered for two or three days even in hottest summer they have recovered quickly and bloomed as though they had never been moved. When transplanting marigolds or moving them like this, always plant much deeper than before as they root up and down the stalk thus giving a more compact, bushy plant. Tall marigolds grow to 3 to 4 feet and should be spaced 18 inches apart. Medium growers, grow to 2 or 2½ feet; space 12 to 15 inches apart. Dwarfs, needed for close effect, 6 inches apart. Varieties which are my favorites among the tall sorts are the 'Climax' series, 'Hawaii,' 'Gigantea,' 'Sun Souffle' and 'Mary Helen,' although of all of these I love the 'Toreador Climax' the best for its bright orange color so beautiful in fall weather. Of the medium growers I like the 'Red and Gold' hybrids and 'Spun Yellow.' 'Yellow Nugget' looks as though it is going to be excellent. For the dwarfs I particularly like 'Brownie Scout' for the edge of my perennial border alternated with plants of 'Midget Blue' ageratum. Other dwarfs I would not be without in my summer garden are the 'Petite' marigolds and the little one known as 'Signet' marigold.

MATRICARIA (FEVERFEW) ☐ Although this little flower which looks like a small button chrysanthemum is a perennial, I like to use it as an annual. Sown indoors in March it germinates in 5 days. Outdoors in May, 7 to 15 days. Needs warmth for germination. These bloom until hard frost and are fine for borders and edging. In hot dry weather they do suffer from red spider-mites. A good forceful spray from the hose routes these little "devils" usually. Blooms all summer to frost if started early. Grows 12 to 15 inches tall; space 10 inches apart.

MATHIOLA (STOCK) ☐ Needs coolness for germination. Sown indoors in February germinates 3 to 5 days; outdoors early spring, 10 to 20 days. Should be planted in autumn in the South as flower buds will not set if plant is not sufficiently large before nights

91   ARCTOTIS GRANDIS. *Bodger Seeds, Ltd.*

92   NASTURTIUM 'MOONGLEAM.'
Bodger Seeds, Ltd.

93   COSMOS 'GOLDCREST.' *Bodger Seeds, Ltd.*

94   CLEOME 'PINK QUEEN.'
Bodger Seeds, Ltd.

are over 60 degrees. Beautiful spikes of flowers in white, rose or lavender. Prefers full sun except in regions of hot summers. Will do fairly well in 6 hours of sunshine. 15 to 18 inches tall; space 12 to 15 inches apart. In every packet of double flower seeds some plants will show single blooms. This is a characteristic of this plant.

MIGNONETTE ☐ Needs warmth for germination indoors in April; germinates in 3 days; outdoors in May 5 to 10. Very fragrant orange flowers. Old-fashioned favorite. Prefers full sun but will grow in part shade although it will become spindly in shade. Resents transplanting. Best sown where it is to bloom.

MIMULUS (MONKEY FLOWER) ☐ Needs coolness for germination. Seed is very fine and is best started indoors in February with germination in 10 days. Transplant seedlings in little clumps and divide later when large enough to handle easily. Plant in garden after all danger of frost has passed. Likes cool weather and light shade. Good in upper New England and upper northern states. Fine winter bloomer for the lower South. 15 inches high, space 8 to 10 inches apart.

MIRABILIS (FOUR-O'CLOCK) ☐ Sow indoors February; germinates 5 days; outdoors late spring, 7 to 15. Needs warmth for germination. Also called Marvel of Peru, this plant produces a tuber which may be taken up and stored like you would a dahlia. Self-sows freely. Is perennial in areas of mild winters. Can be started in coldframe in March in North. Grows 2½ to 3 feet tall; space 12 to 15 inches for good effect.

MOLUCELLA (SEE BELLS OF IRELAND)

NASTURTIUM ☐ Most everyone knows this old-fashioned flower. There are bush and trailing sorts producing small trumpet-shaped flowers in yellow, mahogany, orange and gold. Prefers sun and not too rich soil. Sow in autumn in deep South for winter bloom. Germination 7 to 10 days outdoors planted in mid-May in the North. To 15 inches high; space 15 inches apart.

NEMESIA ☐ Plant outdoors where it is to grow. Prefers to be cool for good germination. May 1st planting in the North germinates 5 to 10 days outdoors. Likes cool climate and moist soil. Does not like hot dry places. Good for winter bloom in lower South and California. Can be started in coldframe under glass in March. Has lovely, little blue flowers. Good in rock gardens. Grows 12 inches; space 6 to 8 inches apart for good effect.

NEMOPHILA (BABY BLUE EYES) ☐ This charming little plant should be grown in more gardens. The foliage is fern-like and the 1-inch flowers in heavenly blue are up-facing. Grows 6 to 10 inches high and is good in rockeries. Self-sows freely. Although it is said to not like dry weather, it has done well in my garden through several warm, dry summers.

NICOTIANA ☐ Sow indoors April, warmth for germination in 5-7 days; outdoors late spring, 14 to 18 days. Seeds very fine. Do not cover. Thrives in hot sun but will bloom in semishade. Self-sows readily but does not come true to color. Grows well from Maine to Florida and all parts westward; in the deep South as well. Except for variety 'Lime Sherbet' I plant my seeds right to the garden in May. Flowers on variety 'Daylight' and 'Lime Sherbet' remain open all day. Both of these are good for cutting. 15 to 18 inches tall; space 10 to 12 inches apart. The old-fashioned white has delightful evening fragrance.

NIEREMBERGIA (CUPFLOWER) ☐ This is a nice edging or bedding plant but does better in cool places. Will bloom in part shade. Needs long growing season so should be started in February or March indoors with germination in 7 days. Foliage fine and fern-like; flowers 1 inch across in a pretty shade of blue. 6 to 8 inches tall; space 3 to 4 inches apart for best effect.

NIGELLA (LOVE-IN-A-MIST) ☐ Needs warmth for germination. I prefer to start this one outdoors in May; germination in 10 to 15 days. Old-fashioned flower in blue and lavender shades with fuzzy green "veils" over the flower. Foliage is fern-like. Does not seem to mind full, hot sun but needs to be watered in time of drought. Is grown especially for interesting seed pods which are nice for dried bouquets. To 15 inches tall; space 8 inches apart for best effect.

PAPAVER (POPPY) ☐ The most popular annual poppy is the variety Shirley. Comes in both double and single forms. I prefer to start this outdoors in May with germination in 10 to 15 days. This has a short blooming season. Resents transplanting although can be moved if kept well watered and shaded for a few days thereafter. Does not like too much heat or dry weather. Self-sown poppies in the North are much larger and sturdier and bloom more profusely because they start to grow in the fall and rosettes live over the winter and come into bloom by mid-June. Planted in mid-May they start to bloom in early July. Very good for overplanting tulip bulb plantings. Two feet tall; space 12 inches apart.

PERILLA (FALSE COLEUS) ☐ Sow indoors April; germination 4 to 6 days. 15 to 20 days outdoors in late spring. Needs warmth for germination. This plant is excellent for contrast in bed or border as its foliage is dark reddish purple. Is lovely with gray foliage plants. I like to have it throughout my perennial border to give contrast to foliage of early blooming perennials. Self-sows readily. Resents transplanting but will move with care; expect wilting for a few days. Pinching when 6 inches high insures a good bushy plant. Has a pinkish spike of flower. Grows 15 to 18 inches high; space 10 to 12 inches apart.

PETUNIA ☐ Sow indoors in heat; 4 to 7 days for germination; outdoors late spring 10 to 15. Petunias are one of the best loved flowers in the country for bedding and borders. There are lovely varieties which have been hybridized for us by the growers. The fringed and double varieties should be started indoors in February or March as the seed is fine and very valuable. Do not cover seed. Petunias are one of the few plants which germinate best in sunshine if planted indoors. We start ours indoors in February and transfer to flats as soon as large enough to handle. Even bedding varieties are best started early if one has the facilities. If they start to grow spindley, pinch out the growing tip to make them grow side branches. Very early spring sowing is advised for the lower South. Prefer full sun but will do fairly well with six hours ·of sunlight. In desert regions of the West they are good for winter and spring bloom, blooming from October to May. Can be started in flats in coldframe in April in the North. Grow 10 to 15 inches tall; space 10 to 12 inches apart. Study catalogs for varieties—they are numberless.

PHACELIA (BEE'S FRIEND; SEE EUTOCA)

PHLOX (ANNUAL) ☐

Needs coolness for germination. Indoors in April germination in 7 days; outdoors in late spring, 10 to 20 days. My favorites are varieties *Drummondi* and 'Twinkles.' Very good bedding plants coming in shades of rose, crimson, scarlet, pink and violet. Good for fall sowing in areas of mild winters. Does best where summers are not too long or hot. I prefer to sow mine to garden directly where they are to grow. Grows 12 to 15 inches high; space 10 inches apart.

PINKS (SEE DIANTHUS)

POLYGONUM (PRINCESS FEATHER) ☐

Germinates indoors in March 8 to 12 days; outdoors in May, 15 to 20 days. Very interesting accent plant with large pale green leaves covered with sprays of pink flowers. Resents transplanting and will wilt for a day or two after moving. Grows fairly large, 3 to 5 feet tall; space 20 inches apart.

PORTULACA (ROSE MOSS) ☐

This is another annual which nearly everyone knows. Has needle like foliage and is low and spreading covered with white, yellow, light orange or rose colored flowers which close in the afternoon. Needs warmth for germination which occurs in about 10 to 15 days. Grows quickly and comes into bloom within four to six weeks. Loves heat and drought. Very good in areas of hot, dry summers. In cooler climates such as upper New England start indoors in late March. Grows well everywhere in the country; 4 to 6 inches high; space 4 inches apart for solid beds. The new double forms are especially good.

POPPY (SHIRLEY, SEE PAPAVER)

RUDBECKIA (GLORIOSA DAISY) ☐

This is the hybrid and improved form of the old "black-eyed Susan." It is a bold and beautiful flower in bright gold; some tipped with mahogany. There is a double yellow form which is also very attractive. Foliage is fairly disease free. Grows extra well in full sun and rich soil. Blooms all summer to hard frosts. This is also a flower I like to use throughout my perennial border to "stretch" the blooming season. Self-sows readily. Resents transplanting and will wilt for a day or two. Perennial in areas of mild winters but often lives over in our garden if we are fortunate enough to have a snow cover most of the winter. I like to start this indoors in late February or March with germination in 6 days. Outdoors germination is had in 20 to 25 days. Barely cover seed. Can be started in coldframe in March. Grows 3 to 4 feet; space 15 inches apart.

SALPIGLOSSIS (PAINTED TONGUE) ☐ Needs warmth for germination. Indoors in late March germination in 7 days; outdoors in May, 15 to 20 days. Seeds are very fine. Do not cover. Resents transplanting except when quite small. This is one of my favorite annuals. Flowers are trumpet-shaped in gorgeous deep colors many with striped throats; blue, garnet, orange and other dark, rich shades. Gorgeous in bloom. Cuts well for bouquets. Grows 15 to 18 inches high. I like to space mine but 8 inches apart for best effect.

SALVIA (SCARLET SAGE) ☐ Needs warmth for germination. As it needs a long growing season to come into bloom best sown indoors in March. Germinates in 6 days. Outdoors in late spring germinates in 15 to 20 days. Transplants well. Tall varieties space 12 inches apart; low varieties 10 inches apart. Closer for solid effect. My favorites, because they come early, are 'St. John's Fire,' 'America' and 'Bonfire.' This salvia also comes in rose, purple, white, salmon. Many gardeners are not aware of this as visitors to our garden seeing them have often remarked that they had not known that salvia was available in such pretty shades. The newest variety 'Snow Tips' does not do well in full sun in my garden but was lovely in part shade. If the bright red of the scarlet sage does not look right in your garden, try some of these pastel varieties.

SALVIA FARINACEA ("BLUE BEDDER" OR "BLUE SALVIA") ☐ This variety is really very easy to grow and has lovely spikes of blue flowers with gray foliage. Needs a long growing season to come into bloom so needs to be started indoors in February. Germination in 7 days indoors; 15 to 20 outdoors in late spring. Spikes of flowers dry well for winter bouquets. This variety is perennial in areas of mild winters and has often wintered over here in Connecticut. It does not start to grow until mid-May from wintered over plants, so if you want to keep it, be sure to mark where it is growing so that the crowns will not be disturbed before it starts to grow. I personally think the nicest plants are the ones started anew each year. Grows to 3 feet; space 18 inches apart.

SCABIOSA (PINCUSHION FLOWER; ALSO MOURNING BRIDE) ☐ Needs warmth for germination. Indoors in March 7 days; outdoors 10 to 15 in late spring. I prefer to start this outdoors where it is to grow. Does well except in the hottest climates. Flowers are globes of pretty shades of blue, white, rose and purple; grand for cutting. They seem to prefer crowding for good effect. Grows 2½ feet tall; space 10 to 12 inches apart.

SCHIZANTHUS (BUTTERFLY FLOWER) ☐ This used to be considered strictly a greenhouse flower but I have been growing it outdoors as an annual in my garden for years, planting seeds where they are to grow in May with germination in 15 to 20 days. Plants are covered with yellow flowers over fern-like foliage. May be started indoors in March with germination in 4 to 6 days. Grows 15 inches tall; space 8 to 12 inches apart. Good for winter bloom in California, Arizona and Florida.

95   TETRA MIXED SNAPDRAGONS.
Bodger Seeds, Ltd.

96   CLOSE-UP VIEW OF ROSE MOSS OR PORT-
ULACA IN GARDEN.   *Bodger Seeds, Ltd.*

97   MARIGOLD 'GOLDEN JUBILEE' HAS DE-
SIRABLE HEDGE-TYPE GROWTH.
Bodger Seeds, Ltd.

98   PETUNIA 'SNOWSTORM' IS FRAGRANT.
Bodger Seeds, Ltd.

SNAPDRAGON (SEE ANTIRRHINUM)

STATICE (SEE LIMONIUM)

STOCK (SEE MATHIOLA)

STRAWFLOWERS (SEE ACROCLINIUM)

SWEET PEA ☐ Plant out of doors as soon as the soil can be worked. Needs cold for good germination. In many places sweet peas are planted in trenches in the fall and after they have started to grow in spring, the trenches are filled in. Needs very rich soil and a fence to climb on. Does not like hot, dry weather. Climbs 3 to 4 feet; space plants 3 inches apart. Flowers are very fragrant and good for cutting. This is another flower which the hybridizers have improved greatly and where they grow well are delightful. Best where summers are cool such as upper New England and New York and in the northern tier of the country; or in winter in the south where days and nights are frost free. Dwarf sweet peas are available with flowers typical of the taller growing varieties. Growing to 12 inches they bloom earlier and the 'Bijou' varieties come in separate colors. Space them 10 inches apart. They prefer cool weather and moist conditions to grow well. The drought we have experienced the past few years has made it impractical to grow them in our garden. Started in fall in the lower South they perform beautifully during the cool winter days. An all-America Selection for 1967, the 'Knee-Hi' sweet peas grow to 2½ feet tall. These have been bred for their resistance to heat and drought and should do well when these conditions prevail. Fine for bedding. The flowers are carried on long stems and are very fragrant.

TALINUM (JEWELS OF OPAR) ☐ Needs warmth for germination. Indoors, March, 5 days; outdoors late spring, 10 to 20 days. We have started these in March indoors for early bloom but they do well planted directly to the garden in May in our section of the country. This is a most interesting plant. Foliage is absolutely disease free, sturdy and beautiful green. Tiny rose-colored flowers are carried on high thin stalks; opening only in the morning. Following the flowers are red bead-like pods which are fine for drying. Does not mind heat or drought. Interesting and unusual. To 18 inches; space 15 inches apart. Self-sows.

TITHONIA (MEXICAN SUNFLOWER) ☐ Plant indoors in April with germination in 5 days or outdoors in late spring with germination in 10 to 15 days. I prefer to plant this directly to my garden. Endures heat and drought. Foliage is velvety gray and flowers are brilliant orange daisy-like. Very striking. Tall forms grow to 6 feet and should be spaced 24 inches apart. The so-called dwarf form 'Torch' grows to 4 feet and I space it 18 inches apart. I grow this flower every year in my garden because of its brilliance.

TORENIA (WISHBONE FLOWER) ☐ Needs warmth for germination and long growing season to come into bloom. Germination 10 days indoors in February or March. Good for shade. Low grower with pretty blue and white pouch like flowers.

Likes moisture. Does not like much sun or heat. Grows 8 to 10 inches; space 6 inches apart.

VENIDIUM (MONARCH OF THE VELDT) ☐ Needs warmth for germination. Indoors, March, 5 days; outdoors late spring, 10 to 15 days. I prefer to sow seeds directly to garden where they are to grow. These are fine plants for hot, dry places but they need full sun. The flowers are daisy-like, cream, yellow, salmon, cerise and orange with zone of black-purple. Grows 2 to 2½ feet tall; space 15 inches apart.

VERBENA HORTENSIS (HYBRIDA) ☐ Needs warmth for germination. This old-fashioned flower is known to all but the most inexperienced gardeners. The new hybrids do not sprawl like the old ones and the colors of the flower heads are clear and sparkling blues, lavenders and rose shades. Needs long growing season to come into bloom. Start indoors in March in the North and in mid-May out of doors. Germination is slow, 15 days indoors; 21-30 outdoors. Blooms from early summer to hard freezes. 'Sparkle' and *grandiflora* varieties are very good.

ZINNIA ☐ Needs warmth for germination. Indoors in late April 4 to 7 days; outdoors late spring, ·7 to 15 days. Zinnias may be started in flats in late April for setting out in mid-May in our locality. Started indoors too early they tend to become spindly and do not become bushy plants. I like to give zinnias at least one transplanting before placing them into the garden. However, except for those I want to plant for extra color in my perennial border, I always plant zinnias directly to the garden. They germinate quickly and grow rapidly and are always in bloom by mid-July from seed sown May 10th. While zinnias do well on most any soil they are not at their finest except in well enriched soil and with adequate water. When transplanting, set the plants deeper than they were in the flats or if using "thinnings," these take hold better when set as deep as possible in their new locations. My favorites are the 'State Fair' and 'Zenith' zinnias; variety 'Will Rogers,' a brilliant, clear red; the new 'Envy,' the pale green one which is most attractive and dries well in Borax and cornmeal; the new 'Whirly-gig' zinnias have been excellent in my garden. The Cupids and 'Thumbelina' are always good but my favorite dwarf is 'Pink Buttons.' Zinnias are sometimes subject to a disease which causes black spots on leaves and stems and finally the flowers. We have found that by spraying our zinnias with ferbam before this disease shows up we have practically eradicated it from our garden although for several seasons most of our zinnias were subjected to this fungus before they had reached peak bloom. Mildew can be kept from zinnias by using Mildex or some similar material to prevent this whitish mold which often forms on hot, humid days and nights. This spraying must be done as a *preventative;* therefore should be applied before signs of mildew or at least at the first signs of mildew. Other good varieties of zinnias are 'Burpeana Giants,' 'Cut and Come Again,' 'Burpee's Gigantea,' 'Ortho-Polka,' and for dwarfs, 'Mexicana,' 'Persian Carpet,' and 'Daisy Mae.'

ANNUAL VINES

CARDINAL CLIMBER ☐ Very pretty annual vine with lacy green foliage and dark red flowers having a white throat. Loved by hummingbirds. Will grow to 10 feet. Needs support. Must be started in March indoors for early blooms; germination in 7 days. Sown outdoors in May, germination in 10 to 15 days. Foliage is too light for use as a shade vine for porch or arbor.

CLITORIA TERNATA (BUTTERFLY PEA) ☐ Dark blue flowers with white ring shaped like a large sweet pea. Foliage is light green. Must be started in March to bloom in July in our area. Will grow to 10 feet. Good pot plant for winter bloom if growing tips are pinched in order to form a bushy plant. May be allowed to climb in the greenhouse. Sow in warmth, 65 to 70 degrees with germination in 7 days. Sown outdoors in May germination in 10 to 15 days. Likes rich soil and moisture. Full sun.

COBAEA SCANDENS (CATHEDRAL BELLS) ☐ Fast growing vine will cling by tendrils. Covers a porch in just a few weeks. Foliage is dark green and flowers are urn-shaped in greenish blue or white. Likes good soil and plenty of moisture to thrive. Will bloom in sun or part shade. It is best to start the seed early indoors, planting the seed on edge with a small part of the edge exposed. Germination is had in 10 to 12 days indoors. Outdoors sown in May will germinate in 15 to 20 days. Place plants 15 inches apart for good coverage. This plant is also excellent for the greenhouse for winter bloom or to shade a section of the greenhouse.

CYPRESS VINE ☐ This is a pretty vine with fern-like foliage and trumpet shaped blossoms in scarlet. Start indoors in March for best results with germination in 10 days. May be sown outdoors in May in our location. This is not good for shading porches as the vine is too light and airy. It is good on a fence or in window boxes in full sun. Hummingbirds are fond of the blossoms. Will do well on any good soil, but needs moisture. Space plants 8 inches apart for good effect.

MARBLE VINE ☐ This is an interesting, fast-growing vine which is good for quick cover on fences. Fruits are very interesting, shaped like marbles with white veining. Start early in March with germination in 5 to 10 days. Outdoors in May it germinates in 15 to 20 days. Space plants 8 inches apart for good effect. Does well on most any soil and in part shade.

MOONVINE (IPOMOEA NOCTIFLORA) ☐ This is a member of the morning glory family. It grows quite rapidly but takes a long period to come into bloom. In the North it is best to start early, in late March or April, with germination in 4 days. Pinch growing tips to make a much branched plant. Pot up into 4-inch pots and plant outside when all danger of frost is over. Very good on fences or porches. Flowers are huge, trumpet-shaped and open in the evening. Very fragrant. Likes good soil and moisture. Does best in full sun.

MORNING GLORY (IPOMOEA) ☐ Everyone knows and loves the morning glory. It is a wonderful vine for quick cover of porches, trellises or fences. It needs string or

99   ZINNIA 'BURPEE ROSE.'   *Burpee Seeds*

100   KNEE-HI SWEET PEA 'SAN FRANCISCO,' AN ALL-AMERICA SELECTIONS WINNER FOR 1967.

101   PETUNIA 'SUNBURST' IS A LIGHT YELLOW GRANDIFLORA.   *George J. Ball, Inc.*

102   CLITORIA, AN UNUSUAL VINE.   *Geo. W. Park Seed Co., Inc.*

wire to help it climb if planted where its tendrils cannot twine around a support. It covers quickly and flowers open in the morning. There are some varieties whose flowers stay open all day. Good soil and moisture will make morning glories grow fast. I prefer to start mine indoors either in separate peat pots or sown in seed pan and transplanted to pots. Start in April, in warmth; germination will take place in 4 days. Although authorities assert this seed needs to be soaked to encourage germination I find that it germinates quickly in the vermiculite mix we use. If planted outdoors, perhaps soaking would hasten germination. Mine are potted up when they get their first true leaves to 4-inch pots and the growing ends pinched until planting time out of doors well after the last frost. There are many good varieties of morning glories. I have several favorites. 'Double Blue,' dark green leathery leaves and blue flowers with a white edge; an excellent ground cover. 'Tinkerbell's Petticoat,' which is double, comes in mixed colors; edges of the flowers are frilled. 'Heavenly Blue' is the familiar light blue morning glory with flowers which stay open all day. 'Scarlet O'Hara' has large rose-red flowers and 'Candy Pink' has lovely flowers of a clear shade of pink. 'Gentian Blue' is a good one for part shade. 'Pearly White' is an excellent large flowered white variety. Another choice variety is Japanese Imperial Super Giant; white fringed and an F_1 hybrid. The Japanese morning glories have large leaves and unusual flowers. They should be started in March with germination in 3 to 5 days in warmth and potted up. These make stunning terrace plants if grown in large pots to 10-inch size. Keep the growing ends pinched to make a bushy plant. Feed them every other week with Rapid-Gro to keep them growing vigorously in the pots. They are fine for winter bloom in the greenhouse.

THUNBERGIA (BLACK-EYED-SUSAN VINE) ☐ Sow indoors in April with germination in 8 days or outdoors in May with germination in 10 to 15. Flowers are in salmon, cream or white with dark centers. They are fine for hanging baskets and make excellent ground covers. This is also an excellent greenhouse subject. Grows in any good soil and needs full sun to be at its best.

4. Biennials from Seed

Biennials are plants which, grown from seed this year, live over the winter to flower next season, go to seed and then having fulfilled the life cycle, they die. Some plants we use in the northern sections of our country as biennials will grow as perennials in warmer climes.

In the course of my gardening years I have often heard gardeners make the statement that they cannot be "bothered by biennials;" their only objection to them is their short life and blooming season. While the list of biennials is not long, it does include some of our best loved and some of the most beautiful of our garden flowers. To me, in my June garden nothing is more stately and lovely than the spires of foxglove (digitalis). Canterbury bells when well grown are truly a sight to see. Our perennial border is a mixed one with biennials filling a need for extra color in early summer before the annuals add their gay touches later on. We like to use clumps of white and scarlet sweet William *(Dianthus barbatus)* to perk up the late June border and we enjoy the delicate blossoms of Iceland poppy throughout the summer.

Culture of biennials is exactly like that described for perennials (see chapter 5) and there is no need to repeat these directions here. Our own experiments belie some of the statements often made by authorities in growing these plants, proving that no book could possibly serve anything more than as a guide to us in this great country where there are so many varied and in some cases difficult, soils and climates. With the exception of pansies, we prefer to start biennials no later than March indoors or April in the coldframe in order that the plants will be of good size to survive the winter and bloom properly the following year. Some of them, when 3 or 4 inches high, we like to plant to permanent places in the border as they are not at their best if they must be moved in spring. Foxglove is one of these. Listed herein are the biennials with which we have had experience. I hope all gardeners experienced and inexperienced will take the time and "trouble" to grow and enjoy a few biennials in their gardens.

ALTHEA (HOLLYHOCK; SEE ALSO UNDER PERENNIAL) ☐ Many authorities list hollyhock as biennial. In my garden they prove to be a short-lived perennial usually living three or four seasons. Annual sorts are available also and this makes it necessary to check the catalog description to be sure which variety you are growing from seed. In some sections the perennial ones offered from seed will die after the second year, although hollyhocks self-sow readily. These are old-fashioned plants growing 4 to 6 feet tall with long spikes of large flowers in many colors and should be placed 18 inches apart. Variety 'Indian Summer' is biennial in my garden. Others I have grown are 'Fordhook Giants,' 'Powderpuffs' and 'Triumph.' They do best on good rich soil and with full sun but will suffer in time of drought. Start indoors in March; germination in 7 days; outdoors, 10-15 days.

BELLIS (ENGLISH DAISY) ☐ These charming little plants are good for rockeries and borders. They prefer full sun and good rich moist soil. Plants form low rosettes of leaves from which the flowerhead springs. They do well in protected gardens in our area but sometimes do not survive the extremes of temperatures we experience in our present garden. Start indoors in March with germination in 5 to 7 days. Outdoors in coldframes in April or May with germination in 10 to 15 days. Grows 6 to 8 inches tall; space 6 inches apart for good effect.

CAMPANULA (BELLFLOWER OR CANTERBURY BELL) ☐ *Campanula medium* is the well known Canterbury bell. Flowers are somewhat trumpet-shaped in luscious shades of pink, rose or blue on many branched stems. The cup-and-saucer variety is especially beautiful. They need a deep, rich soil to be at their very best. They do not like drought conditions. These we prefer to plant in permanent places when leaf rosettes are 2½ inches across as they do not perform at best if moved in early spring. Unfortunately the crowns of these plants are one of the favorite winter foods of the numerous bunnies who frequent our garden, so we have had to give up growing them. Sow in early March indoors with germination in 14 days; outdoors in coldframe April, germination 20 to 25 days. Grows 2 to 2½ feet tall; space 15 inches apart. A row or border of these plants in June is an unforgettable sight.

CHEIRANTHUS (WALLFLOWER) ☐ Varieties *C. Allioni* (Siberian wallflower) and *C. cheiri* (English wallflower) are grown by many of my friends whose gardens are protected but these do not live over to bloom in my garden. A new variety of Siberian wallflower called 'Apricot' survived one winter and bloomed beautifully the next June. Wallflowers have orange or golden very fragrant flowers. They grow 15 to 18 inches high and should be spaced 12 to 15 inches apart. Sow in March indoors with germination in 5 days; outdoors in coldframe in April with germination in 10 to 15 days. *C. kewensis,* often called the winter-blooming wallflower, has gold and violet flowers but should be grown only where winters are frost free.

DIANTHUS BARBATUS (SWEET WILLIAM) ☐ Who does not love this old-fashioned fragrant flower which grew in our grandmothers' gardens? The foliage differs from that of the spice pinks (dianthus) although they are in the same family. Leaves and crowns are dark green instead of the typical gray narrow-leaved of the pinks. Flowerheads are large, made up of a composite of small pinks. Some are solid color and some are bi-color. They grow to 15 inches tall; space 12 inches apart. We sow ours indoors in February with germination in 4 to 5 days; outdoors they germinate in 10 to 15 days. Plants are grown on in flats and then placed in nursery rows in our cutting garden until the following April when they are put into permanent places in the perennial border for late June bloom. We like to use clumps of white and 'Scarlet Beauty,' placed together, throughout the border to "perk" it up at a time when early June perennials have finished and the late ones not yet started. Other good varieties are 'Newport Pink,' 'Crimson Beauty' and 'Copper Red.'

DIGITALIS (FOXGLOVE) ☐ Foxgloves are gorgeous plants. From large velvety basal leaves rise gorgeous spikes of tubular shaped flowers in cream, yellow, white, often spotted, strawberry and purple. Varieties which I have grown and found more than satisfactory include Shirley hybrids, *gloxiniaeflora* Excelsior and *monstrosa*. *D. mertonensis* with strawberry-colored flowers is perennial in many areas but does not usually live beyond the second year in my garden. All foxgloves do well in good garden soil but need copious water in times of drought. They will bloom well in full sun or where they receive only six hours of sun a day. Foxgloves grow to 3 feet; space 15 inches apart. Easily raised from seed. In order to have good sized plants before fall they should be started no later than March 15th indoors with germination in 7 to 10 days. Outdoors they may be planted in April in a covered frame. Seeds are fine and seedlings quite fragile at first. I prefer to plant mine in the permanent places no later than the first of September. They can be moved in early spring but their blooms will not be as satisfactory as fall planted ones. Foxgloves should never have mulches placed over their leaves but instead the mulch should be tucked *under* the leaves after hard freeze in order to keep the ground frozen and prevent heaving which will fatally damage the plant.

GILIA RUBRA ☐ Although this is often listed as an annual in books, I have found it to be a hardy biennial. This is really a gorgeous flower growing on long spikes with heads of myriad flowers in orange, red and gold. One of my friends never fails to win blue ribbons with this in June flower shows. Start seeds indoors in March with germination in 7 days; outdoors, 10 to 15 days. Grows to 4 feet; space 18 inches apart. Foliage is fern-like. Will bloom for a long period if seedheads are kept cut. Self-sows readily and is not fussy as to soil but needs full sun.

LUNARIA (HONESTY) ☐ Also called "silver dollar" or "money plant." These plants are not seen much in gardens any more although they do self-sow readily. Flowers are violet-colored and quite pretty on much-branched plants 2½ to 3 feet tall that should be spaced 15 inches apart. Seed pods are flat, shaped like silver dollars. The outer shell should be rubbed off as the under skin of the pod is silvery. Very good for winter bouquets. They are not particular as to soil and will grow in sun or filtered sunlight. Grows quickly from seed started indoors in March with germination in 4 to 5 days; outdoors, 15 to 20 days.

MYOSOTIS (FORGET-ME-NOT) ☐ Varieties 'Alpestris' and 'Bluebird' are excellent for blooming in early spring with tulips and English daisy (bellis). Plants grow 6 to 8 inches tall with typical deep blue flowers. Will do very well in shaded areas as they bloom before the leaves have opened on deciduous trees in the Northeast. If kept moist they will self-sow. Easily grown from seed started in March, with germination in 4 to 6 days; outdoors 8 to 15 days. Grow 6 to 8 inches high; space 4 inches apart for bedding effect.

PAPAVER (ICELAND POPPY) ☐ This dainty and pretty poppy should be in every garden. It starts to bloom in June and blooms intermittently throughout the summer if seed pods are kept picked. Can be had in mixed colors. A good pure yellow one is 'Yellow Wonder' and for those who prefer pink there is 'Coronaria Pink.' The new 'Champagne Bubbles' is a very good pastel mixture. Grows 12 to 16 inches high with typical poppy flowers on long stems; space 10 inches apart. Easily grown from seed sown in February or March with germination in 5 to 8 days indoors; outdoors, 10 to 15. The seeds are fine and little seedlings fragile. Resents transplanting but does transplant well when quite small if carefully removed with earth ball from the flats. Prefers sun but will bloom where it receives 4 or 5 hours of morning sun. Suffers in time of drought.

PANSY ☐ Everyone knows and loves the pansy. Bright flower faces in early spring are greeted everywhere with delight. The colors are usually deep and rich. Pansy seed should be started in May or June in the Northeast if blooms are wanted for the following spring. In the deep South sow in fall for late winter bloom. Needs cool weather to be at its best. Started indoors germination is had in 5 to 8 days; outdoors 10 to 15. Seedbed or coldframe should be shaded until germination, then given strong light. Too much hot sun will kill the seedlings. Keep seedbed moist at all times. Transplant the small seedlings to other frames or seedbeds. In cold sections of the country after the ground has frozen in early winter, mulch with salt hay for

103 PANSY, MAJESTIC F¹ HYBRID, WHITE
WITH BLOTCH, WAS THE WINNER OF AN ALL-
AMERICA SELECTIONS AWARD IN 1966.
George W. Park Seed Co., Inc.

winter protection. Pansies do best in deep enriched soil and plenty of moisture. Grow 8 inches tall; space 6 to 8 inches apart. Self-sow readily if conditions are right. In regions with mild winters they are often perennial, but should be sheared from time to time to keep them growing.

VIOLA ☐ Violas are "baby pansies." The plants are smaller and the little flowers nearer to violet size. They come in gorgeous shades of crimson, blue, yellow, gold and brown. Grow the same as pansy. Violas are usually hardier than pansies and self-sow readily. To 6 inches tall; space 4 inches apart.

5. Perennials from Seed

It is often said by horticulturists that while annuals are the mainstay of summer gardens, perennials are the backbone and I certainly concur. Perennials live through the winter and start to grow in very early spring. My delphinium and lupine plants start showing new growth in early April when the daytime temperatures go over 40 degrees. What a thrill to walk along the border and see them starting new growth for another season! At this time also those perennials such as candytuft, arabis and Oriental poppy which are somewhat evergreen start to fatten up and turn brilliant green and buds show just about the time we are thinking of getting our annual seeds into seed pans. The main bloom of perennials comes in June but some of them continue through the summer. When the biggest burst of perennial bloom is over the annuals are coming along to keep the summer garden show going.

The hardy herbaceous perennial is a plant which dies to the ground after frost yet whose roots and crowns live through the winter and sprout again in the spring. These should not be confused with "woody" perennials which are shrubs and trees whose trunks and branches become leafless at certain seasons but which live for many years. Some of the flowering plants we use in perennial beds and borders will outlive the gardener who planted them. Peonies, dictamnus (gasplant), platycodon, baptisia and Oriental poppies are examples of long-lived perennials. Others such as lupine, delphinium and columbine tend to die out in three or four years depending upon the weather and the soil conditions where they are grown.

Outside the window-wall in our dining room are rock outcroppings shaded by venerable apple trees which show the patterns of the work of the yellow-bellied sapsucker. Under these, in earliest spring, the rock cress (arabis) shows its white blossoms along with the silvery spotted leaves and the pretty pink and blue blossoms of the leadwort *(Pulmonaria saccharata)*. *Primula denticulata* also opens its delicate lavender blooms and is followed by species tulips, pansies and forget-me-nots. Mounds of basket-of-gold *(Alyssum saxatile)* complement the bright gold of the Baltimore oriole as he flits through the apple trees from blossom to blossom inspecting them for the insects which make up the bulk of his food. In late summer this area is in shade but plaintain-lily (hosta), maidenhair and spleenwort ferns and impatiens give change in texture and bright color. Coleus also lends its beautiful brocade to this planting.

Forty feet or more from this terrace our perennial border begins with doronicums tossing gay, gold daisy blooms along with daffodils and tulips. Then iberis (candytuft), columbine (aquilegia), peonies, iris, daylilies, hybrid lilies, Oriental poppies and baptisia, followed by *Campanula persicifolia* (peach-bells), oenothera, gaillardia, sweet William, pyrethrum (painted daisy), lupine, delphinium, early June asters *(Aster subcoeruleus)* and many others. Following these in late June are the biennials sweet William and foxglove which were discussed in the previous chapter; gasplant (distamnus), daylilies, coral bells (heuchera), iris (both bearded and Siberian), and *Salvia superba* and *Salvia haematodes* with spires of purple and blue flowers. Late June and early July bring artemisia, Shasta daisy, yarrow and anthemis with golden blooms, bee-balm, phlox in various colors and shades and the balloon flower (platycodon) in blue, pink and white with interesting balloon-like buds which open up to gorgeous star-shaped flowers. Veronica, globe-thistle (echinops), stokesia (Stoke's aster; lavender) and late daylilies. In August and September we have helenium, physostegia, chrysanthemums, *Salvia azurea* with powdery blue spires and the hardy asters.

To carry through a season of gay bloom and to augment the blooms of the late summer garden we overplant our tulips and daffodils with golden marigolds and bedding dahlias which we grow from seed each season for this purpose.

Along the front edge of the border for its entire length of 325 feet are alternate plantings in groups of two or three of dwarf blue ageratum and dwarf marigolds in mahogany and gold. This gives a riotous array of gypsy-ish colors which we dearly love, until the first hard freeze in late September which ends our gardening season.

In this border, not including bulbs, tubers and corms, there are seventy-five different kinds of perennials of which some forty were grown from seed. Some of these are plants ten or more years old started in our coldframes long before we owned a home greenhouse. The average gardener does not usually have a garden budget sufficiently large to purchase all the perennial plants desired. For a small budget, growing them from seeds is not only inexpensive but tremendously thrilling. Patience is needed, however, in growing perennials from seed for most of them do not come into bloom until the second season. From one 50-cent packet of delphinium seeds, for instance, one can obtain thirty to fifty plants; quite a substantial savings compared with the usual price at the garden center! The satisfaction stemming from such an experience is most rewarding. There is always new adventure in every new package of seed!

Many perennials are easily grown from seed, most of them coming into bloom as I have pointed out the second year after sowing. Seeds of perennials are planted as directed in chapter 2. In the following encyclopedia of perennials, instructions for sowing specific plants will be discussed. When we grow perennials from seed, after hardening them off, they are transplanted to nursery rows until large enough to be placed where wanted in flower beds and borders.

There are some perennials which resent transplanting after they have attained an appreciable size and if possible these are planted directly from plant bands, flats or peat pots to permanent places in bed or border. Any special treatment needed by different varieties will also be found under the name of the plant in the encyclopedia at the end of this chapter.

In preparing to transplant a mature plant from nursery row to our border we dig overly deep, breaking up the soil in the bottom of the hole to enable the roots of the plant to reach down since most perennials have extensive root systems. Peatmoss or compost plus dried cow manure and bone meal are thoroughly incorporated with the soil already removed from the hole. A layer of this mixture is first placed in the bottom of the hole, then the plant with root ball intact, is lowered to the proper depth, that is, the crown of the plant should be about even with the soil level of the border. The soil is then filled in around the roots leaving a shallow saucer for immediate and deep watering after which the remaining soil is spread around the plant.

If the home gardener has no facility such as a coldframe or is not able to start seeds indoors, perennials may be sown to an outdoor seedbed which should be prepared as previously discussed in chapter 2. While authorities disagree on the necessity of enriching the soil of these outdoor seedbeds we have found that this treatment is beneficial. For an outdoor seedbed I prefer one slightly raised and protected on the sides and ends by boards, although many of my friends have been successful just planting the seeds as I do my annuals. The rows, however, can be as closely spaced as 12 inches and seedlings should be thinned to 6 inches between plants for small-growing varieties and 12 inches for larger varieties.

If you use the side board method the bed can be shielded by a make-shift cover for the protection of the seedbed until germination. If you live where there is a snow cover most of the winter this will be all that late-fall-planted seed would need. If, however, you live where the weather is change-able, I would suggest a temporary plastic screen cover or at least a canopy of burlap or unbleached muslin. This cover should be 4 to 6 inches above the bed and the gardener should make sure it never rests on the seedbed. When good germination prevails this temporary cover should be removed. In the case of all fall-sown seed do not become impatient if germination is not prompt in early spring. One of my young friends remarked to me in early May one year that delphinium seed which she had planted in the late fall had not germinated. We had had the driest spring on record so I suggested that possibly the weather had not been conducive to good germination and to be patient a little longer. Some weeks later she was happy to report that she had found many little delphinium seedlings among the weeds which she had allowed to grow in the rows. After weeding, cultivating and feeding she was rewarded with many fine delphinium plants. There should be a lesson here for the inexperienced home gardener. Do not give up too soon. Keep your seedbeds and nursery rows weeded to provide optimum growing conditions for your plants and do not by all means become impatient and expect fussy perennials to sprout like weeds. Some perennials are not truly difficult from seed but do need special handling for good germination and I shall try to share with you my experiences in growing these plants.

Soils are prepared for perennials as indicated in chapter 2 under prepara-tion of soil for the garden. It would be advisable, if possible, to work the soil for perennials as deeply as 12 to 15 inches in order to provide an adequate depth of soil for roots to become established. Peatmoss and/or compost mixed with shredded dry cow manure should be added in as large a quantity as possible and thoroughly mixed with the soil. Addition of one pound of bone meal to each 25 square feet of soil will also be beneficial. If the pH shows a reading of below 6.0 the addition of five pounds of lime to each 100 square feet will also be helpful. Once planted, perennials need a minimum of care and will bloom for years. Although most authorities assert that perennials can be planted at any time except when the ground is frozen, and I am sure this is good advice in those regions where fall is late and lingering, in our own area, we generally prefer to do our planting in spring. Exceptions to this are iris which are moved immediately after the flowering period and Oriental poppies and Madonna lilies which are best moved during the dormant period which is August in our location. Some perennials once planted to bed or border should stay in the permanent places indefinitely. Examples of such perennials are peonies, platycodon, Oriental poppies, baptisia and dictamnus.

Such perennials as phlox, Shasta daisy, coral bells, helenium, hemerocallis (daylily) and others of similar growth habit need dividing every three or four years. These should be lifted and young shoots around the edges replanted, discarding the woody centers. It is always good practice to add peatmoss and bone meal to the new planting area before replanting divisions of newly divided plants.

When planting a new perennial border, particularly if using seedling plants which you have grown for the purpose, all plants should be mulched *after* the first hard freeze. The soil needs to be *kept frozen* so that there will be no alternate freezing and thawing which disturbs the roots and often results in the loss of the plant. Place mulches around the crowns of plants. Lift the leaves of such evergreen plants as Oriental poppies, campanulas, doronicum and tuck mulch under the leaves of the crowns. Many mulches are available; peatmoss, buckwheat hulls, cocoa bean hulls, shredded bark, salt hay and sawdust are some in common use. Be sure to apply an all-purpose fertilizer such as 5-10-5 and water in well if using sawdust for a mulch as the sawdust will remove nitrogen from the soil as it starts to disintegrate. After the mulch is in place over the frozen ground, the addition of evergreen boughs if available helps to protect the newly placed plants. Heavy mulches and evergreen boughs should be removed gradually in early spring as the weather warms up. A layer of mulch may be left over the soil around the plants throughout the growing season. This will keep soil moist and cool and discourage weeds.

Tall perennials should be staked to prevent their being broken off by the wind. Others might sprawl if left without support of some kind. I like to start this process early in the season, providing bamboo stakes and soft twine. If staked in ample time plants stay upright and natural looking. If one waits until the plants are toppling over, the staking has to be done in such a manner that the plant no longer looks graceful and attractive.

Remove faded flowers immediately to prolong the season of bloom of all perennials. Seed producing reduces the energy of the plant. If the seeds are wanted for propagation, only two or three flowerheads should be permitted to go to seed and these should be removed as soon as they have become brown and dry, but before pods or capsules have broken open. Waiting until these open might result in loss of the seed contained therein.

In late fall, after frost has put the garden to sleep, cut back the perennials to about 4 inches from the ground and give them a feeding of shredded dry cow manure. Like many old-fashioned cooks, I am afraid I am not very scientific about this feeding. I take a bucket of dry manure and one of bone meal with me to the border and spread a layer of about a half inch of the dry manure and over this sprinkle a "snow" of bone meal. Although this haphazard application may be inadequate or overgenerous many visitors to our garden when my perennials are blooming remark, "You must have very good soil"—so I must be "doing something right!"

PERENNIALS TO GROW FROM SEED

ACHILLEA (YARROW OR MILFOIL) ☐ Easy to grow perennials and not fussy as to soil. Germination indoors February to March 5-7 days; outdoors, 10 to 15 days. *A. filipendulina* with stiff yellow heads is the most well-known achillea. These dry well when hung up-side-down and are excellent in winter bouquets. Need to be divided every three years. *A. millefolium rosea* is more dwarf growing and spreads quite rapidly. Foliage is fern-like, gray-green. Variety 'The Pearl' grows rather tall and sprawling with small white pom-pom like flowers. *Filipendulina* grows to 4 feet; space 24 inches apart; *millefolium* to 18 inches; space 18 inches apart; 'The Pearl' grows to 3 feet; space 18 inches apart. Most varieties bloom June to August. Do well in dry situations.

ALTHAEA (HOLLYHOCK) ☐ Everyone knows this old-fashioned flower with tall spikes of large flowers single or double in shades of red, rose and white and purple. Easily grown started indoors in February or March; germinates in 7 days; outdoors, 10 to 15. Grows 3½ to 5 feet tall and should be spaced 18 inches apart. Does well on any good soil. Self-sows readily. Blooms in June.

ALYSSUM SAXATILE (BASKET-OF-GOLD) ☐ Silvery foliage sprays of bright gold flowers blooming with daffodils and tulips. Very hardy; good for both rockeries and borders. Start indoors in February or March with germination in 5 days; outdoors, 7 to 10. I prefer to start mine in early February to have good sized plants to set out in May or June. Blooms second season. Clumps will increase in size over the years. Some in my flower border are eight years old. Must be sharply cut back after blooming to keep clumps in good condition. 10 to 12 inches high, space 15 inches apart.

ANCHUSA (BUGLOSS) ☐ These have bright blue flowers in forget-me-not style. *A. mysotidiflora* blooms in May. Heart-shaped leaves. Seed needs pre-freezing treatment for good germination. I place mine in cold-frame for four weeks in February and

104 PREPARING TO MOVE A TWO-YEAR-OLD PLANT OF PACIFIC GIANT DELPHINIUM FROM THE AUTHOR'S NURSERY BED TO THE MAIN BORDER.

105 PLANT REMOVED, SHOWING AMPLE ROOTBALL. THE BALL WILL BE INTACT IF SOIL IS MOIST AND REASONABLE CARE IS USED.

106 PLANT SET IN ITS LOCATION IN THE BORDER AT THE PROPER DEPTH IN AN OVER-SIZED HOLE TO ALLOW FOR VIGOROUS ROOT DEVELOPMENT.

107 WELL FIRMED-IN WITH A SOIL BASIN FORMED, READY FOR A GENEROUS SOAKING.

March and then bring inside. Blooms second year. Lovely in rockeries and in semishady spots; 12 inches tall; space 10 inches apart. *A. azurea italica* 'Dropmore' is very easily grown from seed sown indoors in February with 7 days for germination; outdoors, 10-20 days. Very spectacular plant, growing 3 to 5 feet tall, with many branches covered with large blue flowers in June. New shoots are late appearing in spring; be sure to mark it well so that early cultivation will not damage crown. Space 18 to 24 inches apart.

ANEMONE PULSATILLA ☐ A purple cup-shaped flower with fern-like foliage blooms in April and is very hardy. Sow in seedpan in February or March and give pre-chilling in coldframe for 5 to 6 weeks before bringing indoors to germinate in 21 days. Grows to 8 inches, space 6 inches apart. Excellent in rockeries. *A. japonica* is not realiably hardy in my own garden although it grows well in northern areas if protected. Pretty single flowers blooming in September rise on tall stems from a low rosette of foliage. Sow as *A. pulsatilla* but it germinates in 15 to 21 days after pre-chilling period. Grows 12 to 18 inches tall; space 12 inches apart. Prefers full sun and good soil.

ANTHEMIS (GOLDEN MARGUERITE OR ANTHEMIS DAISY) ☐ Easily grown perennial with fern-like foliage and yellow daisy-like flowers about 2 inches across. Blooms over a long period in summer. Self-sows readily, blooming first season from seed. Start indoors in February or March with 5 days for germination. Outdoors, 7-15. Grows to 2 feet; space 12 to 15 inches apart. Will thrive in hot dry places and in poor soil.

AQUILEGIA (COLUMBINE) ☐ Varieties *chrysantha*, long-spurred yellow; 'Mrs. Scott Hybrids' and 'McKana Giants' are excellent for borders. Dwarf varieties 'Biedemeir' with upturned flowers and *flabellata nana alba* are good for rockeries. Start indoors in February with germination in 10-12 days; outdoors, 21 to 30. Tall sorts grow 18 to 20 inches; space 12 to 15 inches apart. Dwarfs grow from 8 to 12 inches; space 8 inches apart. All do well in good soil but suffer in dry weather. Self-sow readily but do not come true from seed.

For *A. canadensis* and *A. coerulea*, see Wildflower chapter.

ARABIS (ROCK CRESS) ☐ This little low growing gray-leaved plant with small white flowers produced profusely in April in my garden is extremely hardy. Easily grown from seed started indoors in February or March with germination in 3-5 days. Outdoors, 10 to 15. Grows 4-6 inches tall; space 5 inches apart for good effect. Will bloom under deciduous trees in our area as blooms come before trees leaf out. Fine for rockeries and borders.

ARTEMISIA (DUSTY MILLER, WORMWOOD, SOUTHERNWOOD) ☐ With few exceptions the various varieties of artemisia are grown especially for silvery foliage rather than for the flowers which are small and not showy. For best germination the perennial varieties should be sown in fall in covered coldframe with germination to be had in April or May. May also be sown indoors in March with germination in 10 to 14 days. Tall varieties to 3 feet; space 18 inches apart. Dwarfs 12 to 15 inches high; space 15 inches apart. Most perennial artemisias spread by underground stolons and become pests in small flower beds or borders. A row in the cutting garden is good for use as filler in bouquets. These also dry well for winter bouquets.

ASCLEPIAS (BUTTERFLY WEED; SEE WILD FLOWERS)

ASTER (MICHAELMAS DAISY) ☐ This is the hardy aster which blooms in late August and September. Sprays of blue, or lavender flowers on long stems. Have been hybridized from the native wild aster. Sow indoors in February or March, germination 15 days. Outdoors, 20 to 30 days. Grows 3 feet tall; space 15 inches apart for good effect.

AUBRIETIA (PURPLE ROCK CRESS) ☐ Sow indoors March; germination 5 to 10 days. Outdoors, 21-30 days. Silvery tufts of small leaves covered with purple flowers in early spring 3 inches high; space 3 inches apart. Not reliably hardy in my garden but in a protected spot will live for years. Wonderful in rockeries in full sun. In the North does best on a south slope.

BAPTISIA (FALSE INDIGO) ☐ This is a fine long-lived perennial which can be left in its place without division for many years. Flowers are lupine-like in a light shade of blue; blooms in June. Insect-free foliage makes nice foil for later blooming perennials. Since I have been sowing this seed in our favorite vermiculite mix I have never found it necessary to soak or nick the seed before sowing. Sow indoors February to March with germination in 6 days. Outdoors, 12-20 days. May be sown in fall in open seedbed or coldframe with germination from late April to August. Likes good soil and full sun but does fairly well in part shade and clay soil. To 4 feet tall; space 24 inches apart.

CACTUS (HARDY OPUNTIA) ☐ Hardy sorts do well all over the United States. Good in rockeries. Sow indoors in March in warmth. Germination 14 days. Very good in dry spots. In North likes leafmold, loam and sand combination. Yellow flowers in late summer 12 to 15 inches high; space 18 inches apart.

CAMPANULA ☐ There are tall growing and low growing campanulas. The perennial sorts all need the same conditions for sowing. Indoors February to March with germination in 10 to 14 days; outdoors 20 to 30 days. Seeds are usually fairly fine C. persicifolia and C. pyramidalis grow tall, from 3 to 4 feet, with light blue or white bell-shaped flowers; space 18 inches apart. Very good in perennial border and very hardy although persicifolia (meaning peach-leaved) needs division every third year for best results. Blooms in June in my garden. Does well in semishade but at its best in sun. Varieties C. carpatica and C. garganica both of which I have grown many times from seed are creeping varieties with lovely blue flowers. Carpatica grows 6 to 8 inches tall; space 6 inches apart. Garganica grows 2-4 inches tall; space 4 inches apart. Both of these prefer sun and bloom in early summer and lightly throughout the summer. Will die out in time of drought. Excellent for rockeries.

CENTAUREA (CORNFLOWER) ☐ The two perennial centaureas which I grow are globe or golden centaurea (macrocephala) and montana (also called bluet). Both germinate indoors February to March 10-15 days; outdoors, 21 days. The former has large, coarse foliage with most unusual globe-shaped buds topped by bright golden fluff, beloved by butterflies. Blooms in July in my garden. I have a few of these throughout my perennial border for they are most interesting. The golden seed pods can be cut for dried bouquets after they have opened. To 3 feet; space 18 inches apart. Variety *montana* is a typical cornflower blue. Hardy perennial but needs division every year for best results. Self-sows readily. Blooms in June. 18 inches tall; space 15 inches apart.

CERASTIUM TOMENTOSUM (SNOW IN SUMMER) ☐ This well-known rockery plant which blooms in late May covers itself with tiny white flowers. It is very hardy and long-lived. Likes hot, dry spots. Spreads rapidly thus is a good ground cover. Will grow in poor soil. Sow indoors February to March with germination in 10 days. Outdoors, 15-21. Grows 10 inches high; space 10 inches apart.

CHRYSANTHEMUM ☐ This flower certainly needs no description for it is surely known to even the most inexperienced home gardener. However, not many realize how easy it is to grow from seed and how rewarding. Sow indoors in February or March, germination 5 to 8 days. Outdoors, 12 to 15 days. Seeds of all sorts are available from singles to doubles, earlies to late ones. I grow only the early varieties in my garden because of late September frosts but farther south where frost is late the late varieties perform excellently, all of them blooming the first year from seed. Packets usually contain mixed colors, but that is the fun of growing these fine plants from seed. For good success chrysanthemums need rich soil and water in times of drought. Tall varieties grow 3 to 5 feet; space 24 inches apart. Lower growing varieties 2½ feet; space 18 inches apart. For *Chrysanthemum maximum* and *C. leucanthemum* see Shasta daisy.

COREOPSIS (TICKSEED) ☐ Yellow daisy-like flowers blooming in June and off and on through the season if the seed heads are kept cut. Grows 2½ to 3 feet, space 15 inches apart. Self-sows readily. Likes sun and poor soil. Extremely easy from seed sown indoors with germination in 3 to 5 days or outdoors with germination in 7 to 12 days.

DELPHINIUM (PERENNIAL LARKSPUR) ☐ While most authorities assert that delphinium seed needs to be kept cold for good germination and recommend freezing or no more than 50 degrees, my experience has been that delphinium seed, assuming that it is kept constantly moist will germinate at anywhere from 60 to 80 degrees. I have started them indoors, in windows, in the greenhouse, under fluorescent lights and in coldframes; friends have started them by planting to open seed beds in fall as I have noted elsewhere in this chapter. Sown indoors they germinate in 10 to 17 days; outdoors, 15 to 20. These plants prefer sun, extra rich soil and plenty of moisture to do well. In sections of the country where days are pleasantly warm and nights quite cool and moist they are at their very best. In my garden they rarely live for more than three years. Each year I start a few new ones to replace those lost by winter's ravages. They bloom in June in our area and after blooming are cut down, fed and watered and usually produce a few nice spikes in the fall. Most varieties grow from 3 to 6 feet tall and should be spaced 18 inches to 24 inches apart. I particularly like the Pacific Giants, especially the Round Table Series, Black Knight Series, Blue Bird Series, Percival and Galahad series; the last two are white. The Astolat series are especially

108   GIANT-FLOWERED HARDY HIBISCUS.
Bodger Seeds, Ltd.

vigorous in shades of rose. Belladonna and Bellamosum are old-fashioned very hardy varieties. I have also grown the Wrexham hybrids which do not seem to do as well in my garden as the Pacific Giants. The new Connecticut Yankees did not bloom the first year for me but the second year they grew well and produced new spikes which were in bloom in August when many perennials had finished blooming.

DIANTHUS (HARDY PINKS) ☐ Through the years my husband and I have grown many pinks but unfortunately in our present garden the ever present bunnies consider them the favorite food. They are easily grown and hardy, particularly if the soil is quite sweet (pH of at least 7) and if the weather is not too dry. They prefer full sun although they do quite well with 6 hours of sunshine. For most varieties sown indoors in February or March germination is had in 4 to 6 days; outdoors, 7 to 15. To 12 inches tall; space 10 inches apart.

D. *plumarius:* 6 inches; fragrant, single and double flowers in shades of pink and red. Plant 6 inches apart. Bloom in May.

D. *deltoides* (maiden pink) has creeping foliage and very tiny pink and red blooms in early spring. Grows 1 to 2 inches high; space not more than 3 inches apart.

D. *caesius* (cheddar) gray foliage to 6 inches; space 4 inches apart. This is the lovely little "spice" pink.

D. *allwoodi* is larger than the others and often grown as an annual. Flowers are large and very showy with the typical carnation-pink odor. Blooms in June in my garden if the rabbits do not get it first! Ten to 12 inches high; space 8 inches apart.

D. 'Bravo' is low-growing with unusual bright red flowers. This is also grown as an annual but is perennial over a large portion of the country. To 8 inches; space 6 inches apart.

DICENTRA EXIMIA (SEE WILD FLOWERS)

DICTAMNUS (GASPLANT) ☐ Sow seed outdoors in late fall in open seed beds or coldframes. Germination should take place the following May. Very attractive plant with aromatic foliage and spikes of white flowers in June. Long-lived perennial. A well-grown plant is most attractive in bed or border. Resents transplanting. Small plants should be placed in permanent spots while still 2 to 4 inches tall. Never needs division. Grows to 2 to 3 feet tall; space 18 inches apart.

DORONICUM (LEOPARD'S-BANE) ☐ Yellow daisy-like flowers in earliest spring from rosettes of heart-shaped leaves. Very hardy and is excellent for perennial border because it blooms with the tulips and daffodils and is a fine cut flower. Sow indoors in February or March; germination in 8 days. Outdoors, 14 to 21 days. Can be sown in fall in open seed bed or coldframe. D. *plantagineum* grows to 3 feet; space 20 inches apart. D. *caucasicum* 12 to 18 inches; space 15 inches apart. Easy to grow and not fussy as to soil although plant grows more lustily in rich soil with plenty of moisture. Some authorities claim that the foliage of this plant dies down in late summer, but it persists in my garden although looks dusty and tired in times of drought.

ECHINOPS (GLOBE-THISTLE) ☐ This is an excellent long-lived perennial blooming in July in my garden. Foliage is bold and prickly; flower stems long with three or four globe-shaped steel blue flowers which dry well for winter if cut and hung before the tiny needles open to show the pollen. Light soil and full sun is considered best. Too rich soil will cause too heavy leaf growth. Sown indoors in February and March germinates in 10-15 days. Outdoors, 15-20. Grows 4 ft.; space 30 inches apart.

ERIGERON (FLEABANE) ☐ Also known as midsummer aster. June-blooming perennials to 2 feet; space 15 inches apart. Start indoors in February to March; germiniation in 18 days. Outdoors, 20 to 25 days. There are several lavender varieties which are quite good but the newer variety 'Pink Jewel' has proved to be far superior to the others in my garden. Flowers are larger and the shades of pink clear and lovely. This is a good one for those who like an all-pink garden. Easy to grow and quite hardy.

ERYNGIUM (SEA HOLLY) ☐ Prickly leaves with interesting fluffy amethyst-blue flowers in July and August. Prefers full sun and fairly good soil. Sow indoors in February or March with germination in 18 days; outdoors, 20 to 25 days. Excellent dried for winter bouquet. Best germination is had by sowing in late fall in coldframe or open seed beds.

EUPATORIUM (MIST FLOWER ALSO KNOWN AS "HARDY OR PERENNIAL AGERATUM") ☐ Misty purple flowers blooming in September in my garden. Plant does not begin to show new shoots until late May so should be properly marked so that cultivation will not disturb the crowns. Easy to grow. Self-sows readily. Indoors February to March, 7 days germination. Outdoors, 12 to 18. Grows 2 to 2½ feet tall; space 15 inches apart. Spreads rapidly in bed or border by underground stolons.

FERNS (SEE WILD FLOWERS)

GAILLARDIA (BLANKET FLOWER) ☐ Daisy like flowers in yellow and gold bordered with red. Very hardy. Self-sows freely and blooms the first year. Does well on poor soil and in times of drought. Blooms in June and throughout the summer if seed heads are removed promptly. Start indoors in February or March with germination in 5 days; outdoors, 15 to 20. I especially like the Monarch strain and one called 'Burgundy' which is all wine-red with no hint of yellow. A dwarf variety 'Goblin' growing only to 12 inches is good in the front of the perennial border and in rockeries. Space it 8 inches apart for good effect. Taller varieties grow to 2½ feet; space 12 inches apart.

GEUM ☐ Very pretty single daisy-like flowers in gold or scarlet. Variety 'Mrs. Bradshaw' is the best known. This was perennial in my other gardens which were quite protected. It does not survive the winter in my present one. Blooms in June and July. To 2 feet tall; space 15 inches apart for best results. Start indoors in February or March with germination in 12 to 15 days; outdoors 20-30.

GRASS (BRIZA OR QUAKING GRASS) ☐ Ornamental grass with beautiful seed heads in rosy hues. Very hardy perennial. Does not spread by underground stolons but clumps increase in size each year. Best started indoors as the seedlings look like thin spears of grass. Germination in March within 7 days; outdoors, 12 to 20. Does not mind drought conditions. Seed heads dry beautifully for winter bouquets. Grows to 3½ feet; space 20 inches apart.

GYPSOPHILA (BABY'S-BREATH) ☐ Fine sprays of delicate flowers good for filler in bouquets. Variety *paniculata* has single flowers; *florepleno,* double flowers. Grows 2 to 4 feet tall; space 20 to 24 inches apart. Does well in hot dry places. Blooms in June. Likes limestone soils. Grows rather large and rank in rich soils. Very easy to grow from seed. Start indoors February to March, germination in 7 days; outdoors, 10 to 15.

HELENIUM ☐ This is an old-fashioned perennial which should be in every perennial garden as it blooms in August and September when there are few perennials in bloom. Variety 'Riverton Gem' has daisy-like flowers in old gold changing to red. There are hybrid ones which come in gold, tipped with mahogany. Dwarf varieties such as 'Mound Hybrids' are also available. Very hardy. Easy to grow from seed. Start February to March indoors, germination in 6 to 8 days; outdoors, 10 to 15. Space tall growers 18 inches apart and dwarfs 12 inches apart for good effect. Not particular as to soil but resents drought.

HELIOPSIS ☐ This is another daisy-like flower with insect-resistant foliage. Very easy to grow. Blooms all summer. The new variety 'Summer Sun' blooms the first season from seed. Some of the flowers are double; all of them are of a clear gold. Plants grow to 3½ feet. Excellent as a cut flower. Very hardy but plants do not start to grow until mid-May in my garden. They should be well marked so as not to damage the crowns if working in the border in early spring. Space plants 18 inches apart. Start indoors February or March; germination in 4 days; outdoors, 10-15.

HELLEBORUS (CHRISTMAS AND LENTEN ROSE) ☐ Unusual plant grown for its evergreen foliage and blooms which come in early winter or very early spring. Very difficult from seed. Best sown in coldframe in fall. Sometimes takes two winters to germinate. Seeds from established plants dropped under the plant when ripe may germinate the following spring. Sown in seed pan and placed in coldframe in December, bringing into warmth in April will sometimes break dormancy on older seed. Plants should be placed where they will not be disturbed, in very rich soil, with roots well mulched with peatmoss and the tops in the sun.

HEMEROCALLIS (DAYLILY) ☐ Lily-like flowers on long stems with rushlike foliage, mostly in shades of yellows, oranges and maroon. Will grow anywhere in good garden soil. Bloom over a long period in summer. Not difficult from seed. Can be sown in fall in coldframe with germination in late spring. Also grows readily sown indoors in February or March with germination 10 to 15 days. Outdoors in spring sown in seed bed or frame germinates in 20 to 25 days. Will germinate quite freely under fluorescent light. Seedlings should be protected the first year in a shaded seed bed or lath-covered coldframe and set to nursery rows or places in the garden the next year. Blooms are had in the second or third year depending upon how vigorously the seedlings grow after transplanting. Two and one-half to 3 feet tall; space 24 inches.

HESPERIS (SWEET ROCKET) ☐ Old-fashioned flower in lavender, very fragrant, blooming in May or June. Very hardy and easy to grow. Will do well on poor soil and in semishade. Sow indoors February to March with germination in 14 days; outdoors, 20 to 30. Grows to 3 feet; space 18 inches apart. Some kinds are more biennial than perennial.

HEUCHERA (CORAL-BELLS) ☐ This is a very hardy and popular perennial, with rosettes of attractive leaves with spikes of flowers in rose and pink. Likes good garden soil and should be watered in times of drought. Very easily grown from seed. Best germination is had by sowing in February or early March and giving a pre-chilling period of four weeks in the coldframe, then bringing into warmth with germination in 21 to 25 days. Can be sown in coldframe in fall for late spring germination. Rosettes of leaves 12 inches high; space 15 inches apart. In flower, to 3 feet.

HIBISCUS (ROSE MALLOW) ☐ The perennial varieties of this flower are very showy with shrub-like foliage and huge flowers. In the North growth begins very late in spring after other plants have a good start. Grows 3 to 4 feet tall; space 24 inches apart. Makes good "hedge." Needs to be placed in the back of perennial borden. Grows quite well on any good soil. Blooms late June to July. Sow February to March indoors, germination 12 to 15 days; outdoors, 18 to 24.

HOLLYHOCK (SEE ALTHAEA)

HOSTA (PLANTAIN-LILY) ☐ My grandmother used to call this "August lily" because it usually blooms in that month. One of the finest of plants for a shady area. Foliage is very bold and showy and flower spikes are white or lavender. Does best in rich soil and plenty of moisture. Excellent for shady spots. Seed germinates readily sown February to April indoors with germination in 10 days; outdoors, 15 to 20. Plants grow from 15 to 24 inches tall; space 18 to 20 inches apart. Blooms second year after sowing.

IBERIS (PERENNIAL CANDYTUFT) ☐ Perennial sorts of iberis make mats of evergreen foliage 4 to 6 inches high; space 12 inches apart for good effect. Covered with white flowers in May. Variety *sempervirens* is the easiest to grow from seed, sown indoors in February or March with germination in 6 days. Outdoors, 12 to 18. Excellent for edging or rockeries. Should be sheared after blooming.

INCARVILLEA (HARDY GLOXINIA) ☐ Large lacy-like foliage with spikes of tubular flowers usually in shades of rose. Easy from seed started indoors like the tender, true gloxinia. Needs warmth for germination. Start in February or March; germination 12 to 15 days. Sow in covered frame in late April with germination 25 to 30 days. It is best to winter over plants in greenhouse or under fluorescent lights the first year. Very good in part shade where soil remains moist. Suffers in times of drought. Grows 15 to 18 inches high; space 15 inches apart.

IRIS KAEMPFERI (JAPANESE IRIS) ☐ This iris, also called Oriental iris, does not form a rhizome as does the bearded type, but makes a thick mat of fibrous roots.

Excellent in the perennial border if it is kept moist in early spring until it blooms. Prefers acid soil and six hours of sunshine to be at its best. Huge iris flowers open flat. Grows 3 to 4 feet tall; space 18 inches apart. For best germination give seed a 4- to 5-week pre-chilling in coldframe or in protected spot outdoors before bringing into warmth when germination is had in two weeks. Can be sown in coldframe in fall with germination in spring. Mine were placed in coldframe in late February for 4 weeks then brought into greenhouse. After the seedlings reached 3 inches in height they were transferred to flats and placed in covered coldframes in mid-April and fed every 2 weeks with Rapid-Gro. By July they were placed in permanent spots in the flower border. The second year they were vigorous plants and bloom began in the third season after sowing. For bearded iris see Chapter on bulbs, tubers and corms.

LEONTOPODIUM (EDELWEISS) ☐ Wooly foliage with tiny little white flowers growing 4 to 6 inches; space 3 inches apart. Although seeds germinate fairly well in my greenhouse I have had better results by giving them a sojourn of 3 to 4 weeks in cold- frame in February before bringing indoors to germinate in 10 days. Very good in rockeries.

LIMONIUM (SEA LAVENDER) ☐ Variety *latifolium* is the plant called perennial statice. It sends up sprays of small lavender flowers above fairly large green leaves. The flowers dry nicely for winter bouquets. Not particularly showy as a garden flower although many gardeners like it for its airy beauty. Sow indoors January or February; germination in 10-15 days. Grows 2½ to 3 feet; space 15 inches apart.

LUPINE ☐ This is one of the most beautiful flowers in my perennial border and although it tends to die out in 3 or 4 years, I grow new replacement plants each year. Blooming in June, the flower spikes in cream, blue, yellow and rose are very showy and much admired. Lupine needs a rich soil and plenty of water. Drought will kill it. It has a taproot so resents transplanting except when small. We transfer our plants to permanent places when they are 4 to 6 inches tall. I prefer the Russell varieties and separate named varieties in different colors are available. Although most authorities recommend nicking the seed before sowing, I find it germinates readily in our favorite seedling mix. Sown in warmth in February or March it germinates in 3-4 days. Grows 2-3 feet tall; space 18 inches.

LYCHNIS (MALTESE CROSS) ☐ *L. chalcedonica* is very easy from seed. The plant has dark green spikes topped with clusters of red flowers arranged like a cross hence its name "maltese cross." Very hardy and long lived perennial. If first flowers are cut off promptly before setting seed it will bloom from side shoots all summer. To 3 feet; space 15 inches apart. Start indoors in February or March; germination in 15 days; outdoors, 21 to 30. Not especially particular as to soil, it does prefer full sun. *L. coronaria* or (mullein pink)—gardening friends gave us this lychnis for bloom in our first garden. Leaves are gray and velvety topped with dark rose-red blooms. Blooming time is short-lived in my garden so I do not use it in my perennial border. Self-sows readily. Germination as above. To 2 feet; space 12 inches apart.

109 HOSTA GLAUCA HAS LAVENDER
FLOWERS IN SEASON, BUT MORE IMPORTANT
IS THE RICH BLUE-GREEN, VEINED FOLIAGE.
                              Paul E. Genereux

LYTHRUM (PURPLE LOOSESTRIFE) ☐ Sow indoors February or March; germination 7-15 days. Outdoors 15 to 20. This import from Asia is found growing all over the Northeast in meadows and moist places. I have one large clump in my garden growing from seed brought from Washington's home at Mount Vernon. Bees and butterflies love it. Spikes of lavender flowers are quite showy. To 5 feet tall; space 18 inches apart. Spreads rather rapidly.

MONARDA OR BALM—SEE WILD FLOWERS

MYOSOTIS (FORGET-ME-NOT) ☐ Variety *semperflorens* is very hardy in my garden. One of the few plants which does well in shade although it prefers a moist condition. If sheared after the first bloom will bloom again later in the summer. Sow indoors March, germination 7 to 12 days; outdoors, 18 to 20. To 8 inches; space 6 inches apart.

NEPETA MUSSINI (CATMINT) ☐ This is one of the few plants which likes hot, dry places and does not mind poor soil. Low-growing plants with aromatic foliage and pretty spikes of lavender flowers. Best blooming period late May and early June but if sheared will bloom lightly throughout the summer. Easily grown from seed. Sow indoors February; 7 to 12 days for germination; outdoors, 12 to 20. Grows to 10 inches; space 6 inches apart.

OENOTHERA FRUTICOSA (VARIETY YOUNGII) ☐ This is an easily grown very hardy perennial producing clusters of light yellow flowers for 6 weeks in early summer. Because it blooms sometimes when early perennials have finished and later ones have not started. I have clumps of this throughout the entire length of my perennial border. Foliage turns scarlet in late summer and adds a nice accent. Spreads by small rosettes which are easily pulled off in spring if the clumps begin to become too large. Sprays of flowers grow to 15 inches tall and rosettes should be spaced about 4-5 inches apart in a clump for best effect. Indoors February to March with germination in 10 days; outdoors, 15-20. Self-sows readily. Does best in rich soil but will grow anywhere even in part shade.

PAPAVER (ORIENTAL POPPY) ☐ Oriental poppies are quite easy to grow from seed and now that seed of pinks, white, rose and softer pastels are available, more home gardeners should try this beautiful long-lived and hardy perennial from seed. They usually send up a bloom or two the second year. Started indoors in warmth, they germinate in 6 to 10 days. Outdoors, 15 to 20. Seedlings are very small and fragile. Young plants should be protected from the hot sun until well established. The foliage of the Oriental poppy will die down in July and August, sometimes disappearing completely but begins to grow again in the fall. It is wise to mark them carefully so that they will not be disturbed by cultivation or weeding. Poppies may be moved while in this dormant stage without damage. They can be moved in early spring as well although mature plants are usually set back in their blooming period by spring moving. Blooms in June. Does best in good rich soil. To 3 feet; space 18 inches apart.

PEONIES ☐ I do not recommend growing peonies from seed unless one is doing hybridizing work. I have grown tree peonies from seed and find this is an exciting and rewarding plant. The tree peony differs from the garden peony in that it is actually a shrub. In other words the entire plant does not die down to the ground level but hardens its stems like any hardy shrub and new leaves and flowers appear on these stems in mid-May in our locality. The flowers are semisingle and are very large and showy. Seeds need to be frozen to break dormancy so should be planted in the cold-frame for germination the following spring. When 3 to 4 inches high seedlings should be transplanted to nursery rows for a year or two before placing in permanent places where they will live without disturbance for years. Blooms are usually had by the third year. Likes good soil and plenty of water in times of drought. Grows to 4 feet tall and should be spaced 3 to 4 feet apart.

PENSTEMON (BEARD-TONGUE) ☐ Spikes of lovely flowers on long stems above pointed leaves. I love these flowers but they have never been reliably hardy in my garden. Many of them bloom the first year. The Viehmeyer hybrids appear to be hardier; they are beautiful in June. Others which are good in gardens where they are hardier; they are beautiful in June. Likes good soil and full sun. Grows to 20 inches; space 15 inches apart. Very easy from seed sown indoors germinating in warmth 7 to 12 days; outdoors, 12 to 20.

PHLOX PANICULATA ☐ This is the hardy or summer phlox which almost every gardener knows, blooming in July and August in our area. Very hardy plant but needs division every three years for best results. As the colors do not come true from seed and the new hybrid plants offered by nurserymen are so inexpensive I do not recommend growing these from seed. However, if you wish to try your luck with these flowers, seeds should be sown in the coldframe in late fall to germinate in May or June. Grows 4 feet tall; should be spaced 8 inches apart, in clumps. Flowers some in shades of red and rose, pink and white and salmon. Does best in rich soil.

PLATYCODON (CHINESE BALLOONFLOWER) ☐ Lovely blue, pink or white balloon-shaped buds open to star-shaped flowers. Very long-lived perennial and extremely hardy. Blooms in July. Resents transplanting except when small as it has a taproot. Should be left undisturbed in the perennial border for years. Grows readily from seed and self-sows freely. Seed sown indoors February or March germinates in 7 to 10 days. Outdoors 12 to 20 days. Grows 1½ to 3 feet tall; space 12 to 15 inches apart. Taller sorts need staking. Seeds may be sown in fall in coldframe or open seed beds. Plant does not begin to show new shoots until mid-May so should be properly marked so that cultivation will not disturb the brittle crowns.

POLEMONIUM (JACOB'S LADDER) ☐ These are pretty little early spring-blooming plants with airy foliage and sprays of lovely blue flowers good for rockery or front of the border. Not particular as to soil and will bloom in part shade. Seed sown indoors in February or March germinate in 12 to 15 days; outdoors, 18 to 30. Will germinate readily in spring from fall-sown seed in coldframe or open seed bed. Grows 12 inches tall; space 10 inches apart.

PRIMULA (PRIMROSE OR COWSLIP) ☐ Early spring-blooming plants needing a place in a semishaded area where they can be kept fairly moist. Mine do well at my north foundation under mountain ash trees but in times of drought they need to be watered to keep from drying out. Rosettes of dark green fuzzy foliage with clusters of flowers in early May in shades of rose, red, lavender, blue, white and yellow. Varieties I have found particularly hardy in my garden are *P. vulgaris, polyanthus* and *auricula.* Foliage of *P. cashmiriana* (also known as *P. japonicum*) with ball-shaped clusters of lavender flowers in earliest spring dies down during winter while the foliage of the others remains partly evergreen. They need rich soil on the acid side for best results and mulching with pine needles or peatmoss. Although some gardeners freeze the seed for good germination, I find they do well with a pre-chilling period of four weeks in the coldframe in March. Have also had excellent germination in late spring by refrigerating (not freezing) the seed for three weeks prior to bringing to sunny window, fluorescent lights or greenhouse. Germination follows in 21 to 30 days. For best results I prefer to start mine in February in order to have extra large plants by fall. Grow 8 to 10 inches tall; space 8 inches apart. May also be sown in fall in coldframe or open seed beds.

SALVIA ☐ I find perennial salvias very interesting although I do not feel that they are all good subjects for the perennial border, some of them having foliage which is too bold and with not too conspicuous flowers. They are all very easy from seed sown indoors February to March germinating in 5 days; outdoors, 15 to 30 days. For the benefit of the home gardener I want to describe all that I have grown with appropriate comments.

SALVIA ARGENTEA ☐ This is a most unusual plant and one or two in the perennial border will arouse comment. Leaves are fuzzy almost white and quite large about 12 inches long and 6 inches wide. Forms a low rosette. Large spectacular sprays of creamy white flowers bloom in June almost in candlelabra effect. To 2½ feet tall; space 18 inches apart.

SALVIA AZUREA GRANDIFLORA (PITCHERI) ☐ This variety has fine leaves, grows to 4 feet tall with spikes of lovely powder-blue flowers in August. It does not show aboveground until late May in my garden so needs to be properly marked so that it will not be disturbed until it starts to grow. Its only fault is a habit of sprawling and does not lend itself too well to staking. Grows in any good soil.

SALVIA GLUTINOSA ☐ This is an interesting plant with pale green fuzzy leaves. The flower spikes are inconspicuous and the flowers are pale yellow and sticky, hence its name. This, I think would be a good plant for our "wild" area but is too bold and not pretty enough for our perennial border. Grows to 4 feet tall; space 2 feet apart.

SALVIA HAEMATODES ☐ This is my favorite of all perennial salvias. The leaves are rather large and coarse and held close to the ground but the flowers spikes grow to 2 to 2½ feet tall many branched with heavenly blue flowers. Blooms in June. I have won many a blue ribbon in flower shows with this one. Easily grown from seed. Does best in good rich soil and plenty of water in times of drought. Self-sows readily and is easily transplanted in early spring.

SALVIA OFFICINALIS (GARDEN SAGE)—SEE HERBS

SALVIA SUPERBA ☐ This is my second choice of favorite perennial salvias. It also blooms in June with spikes of deep purple flowers and when spikes are cut back as soon as flowers have faded, it will send up a few blooms again in late summer. In my garden this one never grows over 15 inches high and is spaced 12 inches apart.

SALVIA PRATENSIS ☐ This is a rather attractive salvia, sending up its spikes of blooms in mid-May in blue or rose. A row of it is very pretty but the blooms last only a few weeks. Grows to 18 inches; space 15 inches apart.

SALVIA VERTICILLATA, THE LILAC SALVIA ☐ Bushy plants with lilac-blue flowers in long whorls during summer. If flowers are kept cut as soon as faded they will continue to bloom over a long period. To 3 feet; space 20 inches apart.

SAPONARIA (SOAPWORT) ☐ Excellent trailer for rock garden; small leaves covered with pink flowers in May. Easy from seed sown February; germinates 8 days indoors; 15 to 20, outdoors. Self-sows readily.

SHASTA DAISY (CHRYSANTHEMUM LEUCANTHEMUM AND C. MAXIMUM) ☐ Everyone knows this lovely large white daisy which blooms in July. Shastas are the finest of summer flowers for the hardy perennial border and are easy to grow from seed. In my garden the doubles are inclined to die out quickly. All the others only need division about every third year to keep them in good condition. They are easy to grow from seed indoors in February or March with germination 5 to 7 days; outdoors, 15 to 20 days. Grows 3 feet; space 20 inches apart. My favorite varieties are 'Alaska,' 'Floradale Daisy,' 'Marconi' and 'Polaris.' The new variety 'Little Miss Muffet,' a low-growing one to 12 inches, blooms beautifully in one year. The taller ones I like mid-border and 'Little Miss Muffet' toward the edge. May be sown outdoors in late fall in coldframe or open seed bed.

SIDALCIA ☐ Small perennial with hollyhock-like flowers in shades of rose. Grows to 18 inches. Blooms in July in my garden. Space 12 inches apart. Easily grown from seed sown indoors February or March with germination in 12 to 15 days; outdoors, 20 to 25 days. Prefers full sun.

STACHYS (BETONY) ☐ Also known as lamb's-ears. This white wooly-leaved plant is used much for borders in which case the long white stems of blooms with small lavender flowers are cut off when they form. Does not mind drought and poor soil. Plants grow to 10 inches and should be spaced 10 inches apart for solid border; flower stems go to 2 feet tall. Sow February to March indoors with germination 10 to 15 days; outdoors, 18 to 20.

STOKESIA (STOKE'S ASTER) ☐ This is a perennial aster blooming in midsummer in my garden. Grows 12 to 15 inches tall rather in sprawling fashion with many large lavender flowers, in typical aster form. At its best in good rich soil. Start indoors February or March with germination in 15 to 20 days; outdoors, 20 to 35 days.

VERBENA (VENOSA) ☐ This is a lovely verbena with deep purple flowers and it is quite hardy. Start in greenhouse in March with germination in 10 days. Outdoors, 20 to 30 days. Grows to 1 foot; space 10 inches apart.

VERONICA ☐ Perennial veronicas are easy to grow from seed sown indoors in February with germination in 6 days; outdoors, 15 to 20. The speedwell is superior to *spicata* in my opinion as it is a lower growing, although a package of *spicata* will yield white as well as blue plants. Not particular as to soil; very hardy but susceptible to drought. Grows to 2 feet tall; space 15 inches apart.

YARROW—SEE ACHILLEA

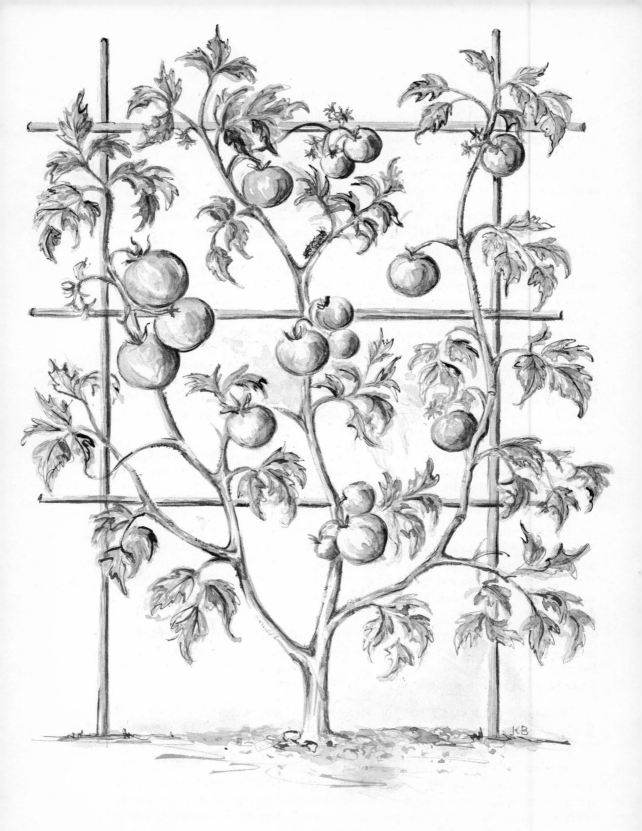

6. Vegetables from Seed

WHEN I was a child my father's work made it necessary for us to move quite frequently and we did not live where we could have a garden, although for three years when I was a very little girl we lived in the manor house of what had been at one time a magnificent estate. There was a kitchen garden where strawberries still bore luscious fruit among grass and weeds. Old peach trees of the white cling variety with a flavor out of this world were still bearing. Fig trees with sweet fruits attracted bees and the grape arbor which shaded the walk to the "summer kitchen" were, despite neglect, laden with fruits each year. My mother had a vegetable garden there and I recall helping to plant the little wrinkled peas which would give us such delicious eating pleasure along with new potatoes in early June and the little white speckled-with-purple lima beans, the "butter beans" of the South which were planted around poles arranged in teepee fashion; easy for children to pick the beans and wonderful for a little girl to escape from six brothers to daydream. I also recall but not with such great pleasure "picking" the potato bugs and knocking them into cans of kerosene. There were no sprays for the garden in those days; at least not in our garden.

My husband's grandmother had a country home where she raised chickens and grew fine vegetables in her kitchen garden. Both of us wanted very much to try to recapture what I like to call "that old timey flavor" of home-grown vegetables but our first garden was not suitable for growing vegetables. The house was built into the side of a little hill which necessitated a number of narrow terraces and there was too much shade even if there had been room for vegetables. We did try tomatoes and the results were satisfactory and I just had to have a row of baby limas—which perhaps gave us one-half dish apiece as its entire crop!

Down the road a little way lived a chicken farmer and as I walked my little dog there I used to drool over the splendid garden he grew. Lettuces literally as large as footballs . . . well, almost as large . . . rows of beautiful peas growing on "brush" cut in winter and pressed to be used for them to climb on. Corn, broccoli and squashes of all kinds and beautiful melons, green beans, lima beans and tomatoes. My husband got into the habit of chatting with the old gentleman and the next summer we were allowed to use a piece of his garden for growing vegetables. Many times we would come down to work to find this kind old man throwing handfuls of well-rotted chicken manure along our rows of vegetables. This was just at the time the Victory gardens were conceived as a patriotic means to supplement the normal sources of food supply. Hundreds of thousands of homeowners created vegetable gardens in back yards and some of them even on the front lawns or on adjacent or community plots to assist in the war effort. Many for the first time realized the superiority of fresh homegrown fruits and vegetables un-obtainable at the local market and experienced the deep satisfaction of accom-plishment of being able to grow their own. A good many of these "patriots" still continue to maintain garden plots and many of their children also grow their own vegetables having learned to appreciate their superior flavor literally at their mother's knee—or father's as the case may be, and they not only insist but know their produce is better than the "store bought" varieties, and no one agrees more than we.

Tremendous progress has been achieved by the truck garden industry since the war to get fruits and vegetables to the market place as nearly in a fresh-picked condition as possible. Better roads, faster refrigerated modes of transportation and plastic packaging all are contributing to better quality produce. California, Florida and Arizona fruits and vegetables of excellent quality are available throughout the nation and reasonably priced during the winter months when agricultural production over much of the country is at a standstill.

With all this crusade by the industry to achieve the quality of garden freshness and the progress which has been made in this direction I have yet to taste the equal of our own home-grown asparagus enjoyed by us for a month or more in the spring or the early June peas which we eat with such relish and appreciation. They truly have that "old timey flavor!" Other crops to be harvested later such as broccoli, cabbage, kohlrabi, eggplant, pepper, tomato, squash, beet and turnips from the garden to the table "within the hour" is a prerequisite that commercial growers cannot ever hope to attain.

Many homeowners even with relatively small plots can devote a small area to a vegetable garden and experience the delight of truly fresh vegetables. A 10- x 15-foot garden, if selectively planted, can yield a surprising amount of vegetables and one twice this size (15 x 20) will take care of much of the vegetable needs of a family of four. Of course the catch phrase is "selectively planted." The "sprawlers" such as vine squash and melons must be avoided and it is unlikely that corn could be suitably accommodated in such a limited space.

The small space consumers such as carrots, beets, lettuce, bush beans, onions, turnip, radish, kohlrabi, spinach and the bush-type summer squash all lend themselves to a limited garden area. Rows and plants can be closely spaced to obtain maximum yields. Many means are available to the enterprising gardener to grow crops *vertically* to conserve space. Tomatoes staked and kept pruned will produce fruit superior to those not staked. Pole beans yield very heavy crops compared to the bush variety. If cucumber (a sprawler) is a must then grow it in the air on chicken wire. Also to gain full use of limited space the very early quick maturing crops such as radish, lettuce, turnip and the quick yielding bush beans will, after harvest, permit second plantings of additional vegetables for a late fall harvest. However, I am straying from my purpose, and the subject of this book, growing plants from seed. There are a great many books on vegetable gardening and much free information upon request from the county agents and the state agricultural stations as well as the United States Department of Agriculture as I have mentioned before in this book. Seedsmen's catalogs contain a wealth of information on varieties, growing habits and on maintaining a vegetable garden, complete with charts.

With vegetables as with flowers and other ornamentals, great strides have been made by the seedsmen of this country to have available for the home gardener seeds of vegetables of extra fine quality and which will grow under many different soil conditions and in the many climates of our various states. As few seeds are planted under ideal conditions, seed treating is a means of protection or insurance that seeds planted under adverse conditions will sprout, grow and produce fine crops. I asked Mr. Joseph Harris of the seed firm by that name, Rochester, New York, if he would explain for the benefit of my readers, in language easily understood by the inexperienced, the reason for treated seeds and I am quoting here his reply.

"In the case of certain kinds such as lettuce, endive, onions, radish, there is normally no special benefit in seed treating and it is not usually done. However, with many other kinds the seed treatment affords protection against soil organisms which tend to attack the seed, especially under cool conditions. A great deal of research has gone into chemicals and rates of application on the important process crop such as peas and corn, and it has been well established that peas, which are normally planted in cold soil anyway, give better stands with treated seed than without. If sweet corn seed is planted in warm soil say around Memorial Day or June, there will be   little difference between the treated and the untreated seed. However, a great deal of seed is planted earlier than this, and with the early varieties in particular, the seed is often planted in April or early May when the soil is quite cold. Under these conditions, the treatment affords very valuable protection. Both peas and corn are treated with Captan, a mild, non-toxic but very effective fungicide.

"In the same way, cucumbers, melons and squash generally benefit from treatment although we do not normally treat all kinds of the latter. Of the greenhouse crops, peppers and eggplant will do all right without treatment if they have a good warm spot to grow, but under cool conditions the treatment is beneficial. We presume you are familiar with 'damping off' which is usually Rhizoctonia and occasionally Pythium and the seed treatment tends to protect against attack by these organisms on the young seedlings, as well as on the seed itself. Of course, even treated seed will 'damp off' when planted in contaminated soil.

"A further class of treatment is the hot water treatment of brassicas and tomatoes. It is possible for these seeds to be carriers of certain seed borne diseases and as a protection against this possibility we carry out the hot water treatment which eliminates alternaria and any possible black rot or black leg on cabbage, cauliflower, etc., and controls Septoria, early blight, bacterial spot and any possible bacterial canker on the tomatoes. The fungicide on these crops after hot water treatment is often recommended but we do not normally treat them, since Arasan is probably the best and it is quite irritating to handle.

"On beans a small quantity of insecticide is used to the Captan seed treatment to guard against the seed corn maggot which used to be quite destructive on beans planted in late May or early June. This maggot will eat right into the seed before it comes up and may destroy the seed entirely or make it grow

110   FOR TYPICAL STRAIGHT ROW PLANTING THE TAUT LINE SERVES AS A GUIDE TO MARK OUT A SHALLOW FURROW. HERE A RAKE HANDLE SERVES THE PURPOSE.

111   SEEDS, SHAKEN FROM PACKET, ARE THINLY SOWN ALONG THE FURROW.

112   RUNNING THE FOREFINGERS DOWN THE ROW PERMITS A GOOD CONTROL IN COVERING SEEDS THE PROPER DEPTH SINCE COVERING DEPTH DEPENDS ON THE SIZE OF INDIVIDUAL SEEDS.

113   FIRMING THE SOIL OVER THE PLANTED SEED ROW WITH THE BACK OF A RAKE— BUT LIGHTLY!

abnormally and never be productive. A tiny fraction of an ounce of Dieldrin per pound of bean seed will prevent this maggot damage, and we use it on all our beans and some summer squash. Despite the name, the sweet corn maggot is not likely to be destructive on sweet corn, but in areas where it has been severe, an insecticide and crow repellent material such as Red Shield can be applied.

"As you will have gathered, the chief value of seed treating is protection or insurance, and under ideal conditions there would be little if any benefit. However, few seeds are planted in such conditions, whether for home use or on a commercial scale."

My husband and I have for a number of years been fortunate to have an area large enough to maintain a rather large vegetable garden amply adequate to grow any of the field or garden crops including the large field pumpkins, a hill of which, when well grown, would itself cover the 10- x 15-foot garden mentioned before. We have over the years as a result of failures and successes developed our own methods and procedures, some orthodox and some unique, to a degree where our failures—and we still have some—are minimal.

Most soils in the northeastern states are lime deficient. Repeated soil tests have revealed a need in our area for an application of lime every other year to maintain a pH of 6.9 which is in the "satisfactory" range for most all vegetable crops. We apply in the early winter after crops are harvested about 5 lbs. of ground limestone per 100 square feet. The pulverized lime will do but being finely milled to a flour like consistency it is dusty and unpleasant to apply. We would not suggest that the inexperienced gardener should follow our example *unless a soil test shows the need* for lime. Some soils are very highly alkaline and the application of additional lime could be disastrous.

Inexpensive, simple soil test kits are available at most garden centers or for a small charge your county agricultural agent or state agricultural station will send you instructions how to take a sample of soil and will test same and recommend the required lime and fertilizers. I cannot stress too strongly the need to determine the basic adequacy of your garden soil by either of the above methods. It can mean the difference between a below average garden and a lush and bountiful one.

The balance of this chapter is devoted to pictures taken in our own garden and an encyclopedia of most of the usual garden vegetables disclosing some of our methods which I hope will guide the beginning gardener especially, to a successful and satisfactory growing experience.

ASPARAGUS ☐ A true, long-lived perennial. Our own bed, now twelve years old, continues to produce thumb-size shoots profusely. Since it requires about 3 years for 1-year-old plants to reach maturity most gardeners prefer to buy rooted crowns. However, seed is available for the "patient ones," and is not difficult. Sow seeds in rows 18 to 24 inches apart in spring after frost date. Thin to 4 inches between plants. The following spring dig the yearling roots, select the most vigorous and plant in a permanent location. Needs rich soil, well limed with applications of either manure and superphosphate or 5-10-5 fertilizer, every spring. We prefer to use shredded dry cow manure and superphosphate for an additional feeding in the fall. Needs warmth for germination. Germinates indoors 7-10 days; outdoors, 10-21.

BEANS ☐ The varieties of beans are endless. Two types, the green or snap bean and the lima bean are of interest to the home gardener. Both types are available either as low growers (bush) or upright (pole). All members of this family require warm weather *and* warm soil. I have found the snap beans a bit more tolerant than the limas which will rot before germination in cold soil. I have resigned myself after many futile attempts at early plantings, that it is useless in our location to plant limas before the first week in June.

SNAP BEANS ☐ Yellow, green and purple yield in about 7 weeks. Sow seed every 4 inches in rows 2 to 2½ feet apart, covering about 1 inch deep and thin to stand 8 inches. We plant short rows (about 10 ft. long) every 2 weeks up to mid-July which provides us with good bean-eating all summer. Germinates in 5-7 days. Good varieties are 'Tendercrop,' 'Bountiful,' 'Topcrop,' 'Butterwax.'

POLE BEANS ☐ Bear in about nine weeks; will produce over a longer season. Grown on poles or a teepee-combination of poles or trellises. Poles should be 7 ft. high or more. Plant six or seven beans 1 inch deep around pole and thin to the three strongest plants. Will germinate in 5 to 8 days. 'Kentucky Wonder' and 'Romano' are good varieties.

LIMA BEANS ☐ Do wait for warm soil and warm weather. For bush varieties sow 1 inch deep in rows 30 to 36 inches apart. Plant seed 6 inches apart and thin to 12 inches. A 60-ft., well-grown row of limas provides us with fresh beans during the season plus a dividend of twenty to thirty boxes in the freezer. Excellent for home gardens are 'Fordhook U.S. 242,' 'Burpee's Fordhook.' Pole limas are handled similar to pole snap beans and are prolific yielders. However, keep in mind that almost three months are required to bear. If you are limited in your garden area try a few poles, either snaps or limas, (if your climate permits) for a real taste treat. Plant 'King of the Garden,' 'Prizetaker' or 'Burpee's Best.' The Mexican bean beetle, although not troublesome to us, can be readily controlled with rotenone dust. Needs warmth for germination which takes 7 to 10 days.

BEETS ☐ A most satisfying vegetable and an easy and disease-free grower *IF* soil is not too acid. We struggled, many years ago to grow beets with no success. Then we learned that beets need a pH of 6.9 to grow well. In acid soil plants are stunted and foliage mottled and curled. After we limed our vegetable garden we never again had

114 CARROTS, BEETS AND ONIONS LEND THEMSELVES TO BROAD-ROW PLANTING. HERE A SHALLOW FURROW, ONE-FOURTH TO ONE-HALF INCH DEEP, IS MADE, HOE-WIDTH, TO RECEIVE A BROADCASTING OF SEEDS. THIS ROW METHOD WILL PRODUCE THREE TO FOUR TIMES MORE CROP THAN THE CONVENTIONAL ALL-IN-A-LINE METHOD.

115 CARROT SEED HAS BEEN THINLY BROAD-CAST ALONG THE BROAD-ROW, LIGHTLY COV-ERED AND TAMPED FIRM WITH THE BACK OF THE RAKE.

trouble growing good beets. We prefer to sow beets in a broad band, the width of a hoe; broadcasting them about 2 inches apart with a ½ inch cover. Thin to stand about 3 inches apart and use the thinnings for good eating. Some folks enjoy the greens (tops) as well as the beet itself. Beets do best in cool weather and can be planted as early in the spring as the ground can be worked. We also plant a row in early July for a fall crop. Beets are excellent frozen for winter use. If planted in mid-March, may take 3 weeks to germinate; in warmth of midsummer 7 to 14 days.

BROCCOLI ☐ This one enjoys cold weather and germinates for us indoors in 4 days and outdoors in 10-20 days. Start early indoors—or sow out doors with ½ inch soil covering as soon as soil conditions permit. Plant in rows 30 to 36 inches apart. Plants grow large and should be planted or thinned to stand 24 inches apart. There are varieties recommended for fall use, such as 'Waltham #29' which when sown in mid-June provide excellent late crops for freezing or for fresh use. The cabbage worm, easily controlled by rotenone dust, is the only pest we have found to be of any consequence. Good for freezing. Varieties 'Green Mountain' and 'Calabrese' are good for an early crop.

BRUSSEL'S SPROUTS ☐ Grown in the Belgium capital for hundreds of years from which the name originates, this is a fall cropper since it takes 4 months to mature from seed and the flavor is much improved by light frosts. Start seed, planted in rows 30 to 36 inches apart, in May and thin to stand 24 inches apart. Cover seed ¼ inch deep. They thrive as do other members of the cabbage family with plenty of moisture during the growing season. Pinching out the top leaves when sprouts begin to show results in larger sprouts to eat fresh or to freeze. Germination in summer in warmth 3 to 10 days. Aphids, controlled with rotenone or malathion and the green cabbage worm also kept in check with rotenone or D.D.T. are the most serious pests. We prefer rotenone since it performs dual control of both pests and is non-toxic and can be applied either in spray or dust form. Good varieties are 'Jade Cross' and 'Catskill' (also known as 'Long Island Improved').

CABBAGE ☐ Here is a vegetable, no doubt resulting from its universal appeal to housewives' shopping instincts, that has been hybridized and cross-bred to a fare-thee-well. There are available early, mid-season and late varieties; small and large headed types, curly leaved, green, purple and even the so-called Chinese (Michihli) Cabbages do best in cool weather with plenty of moisture and being gross feeders respond well to fertilizer application. We prefer planting our favorite variety by seed, in rows 24 inches apart, covered ¼ inch deep as early in the spring as the soil can be worked. Thin to stand 12 to 24 inches apart, depending on the ultimate size of the variety. We also plant an early variety in mid-June for a fall harvest. If planted in late April it may take 3 weeks to germinate. In warm weather it will "pop" in 3 to 7 days. Troublesome pests and their control are similar to those for Brussel's sprouts. Good varieties for the home garden are 'Early Jersey Wakefield,' 'Emerald Cross,' 'Golden Acre,' 'Danish Ballhead,' and 'Savoy King Hybrid.'

CARROTS ☐ Much research and development has been expended on this most popular vegetable. This root crop is sensitive to the physical condition of the soil and refuses to penetrate into a hard compact soil strata. Varieties have been developed ranging from 3 inches long for heavy soil to 10 inches long for deep friable soil condition. Carrots will not thrive unless the pH is at least 6.9. Select the variety which best suits your type of soil. Good varieties for the home garden are 'Nantes Half Long,' 'Tendersweet,' 'Royal Chantenay,' and 'Imperator.' Here again, as with beets, we sow carrots in a broad band the width of a hoe rather than in a straight row furrow. Broadcast seed, in very early spring (or in mid-June for a fall crop) and after germination usually 2 to 3 weeks, thin to stand about 2 inches apart. When carrots are fingerling size (and are they good!) thin again to 3 inches for mature development. A 10-ft.-long row, planted in the broad band method produces a heavy yield. Although the larvae of the carrot rust fly is considered a serious pest in some areas we have never found it necessary to take any preventative measures with this crop. Perhaps I should qualify this statement. When we had an unfenced garden we had to cover them with chicken wire. Rabbits love the tops—and the deer dig them out. As a final caution, if you have seeds left over—and you probably will—do not try to use them next year. Their viability is short-lived and germination will be either very poor or not at all.

CAULIFLOWER ☐ Cauliflower is one of the "tricky ones." Germination occurs in 6 to 10 days in midsummer. Much care is necessary during the long growing period to produce a real quality head. The purple types are easier and delicate in flavor either cooked or served raw as an appetizer or in salads. We have, over the years consistently grown both the purple and white with, I must admit, varying degree of success. If you rise to a challenge then by all means test your skill. Except in those very limited areas where summers are cool, cauliflower is grown as a fall crop. Some sow seed in flats or in a protected bed such as a coldframe and start the plants (requiring almost 2 months) about June 1st which are transplanted to the open garden in late summer. We sow seed ½ inch deep, thinly, in rows 3 feet apart, in early June and when about 1 inch high thin so that plants are about 20 inches apart. As with most of the cabbage family they are voracious feeders and particularly sensitive to a lack of moisture. To assure near perfect heads soil must never be dry and occassional side-dressing with a fertilizer such as 5-10-5, well watered-in is essential. To blanch the heads of the white type pull the leaves up over the curd when it is the size of a 50¢ piece and tie together until head is harvested. Germinates in midsummer in 3-10 days. Insect pests, aphids and cabbage worms are controlled with rotenone. Excellent varieties are 'Snow ball,' 'Snowball Imperial,' and 'Purple Head.'

CELERY ☐ Although we have grown celery with reasonable success it is a long haul (five months) from seed to maturity, requiring much tender, loving care. If you are a patient gardener and are fortunate enough to possess the few basic requirements, you can do as well as the professional gardener. Celery resents hot weather, requires a deep rich organic soil and great quantities of water. Supplemental feedings every 2 or 3 weeks are required to maintain continued and vigorous growth.

Start seed indoors, if possible, in late February for transplanting in early spring to the open garden. We sow seeds directly to the open garden, ⅛ inch deep in a row the earliest that soil can be worked, usually about April 1st, in our vicinity; expect germination in 10-20 days. Thin to 6-8 inches between plants. Hill plants slightly as they grow. Plants can be blanched by covering stalks with runner boards or paper collars for several weeks before pulling. We have never, for lack of time, followed this practice since we feel no appreciable flavor improvement results. Good varieties for the home gardener are 'Green Light,' 'Burpee's Fordhook,' and 'Summer Pascal.' Although not subject to insect pests, our greatest problems were with deer and rabbits. Until we had a fenced-in garden we protected our planting with a wood frame covered with chicken wire.

CHARD ☐ Swiss chard, really a beet, grown for its leaves and easier than spinach, is a highly satisfactory crop and can be sown as early in the spring as the soil can be worked. It matures from seed in 2 months and if leaves are continually harvested will continue to produce tender young leaves all season which can be boiled as "greens" or used in salads as lettuce. Sow ¼ inch deep in rows 18 inches apart and thin plants to stand a foot apart. Seed germinates in 7 to 15 days. As with all leafy crops they respond to ample supplies of moisture. Rarely are insects or disease a problem. Good varieties to grow are 'Fordhook Giant' and 'Rhubarb Chard.'

CHINESE CABBAGE ☐ "Celery" cabbage (we prefer the Michihli strain), like its cabbage relatives, is a cool weather crop and in most areas should be considered a fall crop. We plant seed ¼ inch deep, in rows 24 inches apart and thin plants to 12 inches. Seed sown about July 10 will germinate in 7-10 days, will produce fine heads in late September. Monthly sidedressing with a 5-10-5 fertilizer and plenty of water will keep plants growing vigorously. This is another versatile vegetable that can be boiled, used in salads, or as slaw. Flea beetles and leaf hoppers are pests but are easily controlled with rotenone, sevin or malathion.

COLLARDS ☐ This headless tree cabbage has long been a favorite "green" in the deep South where it can be grown as a winter crop. It will tolerate heat better than most of the cabbage family and here in the Northeast we have planted it any time from early spring to early summer. Seed planted ¼ inch deep in rows 30 inches apart, germinates in 3 to 10 days and will mature in about 10 weeks. Thin plants to stand 18 inches apart using the thinnings as you would chard or spinach. Leaves are harvested as with Swiss chard. Needs plenty of moisture and is at its sweetest after the first frost. Variety 'Georgia' is the best known in the North. Insects, easily controllable, are the same as for cabbage.

CORN ☐ I would guess that *fresh-picked* corn on the cob would, by popular vote, be awarded the winning trophy for taste-worthiness. The varieties are many and varied. There are early, mid-season and late; white and yellow; field corn for stock feeding, pop-corn, Indian corn and others. A northeastern seedsman lists twenty-one varieties. This is not a subject for a small garden unless, of course, your only desire is to grow fresh corn in sacrifice to other more productive crops. Plant corn in blocks to assure good pollination. A block of four 10-ft. rows is more desirable than a single 40-ft. row. Although corn can be planted in a hill system, most plantings are in rows with seed about ¾ inch deep, spaced 6 inches apart and later thinned to 12 inches with the rows 2½ to 3 feet apart. Seed will germinate in 3 to 7 days. Corn is a hot weather crop as is evidenced by the fact that the bulk of the nation's corn is produced in the Midwest. Plant seed after the soil warms up—here in the Northeast mid-May is our starting date, and even then we use an early variety which we have found slightly more receptive to cool soil. If you have the room, make three or four plantings at two-week intervals using early, mid-season and late varieties which will provide a continuous crop over many weeks. Occasionally we have harvested corn from five plantings by using an early (66-day) corn for the first and last crops. Water heavily, when rainfall is deficient, until silk starts to form. When plants are 8 or 10 inches high sidedress with a garden fertilizer, such as 5-10-5, well watered-in. Hill up soil around base of stalks to provide adequate anchorage aagainst heavy winds. The silk turns brown on most varieties when ready to harvest, but this is not infallible. Immature corn is watery— perfect stage is "in the milk" and the too late stage when kernels are tough and starchy. Peel the husk back and press one of the kernels with your thumbnail. If milky juice squirts out it is at its prime. Some people say to have the water boiling before you pick the corn. Perhaps timing is not quite that critical, but the time from the stalk to the pot should be minimum to retain the fresh picked sweetness. Corn ear worm is the chief insect pest which we have found easy to control by dusting the silk tassels weekly with rotenone. If you are in a section frequented by crows I would suggest using a crow repellent. We have used both the liquid (with a tar base) and a dust form which is much easier to handle. However, both are highly effective. Good varieties of sweet corn to grow are 'North Star,' 'Carmelcross,' 'Golden Cross Bantam,' 'Wonderful,' 'Honey and Cream,' 'Iochief,' 'Spancross,' 'Stowell's Evergreen'—all of which we have grown in our garden and can highly recommend. We, living in a rural area, have on occassion suffered severe damage from racoons. They seem to know precisely when the corn is ready and can anticipate a night in advance of when you plan to harvest.

Regrettably, I have no pat preventative or deterrent for this rascal except possibly an alert all-weather farm dog.

CUCUMBER ☐ This hot weather "sprawler," bearing about 60 days from seed, is available in a variety of shapes and sizes from the small gherkins, tiny as a tot's little finger to the club-like "China" reaching 20 inches in length. There are fat and skinny, smooth, warty and prickly types to suit it seems, everyones fancy. Soil must be warm; mid-May is our starting date. Plant 4 to 6 seeds, pointed end down in "hills" (actually slight depressions) about 1 inch deep. After germination, usually 3 to 7 days, leave two or three well-spaced, pulling the rest. We dig a hole at the hill location about 16 inches deep and place a shovel-full of dried or well rotted manure mixed with a hand-ful of 5-10-5 fertilizer. Cover with about 4 inches of soil as a planting bed. Hills are spaced 4 to 6 feet apart, depending on varieties or if space is limited vines can be grown on a trellis or chickenwire. The hybrid varieties are tremendous producers. One hill of three vines supplies us with more than our needs during the entire growing season. Cucumber beetle feeding on the leaves and spreading wilt disease can be disastrous. Many products (dusts are preferable) are available for easy control of this pest. We prefer rotenone since it is non-toxic. Good varieties of cucumbers for the home gardener are 'Triumph Hybrid,' 'Marketer,' 'Tablegreen,' 'Ashley,' 'Burpeeana Hybrid.' For pickling try 'Ohio Mr. 17,' 'Triple Purpose,' 'West India Gherkin.'

EGGPLANT ☐ This heat-loving handsome fruit may not be a universal favorite for its unusual taste but for eye appeal it has no peer. The dark plum highly polished beauty has accounted for a number of our blue ribbons. Since a relatively long growing period is required (70 to 80 days) we start seeds indoors, sometimes slow to germinate (7 to 21 days), 4 to 6 weeks before time to plant. Soon after germination transplant to peat pots which can later be planted out, pot and all. Set plants 24 inches apart, and keep them growing *steadily* to produce top quality fruit. Water deeply weekly if lacking rain and sidedress lightly every month with fertilizer. This is a delightful vegetable. We have a friend who will not eat it but always grows several plants to use the fruit for table decorations, or for "way-out" flower arrangements. Incidentally we consider many eggplant dishes as a real eat-treat. In our garden we have had excellent results with 'Burpee's Black Beauty,' 'Burpee Hybrid,' 'Black Magic Hybrid.'

ENDIVE ☐ This leafy delicately spicy plant grown for salad can be planted from early spring to mid-July in our northeastern area. The latter date produces an autumn crop after most lettuce is finished. Germination can be expected in 7 to 14 days. Sow seed ¼ inch deep in rows 18 inches apart and thin plants to 8 to 10 inches apart. Plants mature in about three months from seed. Good varieties to grow are 'Batavian,' 'Florida Deep Heart,' 'Green curled.' We have never found insect or disease control necessary although aphids and leafhoppers are considered pests. Extreme caution should be exercised in the use of sprays on salad greens since many leave poisonous residues that resist washing. We absolutely refuse to spray such crops.

GOURDS ☐ I hesitated to include this inedible member of the squash family under vegetables but could not resist. Some seedsmen even list it in the *flower section* of their

116   SWEET CORN 'BURBANK HYBRID.'
Burpee Seeds

117   HYBRID CUCUMBER 'M & M.'
Burpee Seeds

118   F¹ HYBRID BROCCOLI 'CLEOPATRA' WAS THE RECEPIENT OF AN ALL-AMERICA SELECTIONS AWARD IN 1964.

119   BUSH SNAP BEAN 'RICHGREEN.'
Burpee Seeds

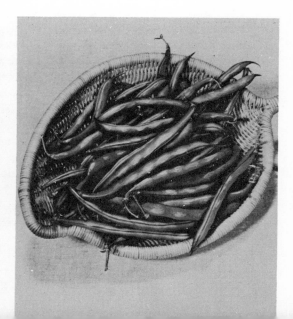

catalogs. Gourds, treated like squash or melons, are available in separate varieties or in mixtures of large and small types. A mixed packet contains many surprises. They are easy to grow—plant a hill, let the vines climb on a trellis, fence or wall. They are fun to watch develop and the smaller, colorful types make delightful fall decoration. Consult your seed catalogs for varieties and descriptions. For fun try 'Turk's Turban,' 'Serpent Gourd,' 'Bottle,' 'Spoon,' 'Striped Pear,' 'Holy Crown' and 'Hedgehog.' Refer to squash for cultural directions.

KALE ☐ This loose-leaved cabbage sports handsome blue-green curly leaves. These are so handsome that many use them in flower arrangements. However, its prime use is as greens boiled as spinach or used raw in salads. Although kale can be grown in early spring it is usually planted in mid-July, when it germinates in 3 to 10 days, for a fall or early winter crop. Taste quality is improved by light frosts and where winters are not severe will frequently live over. Plant ½ inch deep, rows 18 to 24 inches apart, with plants thinned to stand 12 inches apart. Cut leaves as they mature on a cut-and-come again basis for a continuing crop. Good varieties to grow are 'Blue Curled Scotch,' 'Dwarf Siberian' and 'Vates.' Aphids and cabbage worm are the most serious pests but readily controlled with rotenone.

KOHLRABI ☐ This quick grower (eight weeks), with a turnip-cabbage flavor is an easy cool weather crop, germinating in 3 to 10 days. We start seeds in the spring as early as the soil can be worked and again about August 1 for a fall crop. Sow seed ¼ inch deep, in rows 18 inches apart and thin to 6 inches. Harvest when they are about 3 inches in diameter. 'Early White Vienna' is the best type for the home garden in the Northeast. Some like the crispy, zesty flavor in raw slices. We prefer them chunk-cut and boiled tender with a butter or cream sauce. We have never experienced any problems with insects or disease.

LEEK ☐ Because of slow growth, three months plus from seed, this member of the onion family provides fall green onions. The blanched stems have a delicate flavor and are excellent boiled or used in soups or stews. Seed may be sown ¼ inch deep, indoors in flats in early spring, or sown directly in trenches. Seed germinates indoors in 7 to 10 days and outdoors, 8 to 14 days. Rows are set 18 inches apart and plants 3 to 4 inches apart. Trench should be about 6 inches deep and as the plants grow, hill up soil around the stem. As with all onions, water regularly and harvest before hard frost. Variety 'Elephant' and 'Broad London' are recommended for home gardeners. Rarely is it necessary to protect leek against insect or disease damage.

LETTUCE ☐ Probably the most popular home garden product. It will do well on moderately rich soil, responds to light side-dressings of fertilizer occassionally but insists on plenty of water to produce fat turgid leaves and well formed heads. There are many varieties of the three basic types; the loose-leaf such as "salad bowl," Cos or Romaine, and the heading types which include both the loose head and the hard crisp iceberg types. Most varieties germinate in 5 to 7 days. The loose-leaf varieties mature in about 7 weeks from seed but the heading types take up to 3 months. All prefer cool weather, but some varieties have been developed to withstand reasonably hot weather.

Select several types and varieties from your seed catalog, to assure a continuous supply all summer. Do try 'Ruby,' a dark red loose-leaf type for a colorful salad. Sow in early spring, in rows ⅛ inch deep, with rows 18 inches apart. Thin when small to stand 6 to 12 inches apart, depending on ultimate size of plant. For loose-leaf varieties grow 'Oak Leaf,' "Simpson,' 'Salad Bowl,' Matchless,' 'Ruby,' 'Slobolt.' For heading we like 'Bibb,' 'Dark Green Boston,' 'Fulton,' 'Great Lakes 659.' *Remember the lettuce secret; plenty of water.*

MELONS ☐ The melons, whether they be muskmelon (cantaloupe) or watermelon, have three basic needs; adequate room, warm weather and plenty of water. Most of them take about 3 months to mature from seed. Wait until the soil and the nights are warm, plant seed in "hills," 6 to 8 feet apart to suit the variety. We, as with squash and tomatoes, place a shovelful of manure mixed with a handful of fertilizer 4 inches under the surface. Plant 5 or 6 seeds ½ inch deep in a 12-inch-diameter hill (actually a slight depression) placing pointed end of seed down. Most varieties germinate in 4 to 7 days. Thin to the two or three best-placed seedlings and start your regular watering routine if rain is lacking. Keep area free of weeds and side-dress monthly with a cupful of commercial fertilizer, well cultivated and water in. If you have the room, try one of the newer F_1 hybrid musksmelons. I guarantee you will be amazed at the sweetness of your home-grown produce compared with those available at the market place. Excellent varieties of cantaloupe for the home garden are 'Delicious 51,' 'Iroquis,' 'Harvest Queen,' 'Gold Star,' 'Honey Rock,' 'Pennsweet.' For warm climates try 'Golden Beauty Casaba' or 'Honey Dew.' Watermelons we can recommend for the home gardener are 'New Hampshire Midget,' 'Sugar Baby,' 'Tetra No. 2,' 'Summer Festival,' 'Burpee's Fordhook Hybrid.'

OKRA ☐ A popular vegetable in the South, where it is more frequently called gumbo. Used as a vegetable, but more often in soups where its gummy quality provides both flavor and thickening. The strange attractive fruit, in both the green and dried stage, is used extensively by flower arranging friends whom I must admit end up with most of our crop. Seeds sown ½ inch deep in rows 24 to 30 inches apart germinate in 5 to 14 days and mature in 2 months. Thin plants to stand 15 inches apart. This is a hot-weather crop—wait until warm nights and warm soil prevail and water regularly. We have grown 'Clemson Spineless' and 'Dwarf Green Long Pod' with equal success. We have had no problem with insects or diseases.

ONIONS ☐ Onions, and there are many varieties, are sold by seedsmen as plants (by the bunch), as sets (small dried onions) or as seed. We obtain very adequate, and inexpensive, crops of white, yellow and sweet Spanish onions from seed. Plant seed ¼ inch deep in rows 18 inches apart as early in the spring as soil can be worked. Seeds germinate in 7 to 14 days. Thin out the young green onions for table use as they grow, ultimately so that plants are spaced 3 inches apart. Sidedress occasionally with fertilizer and most important keep them growing unchecked by frequent watering. Although seedmen list maturing from seed in about 4 months, our experience is closer to 5 months. Varieties we have successfully grown are 'Sweet Spanish,' 'Utah,' 'Early Harvest,' 'Early Yellow Globe,' 'Yellow Globe Danvers.' Although our onions have never

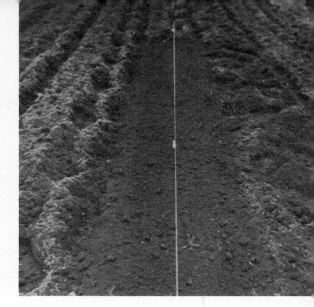

120 THE GARDEN HAS BEEN FERTILIZED AND TILLED. A TAUT MASON'S TWINE IS STRETCHED TO MARK THE ROW.

121 THE ROW AREA ROUGH-RAKED TO LEVEL THE FURROWS RESULTING FROM TILLING.

122 OPENING A FURROW ABOUT TWO INCHES DEEP, THE FULL WIDTH OF THE HOE FOR THE PLANTING BED.

123 THE PEAS HAVE BEEN PLACED, IN THREE ROWS, WITH SEEDS TWO TO THREE INCHES APART.

124 FURROW IS BACK-FILLED USING BACK OF RAKE AS A PUSHER.

been bothered by pests, thrips can be troublesome. Control with malathion but follow the label instructions implicitly

PARSLEY ☐ A member of the herb family and is used both fresh and dried. Although truly a biennial we prefer to grow fresh plants each year. A relatively slow grower so start indoors in early March. Seed barely covered will germinate in about 10 days and can be transplanted to flats or peat pots in about a month. Set out plants about the first week in May (after hardening off) in rows 18 inches apart with plants spaced 12 inches apart. Good varieties to grow are 'Paramount' and 'Extra Curled Dwarf.' Pot up several plants in the fall and put on your kitchen window sill, if well lighted, for decoration and to use as garnish during the winter.

125 SOIL OVER PEAS IS LIGHTLY TAMPED FIRM WITH BACK OF RAKE.

126 A COOL AND WET APRIL PROVIDED IDEAL CONDITIONS THAT BROUGHT THIS SHOWING IN EARLY MAY.

PARSNIPS ☐ Here perhaps is the most unpopular vegetable of the garden. Even the insects avoid it! A slow grower, 120 days from seed, and is accordingly, in our area a fall crop or as far into the winter as they can be dug. Sow seed in late spring, covering ⅛ inch, in rows 2 feet apart and thin plants to 4 inches. Seed germinates in 7 to 25 days. If you wish to extend the season, dig them before ground freezes hard and store in an outdoor pit or in moist soil in the cellar. Good varieties to grow are 'All American,' 'Harris' Model,' 'Guernsey.'

PEANUTS ☐ Not really a subject for northern gardens, but lots of fun. We grow a short row (a single packet) of the 'Early Spanish' variety each summer successfully. Sow seed in hulls 1½ inches deep spaced 8 inches apart in rows 24 inches apart. Germination takes 7 to 15 days. Keep the soil under the plants well loosened. The female flowers on the plant drop their ovaries to the ground to form the underground peanut crop. Dig the entire plant in the fall immediately after the first light frost and hang in a dry place to cure. Several years ago we hung them in the garage to cure and upon checking a week later found that mice had taken every last peanut. Two varieties easy to grow in the Northeast are 'Early Spanish' and 'Jumbo Virginia.' We have never experienced insect or disease damage to our plants.

PEAS ☐ If you have never eaten peas that were cooked within an hour of being picked you have a treat in store for you. They do require more of the gardener's time than most crops but the results are worth the effort. Most of the peas are tall, climbing varieties reaching 2 to 3 feet and require support. There are several that grow only 18 inches, without support, 'Little Marvel' being one which is always included in our garden. We have a dozen ¾-inch-diameter pipes, 5 ft. long and 100 ft. length of 3-foot-high fencing which we use yearly as a pea trellis. Since peas bear in about 2 months the space they occupied can be replanted to such fall crops as lettuce, cabbage and turnips. Plant as early in spring as ground can be worked (usually about April 1st in our area), and you will have early June peas. We prefer to sow as follows: Using a hoe, dig a trench about 2 inches deep the *full width* of the hoe. Sow three rows of seed, or scatter in trench so that seeds are about 2 inches apart. Space rows 30 inches apart. Seed will germinate in 7 to 15 days. We sow a long row but use early, mid-season and late varieties to get succession bearing. We drive pipes about 8 feet apart and fasten by occasional wiring to the 3-foot high fencing. Good varieties for the home garden are 'Little Marvel,' 'Frezonian,' 'Lincoln,' 'Wando,' 'Alderman,' 'Thomas Laxton.' Pea aphids, if prevalent, can be controlled with rotenone.

PEPPERS ☐ Both kinds of peppers, the sweet and the hot are red when mature although the sweet pepper is usually picked and eaten when green. A half dozen plants will provide for the average family. Since it takes about 2½ months to mature after transplants are set out it is desirable to start indoors about April 1st, with germination in about 5 to 8 days and transplant to pots so that they can be set out with no root disturbance. Plants and rows should be about 24 inches apart. We create a soil basin (as we do with squash and tomatoes) around each plant to hold water. Water deeply each week if rain is lacking. Breeders have developed F_1 hybrids which are highly productive and of excellent quality. For the home garden we highly recommend 'Calwonder,' 'Pennwonder,' 'Keystone Giant,' 'King of the North,' 'Burpee's Fordhook.' We have never found it necessary to spray peppers for insects.

PUMPKIN ☐ If you have lots of space, try it. A single hill will cover a space 10 to 15 feet in diameter. They are good eating although our crop, usually one hill, ends up with the neighbor's children for Halloween Jack-o-lanterns. Treat the same as squash, with a shovelful of manure under the hill. Plant 4 to 6 seeds, point down, covered with 1 inch of soil. Seed will germinate in 4 to 7 days. Thin to the two best seedlings. Create a depression around the hill to hold water. Water regularly weekly. For the extra large ones select the large growers and only permit two or three closest to the main stem to grow on a vine by picking off the balance as they form. Good varieties of pumpkin for the North are 'Small Sugar,' 'Young's Beauty,' 'Big Max,' 'Jack O'Lantern,' 'Big Tom.' Insect and disease control same as for squash.

RADISH ☐ The speed of growth of this cool weather vegetable is fantastic. There are many varieties which mature from seed in from 22 to 28 days. Plant succession plantings every 10 days starting in early spring through the cool weather and again in the fall. Sow ¼ inch deep, in rows 12 inches apart, expect germination in 4 to 7 days, and thin plants to stand 1 to 2 inches apart. For the home garden use 'Cherry Belle,' 'Icicle,' 'Early Scarlet Globe,' 'Champion.' This is an ideal vegetable to arouse a child's interest in the magic of growing things.

RUTABAGA ☐ The Swede turnip, as it is sometimes called, is as traditional for Thanksgiving as is turkey. This relatively slow grower, compared to the common turnip takes 3 months from seed and is a fall crop only, but can be left in the ground until a hard freeze then dug and kept for several months in a cool cellar. If you notice those available at the market in late winter you will see that they have been dipped in parafin to prevent drying out. Sow ¼ inch deep between June 15 and July 1st in rows 24 inches apart. Seed germinates in 4 to 14 days. Thin plants to stand 8 inches apart. For the home garden use 'Burpee's Purple Top Yellow,' 'Macomber,' 'American Purple Top.' We find flea beetles particularly attracted to the young turnip seedlings. Dust or spray with rotenone.

SPINACH ☐ A rapid growing leaf crop that almost demands cool weather. Some varieties, such as 'America,' are more tolerant of warm weather. Sow seed in very early spring, making several successive plantings at 2-week intervals. Sow again in late summer for a fall crop. Seed sown ¼ inch deep germinates in 7 to 18 days and matures in 7 weeks, in rows 18 inches apart; should be thinned to 8 inches between plants. Grow 'New Zealand,' 'Hybrid No. 7,' 'Viking' or 'America.' Spinach responds to spraying foliage with water and to feedings of a high nitrogen fertilizer. Infestations of aphids can be forcibly washed off with a hose. Toxic sprays should not be used.

SQUASH ☐ Here is one of the most diversified members of the vegetable kingdom. There are bush and vine types, yellow, green and striped in a multitude of sizes and shapes. The average seedsman's catalog lists from 12 to 25 varieties. The summer squash are bush growers and lend themselves to the smaller garden, although a well-grown hill will span 5 feet across. The winter types, the "sprawlers," are large running vines whose hills should, depending on variety, be spaced 6 to 12 feet apart. Heavy fertilizing and almost a continuous supply of water are the chief ingredients for eminent success with this crop. We bury a generous shovelful of manure mixed with a handful of fertilizer under each hill, covering same with 4 inches of soil. Soil and nights should be warm. Plant seeds 1 inch deep, pointed end down, four to six to a hill and thin to the best two or three well-spaced plants. Germination in 4 to 7 days. Create a soil dike around the hill about 4 feet in diameter to retain a reservoir to

127 CANTALOUPE 'FORDHOOK GEM.'
Burpee Seeds

128 SWEET PEPPER 'TASTY HYBRID.'
Burpee Seeds

129 CABBAGE 'SAVOY KING' WAS AN ALL-AMERICA SELECTIONS WINNER IN 1965.

130 FLOWERING KALE IS A HIGHLY DECORATIVE VEGETABLE, ESPECIALLY WHEN GROWN IN POTS LIKE THESE.

collect rain water or to fill artificially by hose. Sidedress monthly with fertilizer well cultivated and watered in. Pick the summer squash when small and the skin so tender that it can be easily scraped with the finger nail. Let the winter squash fully ripen but harvest before the frost. The winter squash keep well in a cool cellar for months. We have kept 'Buttercup' and 'Hubbard' into April. Summer squash to grow are 'Zucchini Hybrid,' 'Caserta,' 'Cocozelle,' 'Early Prolific,' 'Early Prolific Straightneck,' 'Early Summer Crookneck.' For winter squash try 'Blue Hubbard,' 'Buttercup,' 'Golden Delicious,' 'Butternut' (our favorite), 'Royal Acorn,' 'Table Queen.' We find rotenone good control for bugs and borers.

TOMATOES ☐ The "love apple," a native of the Andes in Peru is recorded in the 16th century and was considered vile and poisonous for hundreds of years. It was not until about 1850 that it became acceptable as being edible. This much maligned fruit, developed to a degree bearing little resemblance to the native plant of Peru has become one of the largest commercial crops in this country. The industry produces close to two billion cans of tomatoes and juice annually. Many varieties are available bearing in from 2 to 3 months after plants are set out. Any good garden soil will suffice, but they are lovers of warm weather and warm and rich soil. Do not attempt to plant out too early, unless under glass or hot-kaps (plastic tents) as they will just stand still. Although a half dozen plants will keep the average family well supplied—and they are inexpensive at the local nurseries—we prefer to grow our plants from seed so that we can select the particular varieties we desire. We usually want to try four or five varieties and end up with 12 to 15 plants which produce lavishly for us, our friends and neighbors. Seed which we start indoors about April 1st, germinates in several days. In about 15 days we transplant to individual 4-inch pots where they continue to grow until about mid-May when they can be knocked out of the pots, rootball intact and planted in the open garden. Plants are set out 5 feet apart, since we let them sprawl, and mulched with grass clippings or hay. If they are staked they can be set 2 feet apart. We place a good shovelful of manure under each plant, but do not let it contact the roots of the plant and set the plants deep, right up to the first branch. Create a soil saucer around each plant to hold a water reservoir. We fertilize plants once when the plants have gotten well started in active growth. Excellent varieties for the home garden include 'Moreton Hybrid,' 'Glamour,' 'Campbell 1327,' 'Jubilee' and 'Sunray,' both with yellow fruit. 'Manalucie,' 'Red Cherry,' 'Yellow Pear' and 'Yellow Plum,' 'Big Boy Hybrid,' 'Burpee's Delicious,' 'Marglobe.' Although tomatoes have many pests and diseases, we find it necessary to dust only occasionally and with rotenone. The monstrous horn-worm shows up infrequently, can be easily located by his droppings and "done in."

TURNIP ☐ A quick (5- to 8-week) cold-weather crop. We plant in very early spring and again about August 1st for a fall crop. Sow seed ¼ inch deep in rows 15 inches apart and thin to stand 3 inches apart. Germination 3 to 7 days. The boiled tops, the "turnip greens," are as popular in the South as are the roots. Varieties to grow are 'Purple Top White Globe,' 'Just Right' and 'Golden Ball.' Flea Beetles are a serious pest on the new growth and should be controlled with 50 per cent sevin or rotenone dust—starting as soon as the seedlings emerge.

7. Herbs from Seed

Many of the plants we grow in our gardens such as annuals, perennials, shrubs and trees are herbs in the true sense of the word but with increased interest in recent years in continental or gourmet cooking the word "herb" is nearly always thought of by home gardeners to mean the "culinary" herb. When we started to garden we used such herbs as creeping thyme as a low plant to grow between the flagstones of our terrace for its attractive tiny foliage and aromatic odor, and we grew the familiar parsley and mint. However, culinary herbs such as dill, basil and chives were not included in our garden plans.

Through the years we have been able to garden in the sun here in Connecticut I have added a packet or two of one or another of the herbs to our vegetable and cutting garden. This past season when along with all our gardening activities I was in the process of writing this book I realized that

I had not had enough personal knowledge of herbs and how they grow, so I immediately ordered collections of seeds of herbs from two of our favorite seedsmen. In spite of the warmest and driest summer on record, these have grown most satisfactorily. It would seem from my experience that herbs do well on any good garden soil prepared as outlined in chapter 2 and cared for just as we suggest for annuals and perennials.

The herbs I have grown and some grown by friends are listed in the following encyclopedia with instructions for growing them. Perhaps inexperienced gardeners as well as those who have not yet had the pleasure of growing these interesting plants will give some thought to starting a small herb garden. Even a small plot 4 by 6 feet will grow all a small family would need. If not grown for use in cooking, herbs are worth growing for pleasant aromatic foliage and some of them for the beauty of the flowers as well. Herbs can be used fresh for garnish in salads and to perk up the flavors of bland vegetables or to add flavor to meats and stews in which case one needs only to nipp off a few leaves when wanted.

To dry herbs for winter use cut off tops of the leafy varieties in mid-summer and wash them off with cold water. Hang them up just long enough for the drops of water to evaporate, then tie the stems together and place in a paper bag with stem ends at the opening and close the bag with a rubber band. Use a paper clip as a hook through the band and place the other hooked end over your line where you are going to hang the herbs to dry, indoors. After 2 or 3 weeks remove from paper bags, crumble the leaves and place on a shallow pan and dry out in the oven with the setting at "warm" or at least not over 100 degrees. Some herb enthusiasts dry them by spreading them out on trays or sheets of hardware cloth covered with cheese cloth and place in a dry area. To dry seed heads allow them to grow until seeds are mature and ready to drop from the plant. Cut seed heads on a very dry day and spread on clean paper (not newspaper). It is better to keep them in the sun the first day as little insects which may have been secreted in the heads will leave as the seeds dry out. Better still, if you are eager to grow herbs for drying obtain a copy of Katherine B. William's *Herbs: The Spice of a Gardener's Life* (Diversity Books, Grandview, Mo., 1965) or Gertrude Foster's book *Herbs for Every Garden* (E. P. Dutton & Co., New York, 1966) both of which give in great detail the proper methods of growing and drying each individual herb. Store herbs in glass jars or other airtight containers in a cool place.

HERBS TO GROW FROM SEED

BASIL, SWEET *(Ocimum basilicum)* ☐ Both green and 'Dark Opal' basil are attractive plants for the garden. I prefer to plant the seed where it is to grow directly to the garden in mid-May. Germination usually occurs in 7 to 10 days. Basil is not difficult to transplant. Grows to 18 inches; space 12 inches between plants. 'Dark Opal' has beautiful deep red foliage and lovely pink flowers and is excellent to use along a walk or as a solid bed for decoration in the garden. Basil is very good to use to flavor tomato juice and tomato pastes.

BORAGE *(Borago officinalis)* ☐ This has pinkish blossoms which turn blue like the perennial pulmonaria. It is an annual and should be planted directly to the garden in early May in the North. Growing to 2 feet it should be spaced 10 inches apart. Germinates in 7 to 10 days. Resents transplanting except when quite small. It is excellent used in tossed salad to add a most elusive flavor.

CHERVIL *(Anthriscus cerefolium)* ☐ Although this plant will germinate in the fall and live over the winter I would advise the inexperienced gardener to grow it as an annual, sowing the seed to the garden in mid-May (in this area). Grows to 2 feet and should be spaced 8 inches apart. Grows quickly and is mature in 6 weeks. Resents transplanting. Fresh leaves can be frozen in small packets after washing carefully. Excellent to flavor egg dishes.

CHIVES *(Allium schoenoprasum)* ☐ This is a perennial plant growing from bulblets. They are really very easy to grow from seed. Mine, started under the fluorescent lights as well as in the greenhouse in the spring germinated in 10 days. The tiny little plants look like fragile spears of grass. When transplanted they wilt slightly. Even during a continued drought they grow very well. Mature plants grow to 12 inches; space 6 inches apart. They are very hardy even in cold locations. Flowers are pretty enough so that chives can be grown as a border or in the rock garden. Fine in salads, egg dishes and sauces of all kinds. Potted up, chives will grow on a sunny window sill in winter.

DILL *(Anethum graveolens)* ☐ This is an easily grown annual with feathery foliage. Blossoms are tiny and pale yellow. Grows to 2½ feet in my garden and germinates in 7 to 10 days planted at the same time as tender vegetables. Resents transplanting. May be spaced as close as 4 inches apart. Self-sows readily. Fine for use in pickling and to flavor meats.

LAVENDER *(Lavandula)* ☐ The only variety of lavender which I have grown is a variety known as *vera* and which in Bailey's *Hortus* is described as a form of *L. spica*. I have had excellent success with germinating seeds of lavender giving a four-week pre-chilling period in the coldframe before bringing into the greenhouse with germination in 14 days. This year sown under the lights the seeds germinated in 15 days with no pre-chilling period. This is a hardy perennial with gray foliage and spikes of

131 BALM OR MELISSA OFFICINALIS HAS A
PLEASING SCENT AND ATTRACTIVE FOLIAGE.
George W. Park Seed Co., Inc.

132 MENTHA PULEGIUM IS AN EXCELLENT
GROUND-COVERING MINT.
George W. Park Seed Co., Inc.

fragrant lavender flowers, which when dried are used to perfume the linen chest and for sachets. Dry easily when hung free in a dry garage or attic.

MARJORAM, SWEET (*Majorana hortensis*) ☐ This is a perennial in frost-free sections of the South but is grown as a hardy annual in the North. Sow seed indoors with germination in 7 to 10 days. Grows to 12 inches; space 6 inches apart. Plants may be potted up and grown in the greenhouse or sunny window over the winter. Adds a delicate flavor to lamb, fish, salads and soups.

MINT (*Mentha spicata*) ☐ This mint is very easy to grow. It is a hardy perennial and spreads by root stolons. Sown indoors seed germinates in 10 to 15 days. It grows to 2 feet and is rather sprawling in habit. Space 12 inches apart. Is at its best in good rich soil. Fine to use for mint jelly and in mint juleps, lemonade and other fruit drinks.

SAGE (*Salvia officinalis*) ☐ This is a hardy perennial in our location and is often grown in gardens for its pretty foliage and spikes of bluish flowers. Seed sown indoors germinates in 14 days. Grows to 2 feet and should be spaced 12 inches apart. Can be sown outdoors in May with germination in 21 to 30 days. Fine herb for dressings for chicken, turkey, pork and for flavoring sausages.

133 PRE-PLANTED TRAY OF HERB SEEDS
PROVIDES A SUNNY WINDOWSILL OF SAGE,
PARSLEY AND THYME.
Farmer Seed and Nursery Co.

SAVORY, SUMMER *(Satureja bortensis)* ☐ This is an easily grown annual being best planted in mid-May in our location directly to the garden where it is to grow with germination in 7 to 10 days. Grows to 12 inches tall; space 5 or 6 inches apart. Good to flavor fish dishes, beans and soups.

SESAME *(Sesamum orientale)* ☐ This herb has whitish colored leaves and pretty pink flowers. Needs warmth for germination and should not be planted into the garden until the soil and air are very warm; about 70 degrees. This would be in late May in our location. Germination will take place in 3 to 7 days. Although they grow 2½ to 3 feet they need but 9 or 10 inches between plants as they do not branch. Seeds are used to flavor breads, crackers and cookies.

THYME *(Thymus vulgaris)* ☐ This is a hardy perennial being of somewhat shrubby growth. Leaves are cut for drying before the blossoms are open. It is easily grown from seed sown indoors with germination in 21 to 30 days. Grows slowly when young. Grows to 12 inches; space 8 inches apart. It needs rich soil. Thyme is used for flavoring soups and poultry dressing.

K.B.

8. House Plants From Seed

It is indeed a rarity to find a home gardener who has experienced the great satisfaction of growing plants from seed or has tended an outdoor planting who is not also interested in house plants.

Most of us, in the North at least, feel the need to have growing plants in the house in order to bridge the long gap between fall frost and spring sowing. Many of my friends, who live in warmer climes than ours, including those who live in Florida, enjoy house plants. To the gardener there is always a challenge in anything and everything that grows. Before we owned a home greenhouse or even heard of fluorescent lights I was growing house plants from seed. My husband accuses me of being the kind of person who always does everything the "hard way." I could not be satisfied to grow something easy like coleus—the first house plants I grew from seed were saintpaulias (commonly called African Violets). The variety was 'Blue Fairy Tale' and was offered in the catalog of one of our favorite seedsmen. The seeds were ordered along with our regular spring order for seeds, planted in a flowerpot of soil and placed in a southern window with a pane of glass over to keep in the moisture. The pane was left slightly ajar to let in a little air. It took about three weeks for the light green leaves to begin to show but I ended up with about twenty plants of 'Blue Fairy Tale.' This variety is quite easy to grow and usually blooms all at once with the blooms held high. It looks like an old-fashioned nosegay for the leaves arrange themselves in pinwheel fashion. After this successful venture in growing house plants from seed we grew begonias, cacti, succulents, coleus and other easy-to-grow varieties. Since acquiring our home greenhouse we have been successful in growing many others, some of them considered quite difficult.

When I decide to try house plants from seed I refer to my shelf of garden books and look up the growing requirements of the specific plants. However, for every houseplant grower there are libraries which carry such books and the various state departments of agriculture have available free, or for just a few cents, pamphlets on the growing of house plants. These are often available at the local offices of the country agricultural agents. Look them up. A wealth of good gardening material is available to the home gardener if he takes the trouble to look for it.

In this chapter I will share with you my successes and failures in growing house plants from seed. Listed and described are the ones which I have grown or those which have been grown by friends and acquaintances.

For most of our house plants my husband mixes up bushels of potting soil in the fall and stores the mix in metal garbage cans with tight lids or in plastic-lined bushel baskets. Plastic pails are also good for storing small amounts of potting soil. We use 2 parts of good garden loam to 1 part each of peatmoss and sand, with a 4-inch pot of bonemeal or superphosphate added to each bushel. This material should be well blended. Small quantities can be blended in a wheelbarrow. Our needs are so great that we find blending the mix on the concrete garage floor most convenient. We store this mix in hampers in the greenhouse under the benches to use as a general all-purpose growing medium. We also store a large metal garbage canful in the cellar convenient to our fluorescent light set-up. A sheet of heavy plastic slightly longer than the top of the can which is held in place by the lid retains the soil moisture for a full winter season. Bushel baskets, plastic bags and buckets could be used as convenient storage receptacles. Try to keep as air-tight as possible to retain the soil moisture. It is most unsatisfactory to work with dust-dry soil and extremely difficult to re-dampen it.

For plants needing a more moisture-retentive soil I sometimes add a handful of vermiculite to each 4-inch pot of soil. For some of the plants grown for foliage I also add a cup of Bacto-peat to each quart of the soil mix.

For growers of house plants who are unable to make up potting mixes, the packaged potting mixes are excellent but I feel that they are inclined to be a little on the dry side. I like to add vermiculite to them for plants which love moisture; or sand for the cacti family. After the plants have become established a feeding of half-strength Rapid-Gro or some other water-soluble fertilizer helps to keep the plant in good growing condition when using packaged mixes. The so-called Cornell or "Peat-Lite" mixture is excellent for house plants if the home gardener feels like mixing his own. This mixture contains vermiculite, peatmoss with added fertilizers. Experiments done recently by scientists working with the distributors of vermiculite have found that while this material was previously thought to have no plant food value, it is quite rich in certain trace elements needed by all plants for healthy growth. Here is the "recipe" for the Peat-Lite mix:

4 quarts #2 grade vermiculite
4 quarts shreaded peatmoss
1 level tablespoon powdered 20 per cent superphosphate
1½ tablespoons 33 per cent ammonium nitrate
    OR (not both)
4 tablespoons 5-10-5 fertilizer

Growing house plants from seed is done exactly as has been previously described. When the little plantlets are large enough to handle I replant them to aluminum loaf pans or flats until large enough to be placed in 2-inch pots, usually when the plants are about 2 inches high. When these pots have been filled with roots they can be shifted to the next larger size until they have attained their full size or have grown to the size desired.

HOUSE PLANTS TO GROW FROM SEED

ABUTILON ☐ Flowering Maple also called Chinese Bellflower. Foliage is green or variegated with small leaves resembling those of maple trees. Flowers are trumpet-shaped and come in pink, yellow, white or rose-red. Needs full sun in winter but needs to be semishaded in summer in the North. Should be kept moist at all times. Will die quickly if allowed to become too dry. Grows to 2 feet or more. Some varieties are excellent hanging basket subjects. Very good for window boxes. Sow seeds in warmth, 70 to 75 degrees, with germination in 18 to 21 days. Needs humusy soil for best results.

AGAPANTHUS ☐ Blue Lily of the Nile. Strap-like foliage with umbels of fragrant deep blue flowers. *A. africanus* grows to 3 feet. 'Peter Pan,' a new dwarf, grows to 18 inches with sky-blue flowers. Blooms in summer. Needs rich humusy soil. Water only lightly in winter. In spring water and feed once a month and give full sun. Sow seed February or March at about 65 degrees for best germination which occurs in 20 to 30 days.

AMARYLLIS, see Bulbs, Tubers and Corms

ANEMONE, see Bulbs, Tubers and Corms

ARDISIA, see Trees and Shrubs

ASPARAGUS ☐ Asparagus Fern. *A. sprengeri* and *A. plumosa* are old-fashioned fern-like plants. *Plumosa* has fine foliage and grows upright. *Sprengeri* has needle-like foliage and is a good hanging basket subject. *A. verticillatus* is a vining type and 'Lace Veil' is similar but with finer foliage. Both grow to 4 feet. They like bright light in winter but not full sun. Give plenty of water. Easily grown from seed sown in warmth (65 to 75 degrees) with germination in 18 to 30 days.

AUCUBA, see Trees and Shrubs

BEGONIAS ☐ These are very popular house plants, the variety *semperflorens* or "wax" begonia being the best known. However, there are many other varieties worth growing. There are the so-called angel-wing or cane varieties, fibrous rooted and rhizomatous ones, the best known of the latter being the "beefsteak begonia" or "lettuce leaf," and the rex begonias. (Tuberous-rooted begonias grown for bedding in the semishaded outdoor garden are discussed in the chapter on Bulbs, Tubers and Corms.) Begonias are easy to grow from seed and many of our seed catalogs list seeds of various varieties under seeds for house plants. Seeds are exceedingly fine. They should not be covered. I have had excellent success using vermiculite alone and our favorite mix described in chapter 2. Begonias need warmth for germination. Under fluorescent lights, placed 6 or 8 inches below the tubes, they will germinate in 14 to 21 days. I have had good germination by placing seed pans 18 inches from lights but germination takes longer; anywhere from 21 to 40 days. In the greenhouse in warmth some have germinated in 7 to 14 days. As soon as germination is had it is well to immediately remove the plastic cover. It is also better to water the seed pan from the bottom so as not to disturb the fine seeds or the little seedlings when they have germinated. Feed the little seedlings ¼ strength Rapid-Gro or Plant Marvel using lukewarm water, when they are about one-eighth inch across. When quite small the plantlets can be transplanted to loaf pans, flats or other containers until they grow large enough for 2-inch pots. For begonias I add a cupful of peatmoss and one of vermiculite to my regular potting mix. Begonias may be given several hours of morning sun except in very hot weather but should be shielded from the heat of the sun. Keep begonias moist but not wet.

BIRD OF PARADISE, see Strelitzia

BROWALLIA, see Annuals

CACTI AND OTHER SUCCULENTS ☐ Most cacti and other succulents are remarkably easy to grow from seed. A mixed packet of each provides a large number of interesting seed sown last year I had many interesting variations of the cactus family, some of which I have not, as yet, been able to identify. From a packet of mixed succulents I had plants of kalanchoe, stapelia, agave, kleinia, crassula, aeonium, echeveria and sempervivum. Cacti and succulents do well for me in the potting soil which my husband mixes for me and directions for which are given in chapter 2, but for these plants I add a cupful of sand and a half cupful of gravel (the kind you buy for your parakeet) to each quart of the soil mix. Cacti and succulents used for house plants show a wonderful tolerance to different kinds of soils. In sowing seeds of cacti and succulents I have had equal success using a mixture of ½ peatmoss and ½ sand or our favorite mix of 1/3 vermiculite, 1/3 milled sphagnum and 1/3 perlite. Some of these seeds are very fine and should not be covered; others are larger and need to be only very lightly covered. They need warmth (70 to 80 degrees) for good germination. Some kinds will germinate quickly within 10 to 15 days; others take 15 to 30 days. Do not be too impatient but give them time. I transplant the tiny seedlings to bulb pots of potting soil mixed with the sand and gravel, placing a number of plantlets in each pot until they have grown large enough to be transplanted to 1-inch pots. Soil should be kept a little on the dry side for the first few days, but enough water should be given to settle the plants into place. About two or three weeks after transplanting I feed my cacti and succulent plants with ¼ strength Rapid-Gro or Plant Marvel. During the winter months these plants need only enough water to keep them from shriveling or going limp. In spring, increase the water and keep them slightly moist and start a regular feeding of plant food biweekly in order to help them to come into bloom. In the winter they may be given full sun but should be shielded from hot sun during summer. Too much sun will result in browning of the edges of the leaves or tips of the cacti.

CALCEOLARIA ☐ Pocketbook Plant. These are florist plants but can be grown under lights or in cool greenhouse. Flowers are pouch-shaped and are yellow or orange with brown spots. Needs to be kept quite cool, not over 60 degrees. They like a good rich potting soil. Keep a little on the dry side during winter but give plenty of water in spring. The fine seed is best sown in summer. Although most authorities assert they need to be cool for germination I have had success with them at 75 to 80 degrees. The little seedlings grow very slowly.

CAPE PRIMROSE, see Streptocarpus.

CARISSA, see Trees and Shrubs.

COLEUS, see Annuals.

CROSSANDRA ☐ Attractive plants with shiny leaves and salmon-colored flowers. Use a good, rich potting soil and keep moist but not wet. Needs a bright, sunny window in winter. Not difficult to grow. Seeds germinate best in warmth (70 to 80 degrees), with germination in 21 to 30 days. Grows quickly.

134 HYBRID FUCHSIA SEEDLING.
George W. Park Seed Co., Inc.

135 HYBRID ABUTILON GROWN FROM SEEDS.
George W. Park Seed Co., Inc.

CYCLAMEN, see Bulbs, Tubers and Corms.

EPISCIA, see Gesneriads, this chapter.

FERNS, see Wild Flowers.

FICUS ☐ Rubber Plant. Attractive plants with bold foliage. They grow well in north windows. Varieties *macrophylla* and *elastica* grow easily from seed. Do not cover seed but press into the seedling mix as this needs light for good germination, and temperatures from 65 to 70. Germination occurs in 15 to 20 days. These plants grow fast and if shifted as each pot fills with roots will grow 2½ to 3 feet tall in a year's time.

FUCHSIA ☐ Fuchsias are small shrubs or trees which grow out of doors in frost free sections of the country. They are very popular as house plants in other areas for unusual and spectacular flowers with colors ranging from white to pink, rose, red, lavender, violet, purple and blue. Some grow upright and some are hanging basket subjects. They like good rich soil and must be kept moist at all times. In hot dry places they need to have the foliage misted daily. The rootball must never be allowed to dry out. They like a few hours of morning sun in winter and should be in a bright place but no sun in summer in the North. In winter they like a cool room, not over 70 to 75 degrees. They should be fed every other week except in fall and the dark days of winter. Seeds of hybrid sorts are available and afford the houseplant enthusiast many beautiful variations. Sow seed under lights, in the greenhouse or bright window with germination in 21 to 30 days.

GESNERIADS ☐ The gesneriad family includes many well-known house plants including the African violet (*Saintpaulia*). Most of them have soft, velvety leaves and most of them grow as easily as the African violet. They need temperature ranges from 65 at night to 75 or 80 by day to grow well. Temperatures under 60 are definitely harmful to all of them commonly cultivated. They will grow well in any good potting soil but for gesneriads I like to add a cupful of extra peatmoss and one of vermiculite to each quart of soil. These plants need to be kept moist but not soggy, nor should water stand for more than a half hour in the saucers under the pots particularly during the winter months. Except in very warm weather they should always be watered with lukewarm water. They are also benefitted by having the dust washed from the leaves using lukewarm water now and then but should be allowed to drain and the leaves dry in a warm spot for several hours before being returned to the permanent locations. They should always be washed off early in the day for cold water standing on the leaves at night is injurious. Sun shining on wet leaves is also detrimental. A few gesneriads form tubers or small scaly rhizomes and these need a resting period. All gesneriads grow well in east windows getting a few hours of morning sun. All are fine to grow under fluorescent lights if the temperature of the room where the lights are burning is never permitted to go below 65 degrees. Included in this section are some of the gesneriads I have grown from seed with fine success.

ACHIMENES ☐ "Nut Orchid" or "Widow's Tears." These are excellent subjects for hanging baskets as they have a sprawling habit. Flowers are produced in profusion and are somewhat trumpet-shaped. They come in shades of rose, pink, red, blue, purple, yellow and orange. Seed is very fine. Do not cover. Sow in heat, 70 to 80 degrees, with germination in 15 to 20 days. Mature plants produce scaly, odd-looking rhizomes. Summer is the normal blooming period for this plant. When it starts to look unhappy it is beginning to go dormant. The pot may be stored in a dry place for four or five months during winter, then brought back into light and watered. If preferred the little rhizomes may be removed from the soil and stored in a plastic bag and repotted when ready to start into active growth. Achimenes likes to be kept moist when in active growth.

COLUMNEA ☐ This is a trailing plant. Some varieties have waxy leaves and some have velvety leaves. They do well in an east window or in a semishaded position but brightly lighted. Flowers are yellow, golden, scarlet or red produced along the trailing branches. Keep moist but not wet. Feed every three weeks when in active growth with ½ strength Rapid-Gro, Plant Marvel or similar houseplant fertilizer. Seeds are small. Sow in heat with germination in 15 to 20 days.

EPISCIA ☐ Trailing plant with hairy, pebbled or fairly smooth leaves. Foliage of many of them has red or silver veins and if this plant never bloomed at all it would be spectacular. Flowers are tubular in shades of orange and red, yellow, pink, or white. I find they will flower better if given a little more sun than the African violet. Mine usually bloom in spring and during the summer months. Keep moist but never wet. When in active growth feed every other week. Seed is very fine. Do not cover but press very lightly on top of seedling mix. Sow in warmth (70 to 80 degrees) with germination in 25 to 40 days.

GLOXINIA ☐ This is a well-known gesneriad with large velvety leaves and gorgeous cup-shaped flowers in many beautiful colors. There are single as well as double flowers. I have grown hundreds of these beautiful plants. Seed is very fine. Press lightly on the seedling mix. Keep at warm temperature (70 to 75 degrees) for best germination, although I have had good results with a nighttime low of 65, and 70 by day. Germination should be had in 15 to 20 days. This plant produces a tuber. They usually start to bloom for me when 6 months old. Keep moist but not wet. After blooming keep in good growing condition until leaves start to turn brown, then store dry for six weeks or until new shoots begin to show. At this time I repot mine to fresh soil. The tuber is best planted ¼ to ½ inch below the soil level. Seeds of the miniature or dwarf forms of gloxinia are usually found listed in the catalogs as *Sinningia,* the botanical name for gloxinias.

RECHSTEINERIA ☐ "Cardinal" Plant. Leaves are large, very velvety and pale green. Flowers are bright red and tubular. Sow seeds like gloxinia. This plant also forms a tuber. Blooms in 6 to 12 months. Sometimes after flowering it takes an extra long rest but signifies its desire to grow by showing green shoots. I keep this one in its pot in the dormant state under the fluorescent lights when it is resting and give it a little water now and then to prevent the tuber from drying out completely. When it starts to grow, I repot and place in the east window. Do not be discouraged if it rests for five months or more. One of mine rested for 12 months, but is now in bloom.

SAINTPAULIA ☐ African Violet. Everyone knows this plant, I am sure. Velvety leaves with pretty violet-like flowers in white, pink, rose, purple and blue. They grow best at temperatures from 65 at night and to 70 or 80 daytimes. While they are supposed to need high humidity, I have never felt the need to worry about extra humidity. They grow equally well on a chest in front of the east window and a table a little away from the west window placed in such a way that hot sun will not burn them. During the summer months morning sun is best for the western sun may be too hot. Protect by shading with a sheer curtain or drapery on the west. Every two weeks or so I wash off my saintpaulias with *lukewarm* water and let dry in a warm shaded place before putting back in the window. When in active growth they are fed ½ strength Rapid-Gro every two weeks, alternated now and then with Plant Marvel and Hyponex. Seed is very fine, almost dust-like. Sow in warmth with germination in 21 to 30 days. I have grown seed of this plant in a sunny window, under the fluorescent lights and in the greenhouse with excellent success. When seedlings crowd each other, transplant into other containers such as aluminum foil loaf pans or bulb pans and let grow to at least 2 inches before potting to 2-inch pots. When small pots have filled with roots transplant to 3-inch pots.

SMITHIANTHA ☐ Temple Bells. This is a lovely plant with dark green velvety leaves overlaid with red. Flowers are on spikes in orange and yellow. This plant also produces a rhizome. Although authorities state that seeds are best sown in April, May or June, I have started them as early as February in 70 degrees with great success. Keep moist and feed every three weeks when in active growth. It usually blooms in winter. After blooming I keep it growing until the leaves begin to look limp; then I gradually withhold water and let the rhizomes stay in the pot until new green shoots begin to show after which I divide them and plant the large rhizome to a 4-inch pot and the smaller ones, two to a 4-inch pot.

STREPTOCARPUS ☐ Cape primrose. The hybrid varieties of this gesneriad have large leaves and tubular flowers in pretty shades of rose, pink and blue. The variety *S. rexi* is a smaller windowsill variety with narrow leaves and pretty lavender-blue flowers. Sow seeds as for African violet in warmth with germination in 21 to 40 days. *S. rexi* is especially easy from seed sown under fluorescent light. One year we were "up to here" in them and had to beg our friends to take them off our hands! If grown in the greenhouse they drop seeds and come up even in the gravel of the benches.

GREVILLEA ROBUSTA, "Silk Oak," see Shrubs.

IMPATIENS, see Annuals.

JACOBINIA ☐ Plume Flower. Large green foliage and stunning flowers in large clusters of pink, red or orange. Blooms in winter or early spring. Likes warmth and full sun in winter. Give this plant extra rich soil and never let the rootball dry out as this is fatal. Grows quickly and easily from seed sown in warmth (70 to 75 degrees).

PELARGONIUM ☐ Geranium. Everyone knows the geranium which is a favorite house plant. A packet of mixed geranium seed affords the houseplant enthusiast much pleasure. Seeds germinate best at 65 to 70 degrees taking from 15 to 25 days. They germinate equally well in a sunny window, under the lights or in the greenhouse. Some seeds germinate more rapidly than others so do not disturb the seed pan when removing plantlets. Mine bloom in six months after sowing. Geraniums need all possible

136 KLAUS NEUBNER, DIRECTOR OF RE-
SEARCH FOR THE GEORGE W. PARK SEED COM-
PANY, INC., INSPECTS THE SEED CROP ON
DOUBLE-FLOWERED WAX BEGONIAS.

137 IMPATIENS 'TANGERINE' IS AN OUT-
STANDING HOUSEPLANT WHICH CAN BE
GROWN FROM SEED.

George W. Park Seed Co., Inc.

sun in winter to encourage flowering. Pot up seedlings into 2-inch pots and shift to larger sizes as the roots fill the pots. Seeds of zonale hybrids, Flowerland hybrids, 'Nittany Lion' and Read's are available and are very good to grow.

POMEGRANATE, see Punica, under Shrubs.

STRELITZIA ☐ Bird of Paradise. Bold plant growing out of doors in California but a popular florist plant elsewhere. Flowers are huge, produced on long stems, resembling a bird. They are most unusual and the color is orange with blue. Likes rich soil and will need to be repotted frequently to keep in good growing condition. It is said that it takes seven years for a plant to come into flower. Some authorities insist that strelitzia will flower when it has attained nine or ten leaves. Mine started two years ago from seed has ten leaves but as yet no flower bud is showing. Seed is shiny, black with a tuft of red. It is best to remove the tuft before sowing as it may contain a fungus disease. Soak seed for a day or two before sowing. Will germinate unevenly in 20 to 40 days. Seedlings are quite large and are potted first in 2-inch pots. Check frequently for growth will not be rapid unless shifted to larger pots as needed.

VELTHEIMIA, see Bulbs, Tubers and Corms.

ZANTEDESCHIA ☐ Calla Lily, see Bulbs, Tubers and Corms.

139   STAPELIA VARIEGATA, AN ATTRACTIVE, SMALL-FLOWERED STARFISH CACTUS WHICH MAY BE CULTIVATED FROM SEEDS. NOTICE THIS MEMBER OF THE MILKWEED CLAN USES THE SAME MEANS OF DISPERSING SEEDS AS THE MORE COMMON RELATIVES.

138   RED AND WHITE HYBRID AMARYLLIS FROM SEED.   *George W. Park Seed Co., Inc.*

9. Trees and Shrubs from Seed

AFTER my husband returned from doing his "bit" in the Navy for Uncle Sam in World War II we realized that our gardening efforts were being hampered owing to the fact that our 90- x 100-foot piece of property could not possibly support another shrub, tree or plant. We came to the conclusion the only way we could indulge our passion for gardening was to obtain a larger piece of land, so we purchased two acres in mid-Westchester County, New York, within easy commuting distance from New York City, where we built a new house and started our second garden. One acre was completely wooded leaving about an acre for house, lawn and garden. The plot was on a corner with a 480-foot frontage, and feeling the need for privacy, we decided to plant a double row of flowering shrubs along the perimeter. As our budget was limited we had to content ourselves with inexpensive 2- to 3-foot-high deciduous shrubs. Since the days when we had lived in a New York City apartment and walked in Central Park for exercise and fresh air, we have been interested in the study of birds. Therefore our deciduous hedge was chosen not only for its flowering habit but for food and nesting sites for birds as well. Besides the usual season-spanning flowering shrubs such as forsythia, weigela, mock-orange (syringa), lilac, deutzia, spirea (bridal-wreath) in early, mid-season and late varieties, we chose witch-hazel for its early bloom, acanthopanax (five-leaved aralia), a large collection of viburnums for flowers (some fragrant) and berries for fall and winter bird food, turquoise berry or sweetleaf (symplocos), photinia (Chinese Christmas berry), coral-berry (symphoricarpos) and many others.

Our planting was so varied that eight years later when we moved to our present four acres in Greenwich, Connecticut, the purchaser of our Westchester place asked me to identify and tag these shrubs as she was not familiar with many of them. I started with 250 tags, feeling this would be more than adequate, but ran out of tags before the chore was finished, as we had planted on the property many other flowering trees and ornamentals. It was at the time that we acquired these two acres and built the new house, that I first became interested in growing trees and shrubs from seed. A friend brought to me some seed pods of the tree commonly called mimosa, but which is actually *Albizzia julibrissin.* This tree has fine foliage and produces feathery balls of pink flowers in late summer, followed by seed pods similar to those of the locust. These seeds were planted in an open coldframe in late fall and how excited I was to find about fifty of them germinating the following spring. From this successful venture I became interested in trying my luck with seeds and berries of various shrubs we had planted on our property. I did not know how I would use them if they grew but could not resist experimenting. A coldframe was prepared in a semishaded spot in the fall when I sowed seeds of the various viburnums, shrug dogwood, flowering dogwood, *Euonymus alatus,* mountain ash, redleaved barberry, rugosa and multiflora rose, taxus and fire-thorn.

Making notes for this chapter, seated at my dining room table on a cool July morning, I am rather awed at how many trees and shrubs we grew from seed and moved from nursery rows to our garden here in Connecticut and which we have enjoyed for many years. How exciting and gratifying to look at these beautiful plants and realize anew the mystery of seed. From those shriveled berries and small brown seeds have grown this lovely greenery which we increasingly enjoy and which to our great delight has attracted so many birds to our garden for nesting and food.

Growing trees and shrubs from seed is not difficult if one exercises pa-tience and follows a few rules. It is necessary of course to study individual needs and growing habits.

A number of seedsmen carry many seeds of interesting trees and shrubs and it should become a challenge to more gardeners to try to grow their own. Seeds of many trees and shrubs may be started in open seed beds shaded by burlap or regular screen, or in coldframes, covered or uncovered. I seem to recall that our first frame had a lath covering but my husband does not remember, remarking that I have tried so many projects over the years he could not possibly bring to mind how I went about that first attempt at growing trees and shrubs from seed. Since that time I have sown seeds of trees and shrubs in our home greenhouse and under fluorescent lights as well as out of doors in a coldframe covered with plastic screening. It is my hope that many home gardeners will be inspired to obtain seed and grow their own trees and shrubs. One of my inexperienced friends last year needed two hundred red leaved barberries to enclose an area on her home grounds and purchased 200 *bare root* plants in June. These must have been out of the ground in storage since the fall before and as might be expected only a few plants lived. Roots of even the most hardy shrubs dry out quickly in the heat of spring and summer. Had this young woman known how to go about it, she could have, for about $1 grown all the seedlings she needed for this project. Mine, planted in the coldframe in the fall, germinated in May and grew to 1 foot the first season. Not all shrubs and trees are so easy to grow nor do they attain that size the first season; but many of them do grow quickly and easily.

Open seed beds for sowing trees and shrubs should be in a location in semishade if possible where the seed bed will receive no more than three to four hours of sun daily. The seed bed should be protected by a canopy of burlap or muslin attached to a light wood frame and nailed to posts at each corner of the bed. Screening such as that used for house screens would be better but the home gardener frequently needs to be ingenious and use make-shift methods especially if the garden budget is limited. Mulching with salt hay would be beneficial for the winter but should be gradually removed in the spring as weather and soil warm up. The canopy should be removed when germination is complete except in the case of evergreens. In my opinion it would be better to use coldframes for sowing seeds of trees and shrubs just as I prefer their use of starting seeds which need alternate freezing and thawing in order to break dormancy.

If I purchase seeds of rare trees or shrubs such as franklinia, I prefer to sow them in a seed pan of sterile mix and start indoors. Should they need freezing to break dormancy, the pans with plastic covers in place are given a few weeks in covered coldframes in mid-winter after which they are brought into the greenhouse for germination.

Sowing seeds of trees and shrubs is exactly as described in chapter 2, and I will not repeat the instructions here.

Small plants in open seed beds can be thinned and left in place for the first winter if mulched after the first freeze. Seedlings in coldframes should be transferred to another frame where they can receive more light, water and feeding and be mulched with salt hay after the first freeze until large enough to be placed in nursery rows the following spring.

Plants in seed pans can be transferred to flats and kept growing just like perennial seedlings and, when large enough, transplanted to nursery rows. Should the trees or shrubs be extremely slow-growing ones, the flats can be placed in covered frames for the winter, but it would be necessary to watch them to be sure the soil in the flats does not dry out on warm days. After a snow cover there is no need to worry, but by early March in our area the warm spring sun melts the snow quickly and the frames heat up excessively and need ventilation during the day. By mid-April the hardening off process should begin so that the plants will be properly conditioned before being placed in nursery rows about the first week in May. Deciduous shrubs should be placed in nursery rows where they get at least six hours of sun a day but evergreen shrubs and trees will need light shading for two to three years especially where hot summers prevail. We kept our evergreen seedlings growing in nursery rows under the shade of tall trees for three years before placing in a sunnier position.

Fast-growing trees and shrubs can, by the second summer, be moved to their permanent locations if desired, or transplanted to other nursery rows in order to retain a small, compact rootball to lessen the shock when eventually set permanently. Evergreens, however, are better moved every second year until at least 1½ feet tall so as to keep them compact and provide a good rootball when moving into permanent spots. If there is no room for new nursery rows, evergreens may be carefully removed with rootball intact, keeping them covered with wet burlap or newspaper to prevent drying out while you are preparing the row for re-planting. Turn the soil of the row over and add peatmoss, shredded cow manure with bonemeal or superphosphate. Thoroughly incorporate these materials with the soil, replant your evergreens or other shrubs and trees and give them a deep watering immediately. *Evergreen seedling must be kept well watered at all times* when weather is hot and dry.

As this book is being written especially for the inexperienced home gardener it does not seem necessary to go into long detail to explain how seeds of trees and shrubs differ in specific needs for germination. However, the home gardener should be made aware of the fact that some seeds are best sown as soon as ripe, mature and fresh, while others need an after-ripening period for germination and still others need a period of freezing to break dormancy. Some of them need to be kept at 40 to 45 degrees for a period after sowing for good germination. For these, seed pans in plastic bags can be kept in the refrigerator for the required time. Fortunately since my husband shares my interest in growing plants from seed he is not at all annoyed or astonished to find seed pans in the refrigerator but I must say that some of my house guests or visitors are a little shocked to find such things in a place where only food and drink are usually kept!

Fruit of trees and shrubs varies. The evergreens such as pine, spruce, hemlock, larch, sequoia (redwood) and cypress will produce cones. Within the overlapping protective covering, papery like seeds are found. Cones should be gathered fresh in the fall when mature. To open the scales place the cones in a warm oven (200 degrees) for an hour. During this warming process the overlapping scales will open and the seeds will fall out or may be easily extracted.

Fruit of such evergreens as juniper (cedar) and taxus (yews) are berry-like, one large seed covered by soft pulp. These should be gathered when well-ripened just as they are beginning to fall from the plant. Because the soft pulp may contain fungus disease, all berry-like fruits should have the pulp removed. I usually rub off this coating and wash seeds and spread on a paper towel to dry. Some authorities suggest soaking the fruit for a couple of days, then crushing the fruit. The pulp floats and the seeds drop to the bottom.

Berry-like fruits containing one large or several small seeds are also found on such trees and shrubs as dogwood, mountain ash, shadbush (amelanchier), viburnum, mahonia, barberry, bayberry, myrtle, ginkgo, black alder, boxwood and firethorn (pyracantha).

Many deciduous trees and shrubs produce capsules which contain a number of seeds. Examples of these are syringa (mock-orange), witch-hazel, sweet gum, sycamore, azaleas, pearl bush (exochorda) and poplar. These seeds should be carefully removed from the protective covering.

Narrow pods containing seeds are found on locust, Kentucky coffee tree, albizzia, golden rain, sophora, poinciana and others of like growth. Seed should be removed from the dry pods when gathered from the tree.

Other trees produce nut-like fruits like those of the oak, walnut, hickories, hazelnut, ironwood and beech.

Some trees and shrubs have large, soft fruits containing many small seeds such as the osage orange and the fig.

Seeds of trees and shrubs differ in their needs for good germination. Some need to be stored dry and planted in spring; others need to be planted in late fall; still others may need a long after-ripening period for the seed to become mature enough to germinate.

We hear much about stratification, a method used by commercial growers to store seed for breaking dormancy. I do not feel that the average home gardener would have the facilities for attempting these methods. In stratifying, seed is stored in moist sand or a mixture of moist sand and peat and kept at 32 to 40 degrees for several months which helps to break dormancy of certain seeds or to keep seed moist during the after ripening period. If the gardener is interested in growing a large number of trees and shrubs from seed he should obtain leaflets and other publications from the United States Department of Agriculture as well as books on the subject before starting such a project. This chapter is meant only to serve as a guide to the home gardener who would like to attempt to grow a few trees and shrubs from seed. As in the preceding chapters, the following encyclopedia reflects my own experiences together with suggestions of experienced seedsmen and others who have successfully grown trees and shrubs from seed.

ABIES BALSAMEA ☐ Balsam Fir. Evergreen hardy throughout the North. Used extensively for Christmas trees. Produces cones 3 to 5 inches long. Likes good soil. Sow when seeds are mature in covered coldframe in late fall or keep in seedpan in seedling mix in refrigerator for 4 months then start under fluorescent light; indoors or in greenhouse. Seeds germinate slowly over a long period of time. Transplant to especially prepared seed beds shaded by lath, burlap or screening for the first 2 to 3 years.

ACER (MAPLE) SACCHARUM ☐ Sugar Maple or Hard Maple. Fine lawn tree grows to 50 feet. Leaves turn gold in fall. Hardy in the North. Grows as far south as Georgia and Alabama to Texas. My favorite among the maples for its excellent growth and gold of the leaves in the fall. Seeds are winged. Sow as soon as ripe in open seed beds or coldframes. Does not germinate well if seed bed becomes too dry. Remove "wings" before sowing. Germination is had in spring following fall sowing.

A. PALMATUM ☐ Japanese Maple. Small-growing decorative maples to 15 feet. Hardy in the North. Seedlings of the red variety will show variation, some red, some green and some green tinged with red. Sow seeds in seed pans of sterile mix and keep in refrigerator for three months then give warmth. Purchased seed may be very dry in which case boiling water should be poured over seeds; let soak 48 hours before sowing.

AESCULUS HIPPOCASTANUM ☐ (Horsechesnut and red horsechestnut). Large trees to 75 feet with luxuriant foliage and conspicuous clusters of flowers blooming in May in the North. Fruits are nut-like contained in a "burr." Sow seed as soon as mature out of doors in open seed beds or in coldframes. Seed will not germinate if allowed to become too dry before sowing. May be stored in damp vermiculite and kept at 45 degrees over the winter and sown in coldframes in spring.

ALBIZZIA JULIBRISSIN ☐ "Mimosa." Small trees to 35 feet with fine foliage like that of the locust. Flowers are fluffy balls of pink produced in late summer and followed by flat seed pods. Hardy as far north as Boston but sometimes winterkills. Grows up again from ground level after being frozen. Likes full sun but will bloom in the shade. Soak seed is warm water for several hours before planting. Sow in coldframe in late fall or indoors February to March.

ARBUTUS MENZIESI ☐ Madrone. Fine tree for California and mild climates. Grows to 100 feet. Produces fragrant white flowers. Fruit is red. Bark splits and sheds like the sycamore. Sow seeds as soon as mature, cover ¼ inch deep. Germinates readily.

BETULA POPULIFOLIA ☐ Gray Birch. Hardy in the North. Grows to 30 feet. Bark is chalk white. Very attractive landscape tree.

B. PAPYRIFERA ☐ Canoe Birch. Hardy tree growing to 90 feet. Bark is chalky white or yellowish. Fruits of the birch are nut-like with a wing. Sow in covered cold-frames in fall. Germination will be had throughout the following spring and summer.

CASUARINA EQUISETIFOLIA ☐ Australian Pine. These are evergreen trees growing in California and Florida where there are no killing frosts. Grows to 100 feet tall. Produces a cone-like fruit. Sow in seed pans or frames in spring. Cover seed ⅛ inch deep. Do not allow seedling medium to dry out. Germination is had in 20 to 60 days.

CEDRUS ATLANTICA (Atlas Cedar) and C. DEODARA (Sacred Indian-fir) ☐ Not reliably hardy north of Philadelphia. Evergreen foliage of *atlantica* is a lovely blue-green. *Deodara* is very hardy on the Pacific Coast. Both are beautiful ornamentals. Seeds should be stored in paper bags and kept dry until spring. Sow seed in coldframes or protected seed beds. Germination occurs in 6 to 8 weeks. Shade young seedlings for at least two years.

CERCIS CANADENSIS ☐ (Redbud or Judas tree). Low-growing tree to 25 feet blooming in very early spring with rosy purple flowers followed by heart-shaped leaves. Fruits are thin pods. Does well in semishade. Soak seed before sowing. Needs warmth for germination. Sow in covered coldframes in fall; will germinate in summer following. I have had success with sowing under fluorescent lights with no pre-chilling period. Fair germination is also had by sowing seeds in seedpans and giving a pre-chilling period in coldframe in March for three weeks before bringing into green house. Will grow to 12 inches the first year. When 2 inches high I pot mine up and keep them growing in shaded frame during the summer being careful never to let soil in pots dry out. Pots are plunged in open coldframe the first winter and mulched with salt hay after ground has frozen hard. Make rapid growth once set to nursery rows.

CORNUS FLORIDA ☐ This is the familiar flowering dogwood which is native from Massachusetts to Florida and west to Ontario and Texas. Lovely ornamental tree with white flowers in late spring. Foliage turns deep scarlet in fall. Red berry-like fruits. Needs a long after-ripening period before becoming viable. Sow in coldframes in late fall. May not germinate until the second spring following. Stratified by placing in seed pan of seedling mix and keeping in refrigerator for four months, then placing pan under fluorescent lights or in greenhouse germination is usually more uniform. Young seedlings grow rapidly in second season after germination. Likes sun and good soil.

C. KOUSA ☐ Japanese Dogwood. This dogwood blooms a month later than *Cornus florida;* in June in our area. It will bloom quite well in part shade. Fruits are similar to the strawberry. The berry should be soaked in water for several days in order to easily separate seed from fruit. Seeds are about one-third smaller than that of the flowering dogwood and each berry contains two or three seeds. They are considered very difficult from seed. Stratify in seed pan of seedling mix in refrigerator for 160 days before placing in window, under lights or in greenhouse. I have never succeeded with seeds of *Cornus kousa* but this year plan to make some experiments, sowing a few without stratifying under the fluorescent lights and placing others immediately in the coldframe. The rest will be stratified in the refrigerator as suggested.

C. MAS ☐ Cornelian Cherry. One of my favorite ornamentals. Small tree sometimes shrub-like growing to 15 feet. In earliest spring its branches are covered with tiny but very bright yellow flowers followed by red cherry-like fruits, maturing in August in my garden. Grows in any good soil. Stratify seed in seedling mix in refrigerator for three months then place under lights or in greenhouse, or in covered coldframe in April.

CRATAEGUS ☐ Hawthorn. Many hawthorns are native to North America. Most of them have spiny branches and the flowers are usually white. The Washington thorn *(C. cordata)* is hardy from Virginia south. Leaves turn scarlet in fall. Fruits are bright scarlet globes. *C. crus-galli,* the cockspur thorn, is hardy in the North. White flowers with red fruits. Does well in sandy soil. Good hedge material for large properties. *C. oxycantha,* the English hawthorn, has white flowers and small red fruits. This has been very slow growing in my garden having been grown from seed twenty years ago, it is now only 12 feet tall. Seeds of hawthorns may be planted in late fall when mature in covered coldframes. Wash pulp from berries before planting seeds. Not all seeds are fertile so planting thickly is recommended. Germination is had throughout following spring and summer, although some may not germinate until the second season.

CUPRESSUS ARIZONICA BONITA ☐ Arizona Cypress. Hardy from Virginia south. Does not mind drought conditions. Evergreen. Seeds best sown in coldframe or protected seed beds in spring, with germination in 6 to 10 weeks. Shade young seedlings from hot sun.

C. MONTEREY ☐ Hardy from North Carolina south. Cones are globe-shaped. Very picturesque evergreens. Sow as Arizona cypress.

ELAEAGNUS AUGUSTIFOLIA ☐ Russian Olive. Hardy in the North. Shrublike tree to 20 feet. Pale yellow flowers followed by yellow fruits which are mature by September. Does well on most soils. Sow seeds when ripe in protected seed beds or covered frames. May not germinate until the second spring. Young seedlings, once germinated grow rapidly.

EUCALYPTUS GLOBULUS ☐ Bluegum. Not hardy in the North; very sensitive to extreme cold. Leaves are blue-green. *E. compacta,* grows to 50 feet or more. Flowers are white blooming from December to May. Seeds purchased commercially germinated in 15 to 20 days in my greenhouse. Foliage is aromatic.

E. CINEREA ☐ "Silver Dollar." Leaves are the size of a silver dollar in whorls around stems. Much sought by flower arrangers. Not hardy in the North but makes large pot plant for greenhouses. Sow as directed for E. globulus.

FAGUS AMERICANA ☐ (Beech). Noble tree very hardy in the North. Nut-like fruits are in prickly pods like the chestnut. Will grow to 60 feet tall.

F. ATROPURPUREA ☐ Purple Beech. Ornamental tree often grown as lawn specimen. Flower arrangers like the beautiful leaves which glycernize beautifully for winter flower arrangements.

F. PENDULA ☐ Weeping Beech. This is a gorgeous lawn specimen with dark leaves and lofty spreading branches. Seeds should be sown in covered coldframes in late fall. If necessary to keep over the winter they should be stored in a cool place in damp sand and protected from the depredations of mice, after which they may be sown as any perennial. Young seedlings grow slowly. Should be transplanted frequently when small to retain compact rootball.

FRANKLINIA ALATAMAHA ☐ Gordonia. This is a very rare but beautiful tree, not reliably hardy north of Philadelphia but does grow farther north in protected areas. Needs acid soil in order to thrive. White flowers almost 3 inches across are produced in July or August. Fruit is a woody capsule. Will tolerate light shade. Purchased seed, given a prechilling period in my coldframe for four weeks in March, germinated in the warmth of the greenhouse in 21 days. Plants were potted up when 2 inches tall and grew to 8 inches the first season. Plunge pots in covered coldframe for the first winter. Add peatmoss to potting mix.

GINKGO BILOBA ☐ Maidenhair Tree. Attractive tree from China with unusual shaped leaves. Very hardy in the North. Leaves turn light gold in late fall. Fruits are yellow and have putrid odor. Good tree for city streets. Seeds should be washed free of pulp and stored dry until spring. Sow in seedpans under lights or in greenhouse in warmth. They germinate in 30 days. Not fussy as to soil.

GREVILLEA ROBUSTA ☐ Silk Oak or Australian Fern Tree. Interesting tree with fern-like foliage, growing quite tall in frost-free sections of the country. Does not mind drought. Grows quickly and easily from seed as any perennial. Is excellent as a pot plant for home or greenhouse. Is a good tree for Florida and southern California.

GYMNOCLADUS DIOICA OR CANADENSIS ☐ Kentucky Coffee Tree. Native tree of New York, Pennsylvania, Minnesota, Nebraska and Tennessee. Broad tree not too tall. Flowers are panicles of white followed by long seed pods. Seeds may be planted when mature in covered coldframe in early winter or kept until spring and sown indoors or in frames. Soak seeds for several days before sowing in spring as they will have become very dry. Not difficult and grows easily.

HALESIA TETRAPTERA ☐ Carolina Silver Bell, sometimes called Lily-of-the-Valley Tree. This is native to West Virginia to Florida and East Texas but is found growing in protected areas in New York State. Low-growing tree with drooping white flowers in May. *H. monticola* is hardy as far as north as Boston. Bark peels like the shagbark hickory. Sow seeds when mature in covered coldframe. May take a second year to germinate.

ILEX AQUIFOLIUM ☐ English Holly. Hardy on the Pacific Coast and from Virginia south but not reliably hardy in the North. Shiny leaves with spines and bright red fruits. This is the "Christmas" holly extensively used for decorations at Christmas time.

I. DAHOON ☐ Found from North Carolina to Florida and Louisiana. Not hardy in the North. Red fruits.

I. CORNUTA ☐ Burford Holly. Leaves are almost spineless. Very attractive with red fruits. Not reliably hardy north of Washington.

I. OPACA ☐ American Holly. Leaves are not as shiny as the English holly. This is a native to Massachusetts south to Florida, Mississippi and Texas. In the North the hollies should be protected from late spring sun and high winds. Foliage is likely to burn and drop off in open locations although it will renew itself readily. Hollies should have rich soil on the acid side and a deep mulch should be maintained. They are not easy to transplant and are best grown in pots until placed in permanent locations. Young seedlings should be shaded from hot sun and winds. Plants should be shifted into larger size pots as needed. They should always be moved with an extra large rootball. Wash pulp from the seeds and as holly needs a long after-ripening season, they should be stored dry and planted in spring in seed-pans under lights or in greenhouse or covered coldframes. Usually germination is not had until the second spring after sowing. Some of my friends have been successful in germinating holly seed by planting in coldframes in late fall as I do my wildflower seed.

JACARANDA OVALIFOLIA ☐ Pretty trees with fine fern-like foliage and lovely blue flowers. Grows in southern California and Florida and other frost-free sections. Seeds taken when mature germinate very quickly. I have grown many of these trees from seed which germinated in my greenhouse in 15 days. They make good potted plants for home or greenhouse. Do well in good potting soil.

KOELREUTERIA PANICULATA ☐ Goldenrain-tree. Fine medium sized tree and is hardy in the northern states but is relatively short-lived. Flowers are bright yellow and produced in summer. Withstands drought. Fruits are a bladdery capsule containing three seeds each. Prefers sun and limey soil. Sow seed in pan of seedling mix and keep in refrigerator for three or four months then place under lights, in sunny window or greenhouse for germination.

LABURNUM VULGARE ☐ Golden-chain tree. Grows to 25 feet tall. Yellow flowers in racemes in summer. Fruits are pods 2 inches long. Not reliably hardy in the North. Store seed dry and sow in spring as any perennial. Seedlings grow fast and the tree blooms when quite young. *L. alpinum* hardy from Massachusetts southward.

LAGERSTROEMIA INDICA ☐ Crape-myrtle. Hardy as far north as Philadelphia. Showy low-growing tree with huge clusters of pink, purple or white flowers in summer.

Sow seeds indoors in early spring or in covered frames. Germination is fairly quick and seedlings grow fast. Frequently bloom the second or third year after sowing. Not fussy as to soil.

LARIX ☐ Larch. This is a member of the pine family but loses its short needles in the fall like any deciduous tree. Fruit is a small cone. Tall-growing trees; very attractive in spring and summer. They grow fast and reach a height of 80 to 150 feet. *L. americana* is also called tamarack or hackamatack. Native from Canada south to Pennsylvania and west to Illinois. Very hardy. Prefers damp soil but will grow on any good soil. *L. europaea* is hardy in the coldest regions. Prefers a light, sandy, well-drained soil. Store seed dry in paper bags over the winter and sow in spring as any perennial. Young seedlings should be lightly shaded for a year or two.

LIQUIDAMBAR STYRACIFLUA ☐ Sweetgum or Redgum. This is one of my best-loved trees. Leaves are shiny and star-shaped. It is a gorgeous shade or specimen tree. Native from Connecticut and New York south. Fruit is a spiny globe. Seeds are small. Likes rich soil and full sun. Seed when mature should be kept in a pan of moist seedling mix in refrigerator until spring and sown as any perennial or may be stored dry through winter and sown in March in greenhouse, with about 20 per cent germination. Will grow to 1 foot the first season. I protect this by growing in open coldframe over the first winter.

LIRIODENDRON TULIPFERA ☐ Tuliptree. Hardy in the North. Flowers are tulip-shaped, green with orange, very spectacular and unusual. Fruit is conelike but the seeds are winged. Grows to 150 feet tall. Difficult to transplant except when quite small. If planted in nursery rows, transplant every second year to keep a good rootball. Sow seeds when mature in fall in protected seed beds or covered frame. Grows quite rapidly from seed.

MAGNOLIA STELLATA ☐ Star Magnolia. Shrubby low tree. White star-shaped flowers in early spring. Hardy north but flowers are sometimes damaged by late spring freezes. Blooms when very young.

M. SOULANGEANA ☐ More shrub than tree-like, although it grows to 25 feet. Blooms in early spring with spectacular blooms in rose, purple or white. Excellent lawn specimen. Mature plants of *soulangeana* should be transplanted when in flower with large rootball.

M. GRANDIFLORA ☐ Bullbay. This tree is not hardy in the North growing from coastal Virginia south. Large, shiny leaves are evergreen. Flowers are huge, of a creamy shade and the fruits are produced in large red clusters.

M. VIRGINIANA ☐ Sweet Bay. Native from Massachusetts south to Florida and Texas. Flowers are white very like the water-lily, blooming in summer. This tree was a familiar one in my early childhood and I think of it with great nostalgia. Prefers swampy soil. Young trees transplant well. Fruits are red. Gather magnolia seeds when ripe and carefully wash all pulp from them. Sow seeds in coldframes in fall with germination the following spring. They should be transplanted to pots as soon as the true leaf appears and shifted to larger pots as they grow. Transplant only in spring when of good size.

MALUS ☐ Apple. The flowering crab apples are charming, low-growing ornamentals and in bloom are a joy and delight. They are relatively disease free and vary in
shape from low spreading, to upright and globe shaped or vase shaped. They flower
in early spring with blossoms of white, pink and carmine, followed by fruits of red
or yellow. Some fruits are quite tiny as small as a pea and the largest are about walnut
size. We have a collection of these trees lining a grassy path. Some are species and
some are hybrids. Among them are 'Carmine' (*M. atrosanguinea*); 'Ioensis' ('Bechtel');
Chinese (*M. spectabilis*); Japanese (*M. floribunda*); 'Almey,' 'Elyii' and 'Hopa.' According to the authorities seedlings of the species come true from seed but those from
hybrids do not. One year I collected specimens from some of our trees at random;
removed the pulp and planted the seeds in our covered frame in fall after the little
apples had been hit by frost. The fruit is very hard and is softened by frost so that the
pulp is easily removed. From this planting we have a number of flowering crab apple
trees, each with a little variation in foliage from dark red to pale green; all with
lovely flowers in shades of rose-pink and red fruits. They bloomed in 4 years growing
rapidly the second season. The seedlings are better transplanted to a second frame
the first year to prevent rabbit damage. I understand that much better germination is
had on crab apple trees by keeping the seeds in a seed pan of seedling mix in the
refrigerator for from 60 to 120 days before sowing. In that case, in our area, I would
plant them, after refrigerating, in my greenhouse or under the fluorescent lights.

MELIA AZEDARACH ☐ Chinaberry tree, but also known as Beadtree or Pride of
China. This is a hardy tree from Virginia southward and grows fine in California.
A small tree, it grows 30 to 40 feet tall. Flowers are lilac and fruit is nut-like, covered
with yellow pulp relished by the birds. It is quite insect free. Seeds germinate quickly
if sown as soon as mature in coldframe or protected seed bed. Grows rapidly.

NYSSA SYLVATICA (MULTIFLORA) ☐ Tupelo or Sourgum, also called Pepperidge
tree. Hardy trees of lofty nature with light foliage. Leaves turn a beautiful shade of
scarlet in autumn. Fruits are berry-like, blue-black. Prefers wet spots but I have seen it
growing on hill tops. Difficult to transplant except when quite small. Makes very slow
growth. Free seeds of pulp and sow in coldframes in late fall with germination in
late spring following. If seed cannot be planted when mature, do not permit to dry
out but store in damp vermiculite in a cool place until spring. May take one year to
germinate.

OXYDENDRUM ARBOREUM ☐ Sourwood or Sorrel-tree. Hardy in the north. Grows
30 to 40 feet although I have heard of specimens that will attain 75 feet. Flowers are
white in panicles in summer. Fruits are grayish capsules. This is a lovely tree for accent
in the landscape for its foliage turns a brilliant scarlet in fall. Purchased seed germinated
50 per cent for me, given a pre-chilling period in the coldframe in March then bringing
into greenhouse. Placed in seed pan under fluorescent lights seeds germinated 100 per
cent. Although this tree prefers an acid soil, the seedlings grow well in a good potting
soil mix with extra peatmoss added. They respond well to feeding while in flats. Grows
slowly. Should be transplanted to covered frame and kept there for the first winter.
Do not let the soil in the frame dry out.

PAULOWNIA TOMENTOSA ☐ Interesting tree from China and Japan but is found in protected woodlands from southern New York south. Grows to 45 feet tall. Spectacular when in bloom with large fragrant lavender flowers followed by oval seed capsules each containing a number of winged seeds. Store seed dry in paper bags and sow in spring as any perennial. Grows fairly rapidly. It should be used where it can be protected from winter winds, or it will winter kill in our area.

PICEA ☐ Spruce. All spruces are beautiful evergreens growing rapidly when well established. Most of them grow easily from seed, which, produced in cones, mature in the fall of the year. *P. canadensis* (white spruce) is more difficult to transplant than the others, at least that has been our experience. *P. pungens,* Colorado spruce, is one of the loveliest of this tribe. The seedlings will vary in that some will be deep blue and others bluish green. *P. excelsa* (Norway spruce) is popular but we find it quite susceptible to red spider and spruce mites. Seeds of these spruces may be planted in coldframes in late fall with irregular germination the summer following. Best germination is had by sowing in seed pan of mix and keeping refrigerated for 60 to 120 days and sowing in spring as you do your perennials. Spruces should be misted regularly to keep down red spiders. Young seedlings should be protected from sun by shading either in seedbeds or coldframes. They should be moved every two years to keep the root ball compact. When planted to permanent places they should be removed with good rootball and kept watered daily for several weeks. The best time for transplanting evergreens is late July and August in our area.

PLATANUS OCCIDENTALIS ☐ American Planetree or Sycamore. Hardy in the North but native in the South. Bark is whitish and peels off giving a shaggy appearance to the trunk. Fruits are one-seeded. *P. acerifolia* (London planetree) is used as a street tree although a fungus disease in latter years causes leaves to turn brown and drop during summer. Sow seed in late fall in protected seed beds or coldframes. Not fussy as to soil.

PINUS ☐ Pine. There are many native pines and these evergreen trees are known to most home gardeners. In most cases the needles are long. They are fairly rapid growing and do well under conditions in most home gardens. They are best transplanted in spring before growth starts according to most authorities. The white pines in our garden we found the most difficult to move. *P. strobus,* the white pine, is one of my favorites for its graceful boughs and branches. It is very hardy in the North. Grows rapidly. Austrian pine *(P. austriaca)* is planted throughout the area where we live. It has a flatter top, longer and heavier needles than the white pine. *P. resinosa,* the red pine or Norway pine, is a handsome tree and not planted often enough. Its needles are very long and lovely. These are all hardy in the North. Remove seeds from cones in fall and sow in seedling pans of mix and keep in refrigerator for 90 to 120 days before placing under lights or in greenhouse or covered frame for germination. Shade seedlings the first two seasons.

PODOCARPUS MACROPHYLLA ☐ This resembles the taxus and is native to Japan but grows from North Carolina south. This is an evergreen. Grows as a pot plant in the North. Flower arrangers love it. The fruit is purple berry-like with one seed. Remove seed from pulp and sow in protected seed bed or frame. Easily grown indoors in seedling mix if given a pre-chilling in refrigerator for 60 to 90 days. Mine were potted up and finally given to friends for accent plants in family rooms. In the southern states seedlings should be given the same treatment as that recommended for other evergreens.

POINCIANA DELONIX OR REGIA ☐ Royal Poinciana. This is a large spreading tree found in southern Florida and southern California. Blossoms in summer with huge clusters of scarlet flowers followed by long seed pods. They lose the leaves during winter months. Not hardy in the North. *P. pulcherrima* (Barbados pride; also called dwarf poinciana) is a dwarfish form of this tree usually growing 10 to 12 feet. I have grown these in my greenhouse with germination in 10 to 15 days. Seedlings grow fast and make good potted plants for the home or greenhouse in the North. Both poincianas freeze at 30 degrees but soon recover.

PSEUDOTSUGA DOUGLASI ☐ Douglas Fir. This is another of my favorites, having soft fir-like needles, not sharp like those of the spruces. It is graceful and foliage is blue-green. Produces cones like other evergreen species. In my garden does well in semishade. Store seed dry in paper bags and sow as any perennial. Seedlings must be shaded in coldframe or protected seed bed for the first two years at least. Not fussy as to soil.

QUERCUS ☐ Oak. Oaks are trees found all over the world and were considered sacred by ancient peoples. They are among our best-loved trees in North America. Botanically they are divided into groups but I feel that should the home gardener be interested it would be well to buy a good book on trees. In this section I will describe a few of our easier grown oaks. *Q. alba* is the white oak and is native from Maine to Florida. *Q. coccinea* is native also from Maine to Florida and west to Minnesota and Missouri. Leaves turn scarlet in fall. *Q. palustris* (the pin oak) is my favorite for use on small home grounds. Graceful and attractive with smallish leaves that turn golden red in fall. Lovely drooping habit. Does not grow too lofty for the home grounds. *Q. virginana,* the live oak, is not hardy in the north but is found native from Virginia to Florida west to Mexico. Beautiful picturesque trees; fine for shade. Fruits of oaks are called acorns. The oils in the nut-like fruits go rancid quickly. When mature keep in moist sand or vermiculite until early winter then sow in protected seedbeds or coldframes. Some germinate quickly; others take a second season to germinate. Cold frame plantings should be mulched after the ground has frozen. In the South, cover the acorns with sand to prevent the nuts from becoming too warm which interferes with their growth.

SCHINUS MOLLE ☐ The so-called Peppertree, and often called Florida Holly by my Florida friends. Grows in frostfree sections and is not hardy in the North. Makes good hedge material. Self-sows readily. Plant seeds in seed pans or protected seedbeds or frames. Germinates quickly and grows rapidly. Can be grown as a pot plant in greenhouses in the North.

SEQUOIA SEMPERVIRENS ☐ These are native to California and Oregon and the West Coast. Evergreen. They have been found to be hardy in sections of New York but are best from North Carolina southward. Cones are oval. Store seed in dry paper bags and sow in spring like you would any perennial. It is best to use purchased seeds as the cones hang on for a long time before seeds are mature.

SOPHORA JAPONICA ☐ Also called Pagoda-tree or Scholartree. These are pretty trees with disease-free foliage similar to that of the locust. Will grow to 50 feet in the North. Flowers are borne in panicles 10 to 12 inches long and are white. Seeds freshly gathered and planted in open seedbeds or coldframes germinate readily in spring. I have three seedlings five years old which have attained the height of 5 feet so assume they are slow-growing in our locality. Very attractive and good lawn specimen.

SORBUS AMERICANA ☐ American Mountain Ash. Hardy in the North and grows as far south as North Carolina. Light foliage like that of the locust with white flowers in spring followed by clusters of yellow fruits in the fall. Grows to 30 feet. Very attractive ornamental.

S. AUCUPARIA ☐ The European Mountain Ash or Rowan tree grows to 45 feet. Hardy in the North. I have had good success sowing sorbus seeds washed free of pulp as soon as mature both in coldframes and open seedbeds. Authorities state that better germination is had by keeping the seed at 32 degrees for a period of 90 days, then sowing.

TAXODIUM DISTICHUM ☐ This is the baldcypress of the South, native from Delaware to Florida. It is an evergreen. Likes swampy spots. Seeds should be sown in seed pans of seedling mix and kept in refrigerator for 60 to 120 days, then sow as any perennial. Grow seedlings like other evergreens.

TAXUS CUSPIDATUS ☐ Japanese Yew. These vary, some of them being spreading and some upright. They are evergreen and used for foundation plantings everywhere. The upright ones make excellent hedges. Unfortunately the deer are very fond of taxus and browse on it in winter. Varieties *hicksi* and *hatfieldi* are good upright varieties. Berries are red and produced in late summer. Remove pulp and store in damp peatmoss or sand for the winter and sow in spring as any perennial. Treat small seedlings as you would for spruces, pines and other evergreens.

TSUGA (HEMLOCK) CANADENSIS AND CAROLINIANA ☐ Hemlock. Both are beautiful short-needled evergreens. *T. canadensis* is very hardy in our area. It is excellent hedge material. Our hedge, 400 feet long, was grown 14 years ago from seedlings. It is kept clipped to 6 feet in height and the sides can be sheared lightly to keep it in bounds. It does not brown out in the center as do some evergreen hedge materials. It is a fine background for our perennial border. Fruit is an oval cone. Seed should be stored dry until spring and sown as any perennial. Little seedlings are fragile and they should be grown in shaded seedbeds or coldframes for two years and then grown in semishade another year or two before placing in nursery beds. They need to be moved every third year to keep rootball compact before placing to permanent locations. Grows rapidly when well established.

SHRUBS TO GROW FROM SEED

AMELANCHIER CANADENSIS ☐ Shadblow, Juneberry, Shadbrush, Serviceberry. This native shrub is covered with white or pinkish blooms in early spring followed by dark blue berries loved by birds. They are very hardy in the North and will grow in most any good soil. In shade they tend to become too tall and sparse. Remove pulp from berries when ripe and sow in coldframe. Seed bed should be kept moist. Germination in spring following.

AMORPHA FRUTICOSA ☐ Indigobush. This shrub is not considered reliably hardy in the North yet mine grown from seed has lived for many years in an exposed area. Foliage is fern-like and the flowers are inconspicuous purple, somewhat resembling catkins. Disease-free, this is a good shrub for the deciduous hedge planting. Grows in any soil. Sow seeds as any perennial in spring. Grows quickly and easily.

ARDISIA CRENULATA ☐ Pretty, low-growing shrub with shiny green leaves and red berries grown mostly in Florida. It is used extensively as a pot plant in northern greenhouses. I have grown many of these shrubs from seed sown in February or March as any perennial in warmth (65 to 70 degrees)

AUCUBA JAPONICA ☐ Gold-dust Tree. Pretty evergreen shrubs grown in the South for foundation plantings. Is not considered reliably hardy north of Washington but I have seen it growing in protected spots in southern New York State. Flower arrangers love to use its foliage in arrangements. Leaves are blotched yellow, hence its name of gold-dust. Likes semishade and moist soil. Fruits are scarlet. Sow in warmth indoors or in greenhouse as any perennial.

AZALEA ☐ There are many varieties of azalea, both evergreen and deciduous. They do well in soils ranging from 4.5 to 6.0 although they are considered to be lovers of acid soil. They need a moist, well-drained location and must be shaded somewhat from full sun especially in the North where late spring suns and winds dry them out. Many of them will have the blossom buds blasted if temperatures go below zero in the North if there is no snow cover. Soil should be well-prepared for azaleas, incorporating large quantities of humus, leafmold and peatmoss. Cottonseed meal or a fertilizer made especially for evergreens are good to use for feeding. Azaleas should be heavily mulched with oak leaves or peatmoss. They should never be cultivated as the feeder roots are quite near the soil level. They should be kept well weeded and well watered at all times. (Botanically the azalea is classified as a rhododendron.) There are azaleas which will grow in nearly all parts of the United States. Some of them are native and many came from Japan and China. *R. mucronata* is the first deciduous native to come into bloom in the North with lavender flowers. In my garden I have the native *R. calendulaceum* or the flame azalea growing among deciduous shrubs with no extra care. Other deciduous ones growing in my garden are Mollis and Ghent. There are many native varieties too numerous to mention. Of the evergreen azaleas there are Kaempferi hybrids, Knaphill hybrids, Exbury strain, Kurume hybrids, Dutch hybrids and others.

140 HYBRID AZALEA FROM SEEDS.
Ward Linton

The only azaleas which I have attempted from seed were taken from a plant of *A. mollis* when the seed capsule was brown in August. The seeds are very fine and almost dustlike. Sown in a pan of my favorite mix and placed in my greenhouse they germinated in 21 days. Under the lights it took them 30 days. I do not cover seed but press it into the medium with my finger tips, but the seed pan of course is covered with plastic until after germination. Purchased seed can be sown in January, February or March indoors or in the greenhouse as you would any perennial. Best germination is had at between 68 and 75 degrees. Flat out seedlings when true leaves have formed just as I described in chapter 2, giving them a soil mix containing extra peatmoss. The first winter in our area it is best to keep the flatted seedlings in a plastic tent either under lights, in the greenhouse or a bright window. The second year the plants may be potted up and plunged into a coldframe shaded by lath or covered with plastic screen and mulched with salt hay after the ground freezes. The third year they may be placed in nursery rows shaded by burlap, muslin or screening and mulched with salt hay. These plants must never be allowed to dry out. Mine are fed half-strength Rapid-Gro every three weeks while in the flats. It usually takes two years for the shrubs to attain 8 to 10 inches of height.

BERBERIS ☐ Barberry. Of the barberries there are two that I feel are worth growing from seed. The so-called redleaf barberry, *B. atropurpurea* with pretty purplish red leaves is most attractive either as hedge material or as a specimen plant. Grown in shade the leaves are much paler and greenish. Remove pulp from seed and sow in fall in coldframe. It germinates in May the following year and grows to 1 foot or more the first year. Pinching out the top when 6 inches tall makes a more bushy plant. Not fussy as to soil.

B. JULIANAE ☐ Wintergreen Barberry. It is hardy in the North if planted at east foundation or in semishade as late winter sun and winds brown the foliage in which case leaves will fall off but new ones soon cover the bush. Mine are growing on an east slope and rarely if ever burn. Fruits are berry-like. Sow seed as for *B. atropurpurea* but shade the young seedlings as an evergreen. Does well in any rich soil.

BUXUS SEMPERVIRENS ☐ Boxwood. Beautiful evergreen shrubs with small shiny green leaves, but unfortunately not reliably hardy north of Philadelphia. The only box I have grown is *B. microphylla* which is hardy as far north as Boston. This grows to 2 feet in my garden in front of a stone wall facing east and shaded in summer by a Japanese maple. Seeds gathered in fall and sown in coldframe germinated readily in late spring. The seedlings were kept in flowerpots in my greenhouse for the first winter and planted to permanent places in May of the following year.

CARISSA GRANDIFLORA ☐ Natal Plum. Thorny shrub with small dark leaves. Flowers are white and fruit is an edible berry. This is not hardy in the North and freezes at 30 degrees but will recover. Wash pulp from fruit and sow as any perennial. I have grown many of these and have some as bonsai in my greenhouse. They are very good for background use or hedge material in Florida. Seed germinates quickly.

CARYOPTERIS INCANA ☐ This charming shrub should be in every garden. It grows 2 to 2½ feet tall with small gray leaves. Blooms in August with fluffy clusters of heavenly blue flowers. It is my favorite of late-blooming shrubs. Seed pods are bluish. Seeds gathered in late fall when pods are mature, planted in covered coldframe germinate freely in late spring. They must be transplanted with care to protected seedbeds or other frames for the first year and must not be allowed to dry out. If these shrubs are planted in foundation plantings mulched with peatmoss, seedlings are often found at the base of the plant in summer. Sometimes in a severe winter this shrub will be killed back to ground level but will grow again from the crown, like any hardy perennial.

CHIONANTHUS VIRGINICA ☐ Fringetree or Old man's-Beard. Large shrub to 10 feet, native from Pennsylvania south. White flowers are produced in profusion in clusters. Does not leaf out until very late spring. Fruits which ripen in September are berry-like, dark blue. Excellent lawn specimen. Sow seed when ripe in covered frame in late fall. Germination usually very slow sometimes not germinating until the second spring.

CYTISUS BROOM ☐ The best known of the brooms is *C. scoparius* or Scotch broom. It is upright growing to 5 to 10 feet with pea-like flowers usually yellow. Scotch brooms are not reliably hardy in the extreme North unless planted in protected areas. The only variety I have grown with great success and no protection is butcher's-broom, obtained from one of my favorite seedsmen. Blooms are yellow with orange tips. Sow seed like any perennial February to March in greenhouse or indoors. Germinates in 15 to 20 days. Resents transplanting except when quite small. Not fussy as to soil.

DEUTZIA GRACILIS ☐ A low-growing one for front of foundation plantings and 'Pride of Rochester,' a tall robust growing variety with double flowers. They bloom in June in our area. Shrubs are covered with flowers during the blooming period. Fruit is a small brown capsule. Seeds are small. Sow seed when mature in coldframe where they will germinate readily in early spring. Not fussy as to soil. Prefer sun but will grow fairly well in part shade.

EUONYMUS ☐ There are many evergreen and deciduous euonymus. Of the evergreen varieties the most well known are *E. vegetus* and *E. fortunei*. *E. kewensis minimus* has very small leaves. Of the deciduous kinds my favorites are "Wahoo" *(E. atropurpureus)*, winged euonymus *(E. alatus)* and the lower more compact-growing *E. alatus compactus*. They all have berry-like fruits. The evergreen varieties are trailing or climbing and the deciduous types are shrubs. Although most authorities assert that these seeds should be stratified in winter at 50 degrees to be planted in spring in coldframes, I have had excellent success by removing pulp and planting to coldframe in late fall. They grow quickly after germinating and are very hardy and can be placed in nursery rows the first season. The deciduous kinds are especially fine for brilliant scarlet foliage in fall.

EXOCHORDA GRANDIFLORA ☐ Pearlbush. This is a hardy shrub to 8 feet with white waxy flowers in late May, followed by rounded seed capsules. It is a very lovely specimen shrub and exceedingly hardy in our location. Seed stored dry and sown in spring under fluorescent lights indoors or in the greenhouse germinates readily and the plants grow rapidly. Not fussy as to soil and will grow in semishade although it becomes a little "leggy" where it does not receive full sun.

HYPERICUM CALYCINUM ☐ Low shrubs with single yellow flowers 1 inch across usually blooming in July and August. This is semievergreen in the south. Sometimes kills to ground level in North but springs up again from the crowns. It is very good in rock gardens. Sow as any perennial indoors in February and March with germination in 20 to 30 days. Not fussy as to soil. May also be sown in late fall in coldframes. In extreme North not reliably hardy unless protected.

ILEX ☐ Besides the holly used for Christmas decorations there are a number of members of this family with evergreen leaves. *I. bullata* and *I. crenata* are often used in foundation plantings. Leaves are similar to box which they resemble. Berries are blue-black. *I. cornuta* which is hardy south of Washington has red berries. Remove pulp from berries and sow in coldframe in late fall with germination in May following. I have also grown these from seed stored dry and planted in March under fluorescent lights with germination in 20 days.

I. VERTICILLATA ☐ Black Alder. This is a deciduous shrub native to Eastern North America. It grows 8 to 10 feet high and produces red berries in the fall which are eagerly sought by migratory birds. It grows readily from seed planted to the coldframe in late fall. This is an excellent shrub for low moist locations.

LEUCOTHOE CATESBAEI ☐ Drooping Leucothoe. These are lovely evergreen shrubs, low growing to 3½ feet in our location. Do well in light shade. Ours, growing under deciduous trees on the north side are completely windswept in winter and while there is some browning of the leaves they quickly recover and bloom each spring with long branches of small white flowers. Fruit is a small capsule and seed is tiny. They prefer a pH of 5 to 6 and appreciate a peatmoss mulch. Store seeds dry and sow as any perennial indoors in February or March. Keep in flats indoors for the first winter, then in shaded lath covered frames for the second winter. Does not like hot sun.

LIGUSTRUM ☐ Privet. There are evergreen sorts of ligustrum from Philadelphia south. 'Regal' and 'Ibota' are hardy north, 'Regal' being used for hedging material. Fruits are berry-like. Wash seed from pulp and sow in coldframe in fall. Seedlings grow rapidly the first summer. Not fussy as to soil. Does well in full sun or semishade.

PHOTINIA VILLOSA ☐ Christmasberry or Chinese Hawthorn. Is hardy in the North but needs protection in extremely cold sections. Attractive shrubs to 10 feet with white flowers in profusion followed by red berries. Should be grown in protected areas to prevent winter-kill. Wash pulp from seed and sow in coldframe in early winter. Sometimes takes a second spring to germinate.

PHYSOCARPUS LUTEUS ☐ Ninebark. Also called gold-leaf ninebark. This is a large shrub with maple-like leaves which have a yellow tinge. They bloom in June and the flowers are followed by clusters of golden capsules containing small seeds. Very hardy in our location and has resisted drought for several years although it is usually recommended for moist situations. Sow seed in late fall in covered coldframes.

PIERIS JAPONICA ☐ Beautiful evergreen shrubs good at north foundation plantings or in partially shaded areas. Likes acid soil 5.0 to 6.0 pH. Blooms in early spring with racemes of white lily-of-the-valley like blooms. Very hardy in our location but buds might freeze in extreme northern areas. Fruit is a capsule; sow seed in coldframes in late fall or store dry until spring and sow like azaleas. Small seedlings should be potted up and kept either under lights, in the greenhouse or in brightly lighted window at cool temperature (55 to 60) for the first winter, then plunged into covered frame for the second season. After placing in nursery rows seedlings should be lightly shaded and should not be permitted to dry out. A peaty soil is best for these evergreens. Mulch well with peat.

P. FLORIBUNDA ☐ Native in Virginia south to Georgia but I have seen it growing in sheltered places in southern New York on the east side of buildings. Sow as directions given for P. japonica. Germination should be had in 60 days if planted in spring indoors.

PITTOSPORUM TOBIRA ☐ Attractive evergreen shrubs growing well in Florida and the Gulf states as well as California. Flowers are white and blooms are produced in clusters at the tip of the branches usually during the winter months. Very good for seaside plantings in mild climates. Sow purchased seed as for any perennial. They will germinate in warmth in 15 to 20 days. This is a fine pot plant for northern sun porches and greenhouses.

POTENTILLA FRUTICOSA ☐ Commonly called by my friends the "buttercup bush." It is hardy, low-growing, very good for the rockery and is good at the foot of the rock walls or facing down taller shrubbery. Blooms in profusion in June and July in our location but will bloom lightly throughout the summer. Not fussy as to soil. Sow seeds in coldframe in fall. Germinates readily in late spring.

PUNICA GRANATUM ☐ Pomegranate. This shrub is hardy as far north as Washington. Flowers are orange-scarlet and very showy blooming in May or June. I have grown the P. g. nana from purchased seeds, sowing in pans of seedling mix in March in our greenhouse with germination in 15 to 20 days. This latter variety makes an excellent pot plant and is eagerly sought by bonsai enthusiasts. Grow as any house plant in good potting soil. Likes sun. Blooms when quite young and flowers are followed by fruits even on small potted plants. Foliage is very fine and attractive.

PYRACANTHA COCCINEA ☐ Firethorn. Thorny evergreen shrubs with spiny branches and attractive shiny green leaves. Flowers are white in clusters and blooms in June in our area followed by berry-like fruits which become brilliant orange. They are eaten by the migratory birds in November in our location. Firethorns will grow 6 to 8 feet and may be trained as espaliers or treated as climbers. While firethorns are not considered reliably hardy they do well on the east and south side of buildings in our area. Prefer limestone soils thriving at 6 to 8 pH. Pyracantha is very easy to grow from seed and I have grown many of them. Wash seeds free of pulp and sow in cold-frame in late fall with germination in May following. I have also kept seeds stored dry over the winter and sown in the greenhouse in March with no pre-chilling period with excellent results. The small plants must be placed in flats until large enough to go into 3-inch pots. By the end of the first summer season they will be from 6 to 8 inches tall. I plunge these pots into open coldframes for the winter and mulch with salt hay after the first freeze. The open frame should have a lath cover if the frame is located in a sunny spot.

RHODODENRONS ☐ There are many native varieties of these broadleaf evergreens such as *R. maximum* (rosebay), *R. carolinianum* (Carolina rhododendron) and *R. catawbiense.* There are also many beautiful hybrid rhododendrons. They are not easy for the inexperienced for they need special care and soil. The soil should be a good loam enriched with humus and peatmoss. The roots of these plants, like azaleas, must never be allowed to dry out. They must be protected from hot sun and bright sun and winds in late winter. Fall planting is advisable for the northern section of the United States although they may be moved in spring with great care. The roots of rhododendrons should be mulched with a 3-inch covering of peatmoss at all times. Seeds whether purchased or homegrown, should be stored dry and sown in warmth in pans of seedling mix like the azalea. The seed is very fine and should not be covered but pressed into the medium with finger tips. Encase the seed pan in a tent of plastic whether sown under lights, in a bright window or in the greenhouse. The little seedlings must never be allowed to dry out and it is best to mist them two or three times a week. When large enough place in flats and keep indoors the first winter at 50 to 60 degrees. The second winter handle as for azaleas.

RHODOTYPOS SCANDENS ☐ Jetbead or White Kerria. This is a very hardy shrub in my garden. The foliage is disease-free and attractive. In late spring it is covered with white blossoms resembling orange blossoms. Fruit is black and shiny berry-like containing one hard seed. Although it is considered difficult to transplant, we have moved quite large ones (to 5 feet) with no difficulty. Not fussy as to soil. Will bloom in sun or in semishade. Sow seeds in late fall in coldframe or keep in pan of seedling mix in refrigerator until February and bring into warmth. If seeds have become very dry before sowing, soak them in water for several days.

ROSA RUGOSA ☐ The everblooming Chinese and Japanese rose which will grow 5 to 6 feet is very hardy in the North and does well in seaside plantings. They root by underground stolons and are excellent for planting on high banks. The flowers are single or semidouble in shades of rose or white. Foliage is somewhat leathery and very spiny. I have grown many of these from seed both from those which have "escaped" (found growing wild) and from hybrids. The fruits are large and berry-like and are called "hips." Seed gathered in late fall, washed free of pulp and planted in coldframes or open seed beds germinates readily in late spring.

R. MULTIFLORA ☐ The so-called "living fence" rose. While many gardeners do not like this, it is one of my favorites for it can be kept trimmed to size if wanted for hedge material. The flowers resemble those of blackberry and on a late June morning a plant gives forth a heavenly rose odor. The hips are quite small and bright red and are relished throughout the winter by birds. It does not tip root as do some of the old-fashioned rambler roses and it does not grow by underground stolons. Placed 2 feet on center plants make an impenetrable hedge. Allowed to grow naturally they will reach to 10 feet and spread to 6 feet wide. It is not recommended for the small home grounds. Sow as for *R. rugosa.*

SYMPLOCOS PANICULATA ☐ Sweet-leaf or Sapphireberry. This shrub is hardy from Massachusetts south but is not seen in many gardens. Flowers are white and very fragrant blooming in May or early June. Fruits are berry-like and sapphire colored and ripen in September. The berries are loved by the birds. My first seeds came from a bush in a bird sanctuary where the caretaker permitted me to take a few to try. Does well on almost any soil unless it is very acid. Seed, sown in the coldframe in late fall germinates unevenly and many will not show until the second season. Treat as any hardy shrub.

VIBURNUM ☐ There are many native viburnums which are found growing all over the country. They are so beautiful that large numbers of them are sold in nurseries everywhere. Among my favorites are these: *V. theiferum,* the Tea viburnum with long pointed leaves and clusters of small red berries which hang on over the winter. A most decorative shrub growing to ten feet when given full sun. Another lovely one which is excellent for the winter landscape and provides food for the migratory birds in early spring is the American cranberry bush, *V. trilobum. V. dentatum,* called arrrowood, has small black fruits and is excellent for nesting and food for birds. *V. dilatatum* is the so-called linden viburnum, the Japanese cranberry-bush. Fruits cover the bush and are bright red. *Viburnum lentago* or nannyberry is a beautiful tree-like one with shiny leaves and blue-black berries which ripen in late September. There are many others, all of them good subjects for the shrub border or for the "wild" garden. None of them are fussy as to soil and all of them are very hardy. Of the decorative kinds I prefer *Viburnum tomentosum,* the double-file viburnum both for its lovely flattened flowers up-faced along the branches and the red fruits in fall, and *V. carlesi* for its beautiful pink fragrant flowers in late May. I have grown many viburnums from seed. Pulp should be washed from seed when mature in the fall and they may be sown in open seed beds or coldframes in early fall. Some will germinate the following spring and others will not show until the second spring following. One authority states that seeds should be gathered early and planted while there are still two months of 50- to 60-degree weather and in the case of late ripening seed, sow in seed pans, keep in warm cellar for two months and then move to covered coldframes or keep in cool cellar to be placed outside in early spring. According to this authority germination will be much quicker and easier than the coldframe method. I give this here for any adventurous home gardener who would like to try his luck with this method.

VITEX AGNUS-CASTUS ☐ Chaste-tree. This is a hardy shrub with pretty foliage bearing spikes of lavender flowers in late summer. In extremely cold locations they will die down to the ground level but will grow and bloom from the roots annually. They are improved by severe prunning in early spring before growth starts. Seed should be stored dry and sown in warmth in spring as any perennial.

10. Wild Flowers from Seed

WHEN I started to write this book, as I sat at my typewriter in my work-room, I gazed out at a huge bucket-crane busily at work gouging out the earth at the foot of a beautiful hill to make way for another super-highway. All spring and summer the whine of the power saws muted the bird song, as they toppled huge and lofty oaks, maples, birch and beech. Bulldozers rolled up the carpets of rhododendron and laurel, which were all, together with trees, gathered in huge piles and burned. For weeks it seemed, the smoke from their fires cast a pall of haze over our garden. The underfloor of the woods was ground to dust and lost for all time the beautiful bloodroot and Dutchman's breeches, trailing arbutus, columbine, hepatica, the little spring beauty and the pipsissewa and striped wintergreen, pink and yellow lady-slippers, the little false lily-of-the-valley, all the lovely ferns; maidenhair, Christmas, osmunda and spleenworts.

Now many months later it is impossible to work in my garden or to hear the birds sing at all while the adjoining land is being denuded of topsoil, subsoil, under-layer and hard pan to supply the ever increasing need for "fill" for the new highway; valuable residential and croplands destroyed for generations. No longer will the meadow lark nest there nor will we hear his wild sweet song on lovely spring days. The field sparrow will no longer be heard bursting into song at midnight to voice his happiness. The pheasant whose clutches of eggs were laid in the field will be seen no more. The goldfinches, tree sparrows and juncos who enjoyed in winter the seeds of the common evening primrose, wild penstemon, mullein and thistle will have to find food elsewhere when the snows of winter cover the land.

Shoulders are shrugged and people say, "What can you do? This is progress!" Yes, it is progress, and in this space age there is little the individual can do to protect the natural resources of this great and beautiful country. Many thoughtful citizens have for years tried, sometimes in vain, sometimes with success to protect naturally beautiful spots from highways, dams and housing developments but the growing population pushes the city out to the suburban areas and the suburban areas swallow up the farmlands, and so it goes.

All over the country, the citizens have formed Open Spaces Committees, urging local and state governments to purchase open lands to be kept forever green and in their natural state so that future generations may appreciate, study and understand the wonders of nature. Like an oasis in the desert, these areas would retain all the native plants, trees, shrubs and wild flowers indigenous to that location so that they might perpetuate themselves and where the wild life of the forests and meadowlands might continue to live and roam.

In many states conservationists have been able to make arrangements to go ahead of the bulldozers and other equipment and dig some of the most beautiful wild flowers and remove them to public parks where they can grow and be protected for years. In other states, horticultural groups have asked for and been given permission to dig wild flowers from areas which are to be razed and have planted them in private sanctuaries in order that they shall not vanish forever as did the passenger pigeon in a byogne era. Wealthy people have donated suitable acreage and wooded lands for Nature Conservancies.

What is a wild flower? I have often been asked to differentiate between wild flower and weed. Sometimes inexperienced gardners do not understand what we mean when we speak of "native" plants. Native plants are those which grow naturally all over the country. Of these there are shrubs, trees, grasses, wild flowers and weeds of all kinds.

Wild flowers could be classified as weeds, I suppose, but let us say that of the weeds, those with unusual and beautiful blooms are what we think of as "wild flowers." Many of our wild flowers have come under cultivation and we have grown them so long in our gardens we do not think of them as wild flowers. Our native trees—maple, oak, birch, beech, tupelo, holly, magnolia, sweet gum and others—are grown and sold by nurserymen and there are large numbers of persons who do not realize that these trees grow naturally all over the country. I have seen city people buy a beautiful piece of property complete with many lovely oaks, maples and dogwoods and then have the bulldozer completely sweep away all the native plants, compact the soil to concrete hardness and then go out and buy . . . what? Maples, oaks, and dogwoods! What a wonderful accomplishment if our populace could be educated to appreciate the native trees and shrubs and make use of them naturally in landscaping.

Wild flowers are difficult to transplant. Over the years only a few dedicated gardeners have been able to transplant them properly and by hard work and determination have been successful in getting them to thrive in home gardens. In order to be successful one must know the needs of the plants, where they are growing in the wild, on what kind of soil, whether on hot, dry spots or in cool shade, at or near water. Many thoughtless people have carelessly pulled them up with insufficient root, attempting to transplant them in areas which could not possibly support them. As a result the wild flowers are rapidly vanishing from the woods and meadowland which as yet have not felt the touch of "progress."

In recent years wildflower plants have been grown by a few dedicated nurserymen and are available by mail-order. If the gardener is careful to follow instructions as to where these plants may be placed they can be made to grow and thrive.

Not long ago it occurred to me that surely wild flowers could be grown from seeds and upon research I found that very little work has been published on this subject and very few gardeners have had experience in growing these difficult plants from seed. However, since a large majority of the flowers we grow in our perennial gardens have been brought to this country from all over the world and have acclimated themselves to new and different environments, possibly if we could become successful in growing wild flowers from seed we might be able to perpetuate these beautiful native plants right on our home grounds. Even the smallest of gardens could take a few. One of my friends has a lofty pine tree in her back yard. She loves it and enjoys it year round but bemoans the fact that nothing will grow under it. Think how heavenly it would be if the pink ladyslipper would bloom there each spring along with the troutlily, partridge berry, striped wintergreen and with the

Christmas fern, the shield fern and bracken and club mosses. Another friend has Jack-in-the-pulpit at her north foundation wall, grown from seeds which she planted there one fall. They have increased through the years with no care at all. The wild blue phlox *(Phlox divaricata)* which we grow in our gardens, gives bloom here too in early spring. At the edge of the deciduous shrub border, bloodroot and spring beauty will grow and bloom for years. Dutchman's-breeches will grow under thick maple shade. In such a location also will grow the beloved trailing arbutus, yellow ladyslipper and the delicate pink one, maidenhair fern and trilliums and the violets.

Our own property seems made to order for establishing wild flowers. We are fortunate in that we have four acres. The house and cultivated gardens occupy the western half of the acreage. An old stone wall of the kind found all over New England divides the property. Abutting the wall are old rock outcroppings and from this the land slopes rather sharply leaving a bank facing east and slanting on down to a meadow-like area.

Along the wall grow maples, hickories, wild cherry, sassafras, white ash, paper mulberry, small elms, wild crab apples. Virginia creeper and wild grape as well as bittersweet climb up into some of these trees. Farther down the slope there are oaks and cedar and maples. As the slope continues there are wild buleberries, many of the native viburnums, among them *Viburnum dentatum* and *lentago* and the shrub dogwoods—red osier, gray and others of this family. Black alder grows here too. There are barberry bushes and wild roses, no doubt escapes from cultivated plants of many years ago. There are also native violets and ferns in variety, common evening primrose, penstemon, New England asters and crane's-bill (wild geranium). To these natives we have added white pine and spruces, Douglas fir and hemlocks and pin oaks, as well as a number of flowering shrubs including bush honeysuckle in variety and the multiflora rose. It would seem to me that here on these two acres are all the conditions we need to start our own wildflower refuge. All we need is ingenuity, time—lots of time—seeds, and strong backs. As this would of necessity be a long-range project, perhaps we could never completely finish it but surely some colonies of our vanishing wild flowers could be established within a few years.

What a fine objective the growing of wild flowers from seed would be for members of garden clubs everywhere. Conservation chairmen and horti-culture chairmen could collaborate on such a project to encourage and inspire every home gardener to grow at least one or two wild flowers on the home grounds.

This past fall, having become enthusiastic about the subject of growing wild flowers from seed, I ordered from a New England grower a number of packets of wildflower seed. Included in the order were bloodroot, pink, yellow and showy ladyslipper, bunchberry, blue and red lobelia, trailing arbutus, closed and fringed gentian. There were no instructions for growing included in the order. I have in my personal library several very good books on the subject of growing wild flowers. While these give explicit details on *gathering* the seed with instructions for immediate planting, there is very little, if anything on the subject of growing seeds obtained from a commercial grower and which of necessity would not be considered "fresh" seed. I have done considerable research on the subject and find the available information meager and lacking in detail.

Each variety of wild flower needs, as does all living things, a suitable environment in which to thrive. The *specific* needs of individual plants will be discussed later. At the moment, it would seem in order to discuss the *general* needs and conditions of this fascinating group of plants.

In northern sections of the United States, reasonably good success has been had by preparing open seedbeds, adding peatmoss and/or compost of oak leafmold, decayed pine and hemlock needles and coarse sand. These materials should be well worked into the upper 6 or 8 inches of soil to provide a fairly fine surface. The seed is sown in rows, properly labeled and dated, in very late fall. In these climates a snow cover from late fall to late spring protects the seeds until warm and wet weather brings about germination.

Here in southern Connecticut we might have no snow cover at all or worse still, first a snow, then a melting, followed by near zero temperatures, which are promptly followed by 50 degrees, then down to low temperatures again, repeated throughout the winter. As most wildflower seeds need to freeze and thaw several times to break dormancy, particularly if they are purchased commercially and are not strictly fresh, a coldframe would give better results in our location than would open and exposed seedbeds. Some successful growers prefer to sow their seeds in bulb pans. An inch layer of sand is placed in the bottom over which a thick layer of garden soil mixed with oak leafmold (which incidentally is now available commercially) and/or peatmoss, together with coarse sand. Over this a thin layer of moist, milled sphagnum moss on which the seeds are sown.

Very fine seeds are not covered but pressed into the moss. Larger seeds may have a light sifting of the moss to cover. Place prepared seed pans in container of water until top shows moist. Be sure to provide each with a proper label giving name of wild flower and date planted. Plunge pots in coldframe up to the rims and as soon as the soil is frozen, cover with a light mulch of salt hay or some other mulch which does not pack. Place cover on frame to protect from rain or snow but leave small opening for air. Propping one end of glass cover up off the frame for about an inch will suffice. Remove cover in late spring after the last frost and do not allow seedling medium to dry out. It may be necessary to shade frame lightly with lattice work or burlap. I like to cover mine with plastic screening. This keeps out the hot rays of the sun but lets in good light. Seedlings of some varieties may be transplanted to semishaded nursery beds as soon as large enough to handle. Others will do better if transplanted to flats and kept in shaded frames for the first year.

We planted some of our wildflower seed in November in one of our frames containing garden soil, peatmoss and sand. This frame is partly shaded by spruce and pine trees on the south side. After the soil was frozen we mulched with salt hay and placed plastic screen cover on frame. By the end of May, the lobelias, both blue and red, had germinated freely. The fringed and closed gentians both showed fair germination. As of late July no germination had occured on the ladyslippers, bunchberry, bloodroot or trillium, but the seedbed will not be disturbed in order to give these a chance to germinate later.

In our own cultivated garden we have grown some of the more common wild flowers for years, starting them from seed as easily as we do our perennials. The seed packets (with the exception of trailing arbutus) referred to containing wildflower seeds from New England were so generously filled that we also planted some of the seed in our favorite mix of 1/3 vermiculite, 1/3 milled sphagnum and 1/3 perlite in aluminum foil loaf pans. These were given a pre-chilling period in the coldframe from January to mid-February and then brought into the greenhouse. Both lobelias germinated profusely and were soon flatted out; the gentians took a little longer but we have half a flat of each and these are growing very well. They are still in the flats but I have been feeding them weekly with ½ strength Rapid-Gro and they are very hardy and fine looking plants.

Seeds of the trailing arbutus were sown in seed pans and placed under the fluorescent lights as well as in the greenhouse. Very foolishly instead of planting these in our favorite sterile mix, I allowed a friend to persuade me to add peat to this mix on the theory that arbutus needs an acid soil to do well. Seeds germinated in four weeks but did not grow and finally damped off. With all the experience I have had starting plants with many diverse needs as to soil, I should have realized that acidity is not necessarily a prerequisite for *germinating* these seeds. In late April I asked the seedsman for more seeds of trailing arbutus and these were sown in the sterile mix and placed under the fluorescent lights. In three weeks they had germinated and when they grew large enough to be seen without the aid of reading glasses I began to feed weekly with ¼ strength Rapid-Gro. The little plants have thrived on

141 A PLASTIC MARKET-PAK, PLANTED, WATERED, TAGGED AND IN A PLASTIC BAG, READY TO BE PLACED IN A BRIGHT LOCATION TO AWAIT GERMINATION.

this treatment. Recently I read in the USDA yearbook for 1961 that seeds of ladyslippers would germinate only under controlled sterile conditions so I shall order fresh seeds and try this method in an attempt to grow these beautiful and vanishing wild flowers.

One lady of my acquaintance has had fair success with wildflower seed by planting her seeds out of doors in areas on her property where she wishes them to grow. The proper places according to the needs of the plant she wishes to grow are cleared of weeds and grass to make a planting area of about a square foot. She removes the top layer of soil and mixes with it decayed pine needles, peat and sand and plants her seed on this. Over the seed she places a mulch which she painstakingly has crumbled from oak leaves. She is rewarded with good stands of her favorites using this method. Another grower of wild flowers plants her seed in flats of milled sphagnum, waters well with a fine sprinkler and places these in open coldframes sheltered by her garage, where snow and rain may fall on them. This method has been quite successful. After germination and when plants are large enough to handle the plants are spaced in flats and kept in the frames for two winters before transferring to their permanent quarters.

The list that follows includes specific requirements for growing some of our most favored wild flowers. I have given their common names with the Latin ones in *italics*. This, in deference to my inexperienced gardening friends who complain that the Latin names of plants are "Greek" to them. However, I do feel that gardeners everywhere should become familiar with the Latin names of plants. Frequently we can find them in our garden dictionaries only under Latin names and most growers prefer to use the Latin names in catalogues. Therefore, it is very important to know more than the common name of the flowers we grow. I do agree with my friends however, that "aquilegia" does nothing for us, but the name "columbine" is like poetry!

BUTTERFLY WEED ☐ *Asclepias tuberosa.* This is a member of the milkweed family. The flower is a gorgeous cluster of reddish orange florets. Very showy. Grows beautifully in my perennial border and in my cutting garden in full sun in the same soil in which I grow all my perennials. It blooms in late summer. Seed can be sown in fall or spring in coldframes. We have never had any trouble with germination, planting the seeds in vermiculite or unmilled sphagnum in seed pans in our greenhouse, under the fluorescent lights or in a sunny window in February. We cover our seed pans with plastic to keep the seedling medium moist until germination begins in 10 days. Plants are easily transplanted to flats, peat pots or plant bands while small. Mature plants are difficult to plant because they make a thick taproot, although we have moved them without damage by lifting with a large rootball. Grows to 2½ to 3 feet; space 18 inches apart.

BUNCHBERRY ☐ *Cornus canadensis.* This is a dwarf member of the dogwood family. White flowers followed by red berries. Grows in deciduous woods and needs rich, moist soil but will not thrive unless the soil is *very* acid, about 4.0 to 4.5 pH. Start in flats in coldframe. The little seedlings do not transplant well. Thin out so that the plants you want will have room to expand. Keep in coldframe for second winter, then turn out entire flat intact for planting in a permanent spot; 4 inches to 8 inches tall; space 10 inches apart.

BLOODROOT ☐ *Sanguinaria canadensis.* White flower of good substance, 1½ to 2 inches in size. Leaves are large and rounded but divided into deep lobes. They are found along shaded roadsides and in woodsy areas with light shade. Blooms in early spring before the leaves on the trees have become full size. They like to be shaded in summer from hot sun. Thrive in rich, moist soil with pH 6 to 7. Grow well under maples if the soil is deep and rich and not too dry. Start in pots or flats in coldframe in fall. Germination occurs in spring usually. May be transplanted to small peat pots or plant bands. Protect over winter with mulch of pine needles. 8 to 10 inches tall; space 8 inches apart. Foliage dies down in summer.

BEARBERRY ☐ *Arctostaphylos uva-ursi.* Evergreen ground cover. Leaves small and oval. White flowers followed by red berries in winter. Likes sandy soil with good drainage. Use coldframe method for starting seeds. Bearberry seeds need an after ripening period before germination. Therefore germination may be very erratic. Do not attempt to transplant the little seedlings but let them grow to a point where flat or pot can be turned out with complete rootball and planted as one unit of small plants. One seedsman recommends subjecting bearberry seeds to 75 to 80 degrees temperature for several weeks and then giving them 40 degrees for three months. 1 to 2 inches, creeping; will spread 2 feet.

BERGAMOT ☐ *Monarda.* Also called "bee balm." *M. didyma* has bright red "ragged robin" flowers. *M. fistula* has purple, pink, or white flowers. May be grown in perennial border or naturalized in meadows. Prefers full sun. Sow seeds as any perennial with germination indoors in warmth in 7 days; outdoors in spring 21 days. Grows 3 to 4 feet tall; space 18 inches apart. Suffers in time of severe drought.

COLUMBINE ☐ *Aquilegia. A. canadensis* blooms in April or May. Beautiful gray-green foliage with red and yellow nodding flowers. Called "wild honeysuckle" by some. Grows as easily as any perennial. Sown indoors in February, germination in 2 weeks. Outdoors in spring 21 days. Can be sown in the fall or fresh seed sprinkled where it is wanted to grow. Blooms second to third year after sowing. *A. coerulea* and *A. flabellata* bloom in late spring. *A. canadensis* grows to 15 inches; space 10 inches apart. *Coerulea* and *flabellata* usually have blue or white flowers and grow to 10 inches; space 8 inches apart. All of these grow in my perennial border. They are also very good in rockeries. *A. canadensis* will do well on hot dry sandy soil and on rocky and gravel banks. Does well in light shade under deciduous trees.

CARDINAL FLOWER ☐ *Lobelia cardinalis;* BLUE LOBELIA ☐ *Lobelia siphilitica.* Bloom in August and September. The former with long spikes of bright red flowers. The blue lobelia is not as showy but its spikes of blue flowers are very attractive. They like the edge of wet meadows. Cardinal flower dies out in our garden in about three years but we have a few blue lobelia which bloom each year under the black walnut trees. Seed may be sown in fall in coldframes, open seedbeds or may be sown in early spring, indoors, with fair germination. Given a pre-chilling period of several weeks in the coldframe in February or March then brought indoors germination is excellent within 18 days. As easily transplanted and grown as delphinium, they will grow in the perennial border. Rosettes of leaves, spikes 2 to 4 feet; space 10 inches apart.

142 CARDINAL FLOWER AND BLUE LOBELIA SEEDLINGS, READY FOR TRANSPLANTING, ABOUT THREE MONTHS AFTER SEED WAS SOWN.

143 THREE MONTHS LATER THE SAME TWO KINDS OF LOBELIA READY TO BE TRANSPLANTED TO A PERMANENT LOCATION.

DUTCHMAN'S-BREECHES ☐ *Dicentra cucullaria.* Bloom in early spring, April or May. Small dainty pendant white flowers with blue-gray, fern-like foliage. A small corm or tuber appears in a short time. These are members of the bleeding-heart family. The foliage dies down during summer. They thrive in deciduous woods with rich soil but not too acid, having a liking for 6 to 7 pH. Does exceptionally well on eastern slopes where they are shaded during summer. Sow seeds in pots or flats in late fall in coldframe. To 10 inches; space 8 inches apart.

GENTIAN, FRINGED ☐ *Gentiana crinita.* Heavenly blue, bell-shaped flowers. Grows about 15 inches tall in my garden although in its native habitat it varies from 6 inches to 3 feet. Space 10 to 12 inches apart. Likes moist acid soil with full sun although it does fairly well at the edge of shady areas. This plant is biennial. Started one year in spring it produces little rosettes of leaves and will bloom the following year in the fall and then die. Sow as any perennial giving a pre-chilling period of 4 to 6 weeks in the coldframe in February or March then bringing indoors with germination in 14 days. Seedlings transplant well when quite small. It has been our experience that they are better transplanted to small plant bands placed in a flat so that there will be no injury to roots when small plants are placed in permanent places in garden or meadow.

GENTIAN, CLOSED ☐ *Gentian andrewsi.* This is the so-called bottle gentian. It blooms in the fall with dark blue flowers which resemble unopened elongated buds. It is a hardy perennial and likes to grow at the edge of woodsy areas in moist, humusy soil. Grows about 15 inches tall; space 12 inches apart. Easily grown from seed if given a prefreezing period like the fringed gentian. Transplants well.

HEPATICA TRILOBA ☐ Flowers are small, pale lavender or pinkish white. Small rounded, lobed leaves. Blooms in early spring. Likes oak woods but does well on banks if in soft woodsy soil. Plant seed in late fall in pots or flats in coldframe. Do not attempt to separate individual seedlings but transplant to other flats in small clumps leaving about 2 inches between clumps. Keep in coldframe over the first winter. Makes very slow growth. When transplanting to permanent quarters be very careful not to injure roots. Grows 4 to 6 inches tall; space 4 inches apart.

JACK-IN-THE-PULPIT ☐ *Arisaema triphyllum.* This is a hardy perennial. Makes a thick tuberous root. Large divided leaves with lily-like hooded flower of mahogany and green. Very showy. Likes acid soil of about 5 pH. Grows well at north foundations or in light deciduous shade in humusy soil. Transplants well. Grows 1 to 3 feet tall; space 15 inches apart.

LADYSLIPPER, PINK ☐ *Cypripedium acaule.* Also called the Moccasin flower. Blooms May or June. Flower delicate pink pouch-shaped. Likes dry slopes under pines. Will also grow in moist soils. Soil must be *very* acid. Soil from under pines or hemlocks is excellent. Very difficult from seed. Plant in early winter in bulb pots in covered frame. If germination is had, do not transplant but turn out of pot or seed pan intact. Mature plants can only be moved if taken with an extra large rootball. To 12 inches. Try growing under fluorescent light in sterile medium.

LADYSLIPPER, YELLOW ☐ *Calceolus parviflorum.* Small Yellow Ladyslipper. When established is not too difficult to grow in the wild garden. Blooms in May or June. Likes moist wooded areas under evergreens and deciduous trees. Does not require as acid a soil as the pink ladyslipper. Sow seed as for the pink ladyslipper. Grows to 2 feet; space 10 inches apart.

SHOWY LADYSLIPPER ☐ *Calceolus reginae.* This is the most handsome of the ladyslipper tribe. Grows to about 18 inches and flowers are white with rosy markings, and look like delicate china. Prefers a moist, slightly acid soil. It must never be allowed to dry out completely. Blooms in June. Grow from seed the same as the pink lady-slipper. If moved, should be taken with an extra large rootball. The new location should be prepared with mucky soil and the hole should be more than large enough to take the rootball. Space 10 inches apart.

MAY-APPLE ☐ *Podophyllum peltatum.* Large leaves up to a foot across. Flower is white and grows under the umbrella-like top whorl of leaves. Fruits are greenish yellow. Likes deciduous woods. Does well under maples. Prefers an acid soil, with much humus. Sow seeds in coldframes or in open seed beds in early winter. Should germinate the following May. Not difficult to transplant. Grows 12 to 18 inches tall; space 12 inches apart.

PIPSISSEWA ☐ *Chimaphila.* This is a ground cover, evergreen which grows by underground stolons. Stems are usually 8 to 10 inches high. Leaves are narrow, 2½ inches long. Tiny pinky-white flowers. Prefers dry, woodsy areas but the soil must be *very* acid for it to thrive. It needs summer shade and will not do well unless a permanent mulch of pine needles or peatmoss covers the roots. It is not easy from seed but may be grown by sowing in bulb pans in late fall and keeping in covered coldframe. If germination is had, keep in the frame for at least two winters. When planting to permanent quarters do not disturb individual plants but turn out entire rootball from pot intact.

SPRING BEAUTY ☐ *Claytonia.* Small white flower in earliest spring. Prefers moist deciduous woods. Will grow well in soil which is neither very acid nor alkaline. Produces a small corm. Not too difficult from seed. Sow in flats in coldframe in late fall covered with glass or plastic screening. Keep watered throughout the year. Grows 5 to 10 inches tall; space 6 inches apart. Foliage dies down after blooming.

TRAILING ARBUTUS ☐ *Epigaea repens.* Evergreen creeper with fragile pink flowers, very fragrant. Leaves oval about 1 to 2 inches long. Does well in light shade. Will not thrive except in very acid, moist and woodsy soil. Can be grown at the edges of woodsy areas and does especially well under pines or hemlocks. Blooms in earliest spring. Soil where it is to be planted should be prepared by mixing with the existing soil, decayed pine needles and oak leafmold and peatmoss. Plants should be deeply mulched with pine needles or peat. Sow seeds in bulb pans in late fall in coldframe. Thin out seedlings and allow those left in pot to stay in frame a second winter before transplanting to permanent quarters. Remove rootball intact in order not to disturb roots. One authority has had excellent success by removing the seedlings in bunches and planting to 3-inch pots of acid soil, plunging the pots in a protected spot where they can be kept watered during the second summer and planting to a woodsy area the third summer. The plants in these pots should never be allowed to become dry or they will die. Have germinated very well under fluorescent lights where temperature is 80 degrees, using sterile seedling mix. Feed with ¼ strength water-soluble fertilizer and keep under lights or in greenhouse first season.

TRILLIUM, WHITE ☐ *T. grandiflorum.* Flowers are white but turn pinkish as they get old. Grows to 18 inches tall with rather large leaves, space 12 inches apart. The purple *(Trillium erectum)* is showy. Both will grow under deciduous trees in woodsy soil. The purple one will also grow under hemlocks. In my garden both of these have succeeded under a wild pear tree at the foot of leucothoe with no care at all. They are mulched only by what leaves fall to the ground and are not blown away by the high winds which sweep our place. Another trillium, seeds of which are available, which is worth a try is *Trillium undulatum,* the painted trillium. This one prefers a more acid soil and more moisture than the others. Seed should be sown in flats in the coldframe in early winter under glass. Germination should be good the following spring. They are not too difficult to transplant as they produce small bulblets.

TROUT-LILY ☐ *Erythronium.* Called dog's-tooth violet. These produce bulbs and are found in moist deciduous woods. Yellow nodding miniature lily-shaped flowers usually spotted with brown; mottled leaves. Fresh seed germinates readily. Sown in coldframe in late winter good germination is had by spring. The foliage of this plant dies after blooming. Grows 6 to 8 inches tall; space 4 inches apart for good effect.

WILD BLEEDING-HEART ☐ *Dicentra eximia.* This is in the Dutchman's-breeches family and is grown in many home gardens. The foliage is attractive gray-green and flowers are pinkish-white borne throughout the summer. Foliage does not die down at all until hard frost. Very good under deciduous trees and in lightly shaded gardens. Good in rockeries. Excellent with trillium. Sow as any perennial. Give a prechilling period of 3 to 4 weeks in February or March in covered coldframe before bringing indoors to warmth. Germination will be had in 6 weeks. Blooms second season after sowing.

WINTERGREEN ☐ *Gaultheria procumbens.* Creeping plant with leaves arranged in whorls around the stem. Pinkish-white flowers followed by red berries. Does well under pines and hemlocks. Needs an acid soil, not too dry. Seed should be sown by coldframe method or by freezing three times in freezer before bringing to warmth of room or greenhouse. Transplant to flat and keep in protected frame through the second winter. Grows 3 to 6 inches high, spreading by underground stems.

WILD GERANIUM ☐ *G. maculatum* is a hardy perennial. Flowers magenta-pink about 1 to 1½ inches across. Grows 15 to 18 inches high; space 12 inches apart. Lobed leaves. Grows at the edges of wooded areas and in the partial shade of shrubs in meadows. Not fussy as to soil. Sow seed as any perennial. *G. robertianum* or "herb Robert" has more fern-like foliage than *maculatum* and has red stems. Flowers are quite small, deep rose in color. Very showy. Self-sows readily and spreads rapidly. Makes a good ground cover in rockeries. Grows 12 to 15 inches tall; space 10 inches apart for bedding effect.

WOOD ANEMONE ☐ *Anemone quinquefolia.* Dainty plant with white flowers. Grows to 6 inches tall. Likes open woods but prefers moist acid soil. Blooms in earliest spring. Seeds sown in pots or flats in coldframes in late fall germinate readily in spring. Not too difficult to transplant. Protect the small seedlings the second winter by transplanting to larger flats and keeping in frame covered with plastic screening before planting to permanent quarters.

FERNS

I feel that I would be remiss if I left this chapter without some mention of growing ferns from spores. Ferns do not produce seeds but on the underside of the fronds are found little brown dots which resemble scale insects. These are the spores. From ferns growing outdoors or on your own plants growing indoors collect the fronds and let them dry. I place mine on a paper towel for a few days then shake them and let the minute spores drop off. There are many ways to grow ferns from spores but since this book is being written for the inexperienced I will tell only of my own experiences. The first spores I collected were planted in a brandy snifter on the top of about 2 inches of equal parts of milled sphagnum, vermiculite and perlite. This was covered with a piece of glass and placed in a window which received strong light. Unlike the reader, I did not consult my book as to what to expect from these spores. After some weeks a light green tinge appeared on the surface of the medium. Now and then I gave the medium a little water by using the bulb spray lightly. Six or eight weeks later I could observe nothing except what appeared to be algae, so considering the whole thing a failure, I tossed it out! Some time later I obtained a book on growing ferns and found that I had thrown away all my ferns!

A small plastic refrigerator dish is good for starting fern spores. I have found I get better results using a *sterile* potting mix. The mix is moistened with warm water and after the spores have been carefully springled over the mix, a "baggie" is placed over the top of the dish, which should be kept in a warm spot, with good light. Ferns do very well under fluorescent light. After about four or five weeks the little green "fuzz" will be showing. This is called the *prothallus.* The prothallus is a one-celled body which puts down a rootlike hair that anchors it to the soil, then by adding one cell to another it enlarges to a heart-shaped body less than ¼ inch in size. From this little "heart" the new fern will grow. From spores sown in December, now in August I can start to transplant the young ferns. During the time that the spores were developing

144 THE SPOTS ON THE UNDERSIDES OF
THESE FERN FRONDS ARE CLUSTERS OF
SPORES, CALLED "FRUIT DOTS."
Larry B. Nicholson, Jr.

145 AFTER FORMATION OF THE MOSSY
PROTHALLUS, CONSIDERABLE TIME USUALLY
PASSES BEFORE TYPICAL FRONDS SUCH AS
THESE ARE SEEN.   *Larry B. Nicholson, Jr.*

into prothallus and from prothallus to heart-shaped bodies, I checked them from time to time to be sure the seedling medium was moist. If the container felt unusually light I knew that I had waited a little too long. I watered the container by removing the "baggie" and giving a light but fine spray from the rubber spray bulb using warm water. When the ferns are large enough to be removed, plant in a good houseplant potting mix with extra vermiculite and peat added to make the soil extra spongy. They can be transferred to flowerpots or aluminum loaf pans or any other container which will contain at least 2 inches of soil. Cover the pans with a tent of plastic to keep them moist. From the looks of my ferns I would say that I will need to keep them under the lights or in the greenhouse through this coming winter before planting outdoors. The variety I am growing is the Ebony spleenwort a pretty rock fern for shady areas.

11. Bulbs, Tubers and Corms from Seed

IT would not seem that this book could be complete if there were no information on growing bulbs, tubers and corms from seed. While it usually takes several years for such plants to mature, the patient gardener feels great satisfaction from such an endeavor. There are many such plants which take so many years to come into bloom it would hardly behoove the home gardener to attempt to grow them from seed. However, of those described in the following encyclopedia my husband and I have known the thrill of accomplishment of growing from seed and bringing to full beauty many of them.

BULBS, TUBERS AND CORMS TO GROW FROM SEED

ACHIMENES, see houseplant chapter.

AGAPANTHUS, see houseplant chapter.

ALLIUM ☐ There are many interesting species of allium. They are in the onion family as anyone knows who has ever grown them, for the foliage has a strong onion odor. Blossoms vary from small clusters like those of *A. cyaneum* with blue flowers and *A. moly* with yellow flowers to the huge globes of *A. christophi*. My husband finds the alliums most fascinating and has a small collection of them. Seeds, whether home-saved or purchased can be sown indoors in February or March with germination in 10 to 30 days. They may also be sown outdoors in covered coldframes in April. Seedlings are tiny, thin grass-like spears and are very fragile but like chives will soon become sturdy upon being transplanted to flats and eventually to the garden.

ALSTROEMERIA ☐ These bulbs with lily-like flowers are hardy as far north as Washington, D. C. Flowers are red, purple and yellow and bloom in spring in the South. Purchased seeds can be sown indoors with germination in 15 to 20 days in February or March. Grow as any perennial in flats until they can be placed to nursery rows in the garden to grow to maturity. Makes a tuberous root. Dr. Salter's hybrids come in shades of salmon, pink, flame and red.

AMARYLLIS ☐ These gorgeous flowers are hardy only in frost-free sections of the south. They are usually grown as house plants or greenhouse subjects in the North. Foliage is strap-like and the flowers are large and trumpet-shaped. Seeds of separate colors are available. A number of good hybrids are also available in mixed colors. Seeds can be sown indoors at temperatures between 60 and 75. The seeds are fairly large and should be lightly covered. Germination begins in 30 days. The mature plant, after flowering, should be kept in good growing condition for several months to nurture the bulb for future flowering. We plant ours to the garden for the summer and re-pot in fall with the top one-third of the bulb exposed after which it is returned to the greenhouse and watered and fed when active growth has started.

BEGONIA, TUBEROUS-ROOTED ☐ These begonias bloom in summer and are used for bedding out of doors. They form a rounded tuber. One year we grew three hundred of these beautiful, showy plants from seed obtained from the originator. They varied in forms from the picotee to the gardenia, carnation and peony flowered. Seeds were sown indoors, some under fluorescent lights and some in the greenhouse with germination beginning in 20 days. The seedlings were fed weekly with ¼ strength Rapid-Gro and when large enough to handle were transplanted to flats, spaced 1 inch apart. By June the roots showed no signs of producing tubers but they were planted to a semishaded bed where they received four hours of sun daily. By August the plants were large and lusty, the flowers gorgeous and full sized. After the first frost we lifted the plants. They had made tubers about the size of a marble.

BELAMCANDA CHINENSIS ☐ This plant makes an iris-like rhizome. It is very hardy in the North. The leaves are iris-like and the flowers lily-shaped on long stems. The petals are orange, spotted with red. It is the popular "blackberry lily." These are very easily grown from seed. We sow ours in a pan of seedling mix and give a pre-chilling period of four weeks in the coldframe in February or March before bringing indoors to germinate in 21 days. Ours bloomed the second season after sowing. They are grown as any perennial.

CALLA, see *Zantedeschia,* this chapter.

CANNA ☐ Old-fashioned flower with bold foliage making a large rhizome. They are hardy only in the deep South where they may be allowed to remain in the ground. In the North they must be lifted and stored like dahlia tubers. We have grown several of the dwarf varieties from seed with excellent success. Although some authorities suggest soaking or nicking the seed and state that it takes at least 30 days for germination, our seed germinated in our seedling mix in the greenhouse in 10 days with no pre-soaking period. Small plants flatted out were set to the garden in late May and they bloomed the first season.

CYCLAMEN ☐ This plant produces a small corm. Flowers are like pretty butterflies over heart-shaped spotted foliage. I have grown a number of the variety *C. indicum* from seed. Sown indoors, under lights or in the greenhouse in temperatures of 60 to 65 degrees it takes at least 6 weeks for a leaf to show as this plant first grows a bulb underground before it begins to send up shoots. Pot into flats or small pots, shifting to larger pots as the plant grows and fills pot with roots. Any good potting soil will do. This plant prefers a cool location with bright light but very little direct sun. Rests after blooming.

DAHLIA ☐ The dahlia is a familiar and popular garden flower. It produces a tuberous root. The tender roots must be lifted and stored over the winter in a frost-free place. Some dahlias produce huge flowers to 15 inches across. The extremely large varieties are not good for flower arranging although spectacular in the garden. Seeds of many varieties are available, and as they all bloom the first year after sowing, they can be exciting and most rewarding. Each year we grow a strain called Fall Festival to fill in vacant spots in our perennial border. This variety has dark, reddish foliage and flowers varying in shades of orange-red to scarlet to a deep maroon. Both foliage and flowers make excellent accents throughout the border. They grow 2½ to 3 feet tall and should be spaced 12 inches apart. I have also grown cactus-flowered, pompons and collarette with excellent results as well as such excellent bedding varieties as the Coltness and Unwin hybrids which grow to 15 inches and can be spaced as close as 10 inches for bedding purposes. The tubers can be lifted and stored in the fall if desired. Seed sown indoors in February or March germinates in 5 to 7 days and can be transplanted when large enough to handle to flats, plant bands or peat pots and planted to the garden after hardening off in mid-May in our location. I have also often sown seed to the open garden at the same time as zinnias and marigolds with germination in 7 to 12 days. These are always in bloom by mid-August.

GLADIOLUS ☐ This flower with spikes of many florets in gorgeous colors is well known as it is nearly always stocked by florists and corms of fine varieties are available in spring for the home garden. The garden varieties do not come true from seed but are fun and interesting to grow. Seeds of some of the hybrids are available. Pods of home-saved seed should be gathered when they begin to open and stored in a cool dry place. Sow indoors in greenhouse in early spring or in coldframe in late April or protected seedbed in May in our location. Seedlings are grass-like. Small cormels are produced the first season and stored cool over the winter and are planted to outdoor beds in late April or early May where they will bloom.

GLOXINIA, see houseplant chapter.

IRIS ☐ This is another familiar garden flower with spikes of entrancing flowers and fans of strap-like foliage. There are many amateur and professional hybridizers. It is my personal feeling that rhizomes of beautiful varieties of iris are available at very reasonable prices, and not many home gardeners are interested in growing these from seed. However, one of my favorite seedsmen offers seeds of spuria, Japanese and bearded hybrids. I must assume then that enterprising gardeners or those working on limited budgets are definitely interested in growing iris from seed. In the chapter on perennials I give instructions for growing the Japanese iris (Kaempferi) from seed. For other varieties instructions are essentially the same. They may be sown in late fall in coldframes or protected seedbeds, or they may be sown in pans of seedling mix and given a sojourn of 6 weeks or longer in covered frames in winter before bringing indoors to grow under lights or in the greenhouse for germination which usually begins in 21 to 30 days. Some growers say they do not disturb the seedbeds the first year if sown in open seedbeds or frames. Most familiar varieties of iris produce a rhizome and need a sweet soil with the exception of Kaempferi which makes a thick mat of fibrous roots and needs a very acid soil to thrive. Home-saved seeds should be harvested when the pod is dry and starting to open and then stored in a dry, cool place until sowing time.

LILIUM ☐ To be perfectly frank, I have never attempted to grow lilies from seed but after doing research on the subject and noticing that the George W. Park Seed Co., Inc., lists a large variety of lily seeds, the new season will undoubtedly find me experimenting. How did I ever miss sowing seed of this interesting group of plants? Seeds of some varieties of lilies germinate immediately, those of others form a bulb underground before sending up a leaf. In his catalog, Mr. Park has some varieties marked with an asterisk and explains that these seeds germinate slowly and may not show until the second spring. For these, I would sow the seeds, when received, in very early spring in a covered coldframe and see that the seedbed did not dry out until germination occurred. For all the others listed in the Park catalog I would sow under lights or in the greenhouse as for any perennial immediately upon receipt of the seed. If the home gardener should become especially interested in the various classes of lilies, which would take up too much time here and which would be beyond the

146 TRITOMA OR RED-HOT POKER SEED-
LING.   *Bodger Seeds, Ltd.*

abilities of this writer to explain, it would be wise to obtain a copy of a good book
on the growing of lilies.

RECHSTEINERIA, see houseplant chapter.

SMITHIANTHA, see houseplant chapter.

TRITOMA ☐ *Kniphofia.* Red Hot Poker. These have thick roots which are neither
rhizoamatous nor tuberous but in my mind they belong in this list. These are not
reliabily hardy north of Philadelphia, although they did live over in our first garden in
southern New York. There are available seeds of a number of hybrids. The foliage of
tritoma is strap-like and the flower is bright orange torch-like produced on a tall spike.
My seed was planted in a coldframe in early spring and the plants bloomed the second
season after sowing. In our present garden they are not hardy but the roots can be dug
and stored like that of dahlia.

ZANTEDESCHIA ☐ Calla-lily. This is a familiar flower and it grows out of doors
in sections of the country where winters are mild. In our location it must be treated as
a house plant. The only one I have grown from seed is a dwarf called 'Apricot Sunrise.'
Seeds are sown indoors, under lights or in the greenhouse and treated as a perennial
with germination in 30 to 35 days. Pot up when about 2 inches tall. Ours spent the
first summer in the open garden and by fall the bulbs were of good size and they
bloomed in the greenhouse the first winter. The upper third of the bulb should be
exposed above the soil level in the pot. We remove bulbs from the pots in mid-May
and plant them directly to the garden, leaving the top third of the bulb exposed as in
the pots. After a few weeks they usually drop the leaves and rest. In the fall they are
dug, repotted and brought indoors to grow and bloom again.

Bibliography

BERNICE BRILMAYER: *All About Miniature Plants for Gardens Indoors and Outdoors.*

L. H. BAILEY: *Hortus.*

MARGARET BROWNLOW: *Herbs and the Fragrant Garden.*

GERTRUDE FOSTER: *Herbs for Every Garden.*

ALFRED C. HOTTES: *The Book of Shrubs, The Book of Trees, The Book of Annuals, The Book of Perennials,* and *How To Increase Plants.*

HELEN HULL: *Wild Flowers for Your Garden.*

H. HAROLD HUME: *Gardening in the Lower South.*

ELVIN MCDONALD: *Miniature Plants for Home and Greenhouse, The Complete Book of Gardening Under Lights, The World Book of House Plants* and *The Flowering Greenhouse Day by Day.*

ARNO AND IRENE NEHRLING: *The Picture Book of Annuals, The Picture Book of Perennials,* and *The Propagation of House Plants.*

ROCKWELL AND GRAYSON: *The Complete Book of Annuals, The Complete Book of Bulbs, The Complete Book of Lilies,* and *The Complete Guide to Successful Gardening.*

EDWIN STEFFEK: *Wild Flowers and How To Grow Them.*

SUNSET BOOKS: *How To Grow and Use Annuals.*

TAYLOR: *Encyclopedia of Gardening.*

UNITED STATES DEPARTMENT OF AGRICULTURE: *Yearbook for 1961, "Seeds."*

KATHERINE BARNES WILLIAMS: *Herbs, the Spice of a Gardener's Life.*

Seedsmen

W. ATLEE BURPEE SEED CO., 370 Burpee Bldg., Philadelphia, Pa. 19132; Clinton, Iowa 52733; Riverside, California 92502.

BURGESS SEED & PLANT CO., Box 1140, Galesburg, Michigan 49053.

BURNETT BROTHERS, INC., 92 Chambers St., New York, New York 10007.

BRECK'S OF BOSTON, Breck Bldg., Boston, Mass. 02210.

HENRY FIELD SEED & NURSERY CO., 19 N. 12th St., Shenandoah, Iowa 51601.

HENRY SAIER, Dimondale, Michigan.

FARMER SEED & NURSERY CO., Faribault, Minnesota.

GURNEY SEED & NURSERY CO., 1448 Page St., Yankton, S. Dakota 57078.

JOSEPH HARRIS CO., INC., 32 Moreton Farm, Rochester, New York 14624.

J. W. JUNG SEED CO., Sta. 8, Randolph, Wisconsin.

EARL MAY SEED & NURSERY CO., 6032 Elm Street, Shenandoah, Iowa 51601.

W. W. OLDS SEED CO., Box 1069, Madison, Wisconsin 53701.

GEORGE W. PARK SEED CO., INC., Greenwood, South Carolina 29547.

PEARCE SEED CO., Moorestown, New Jersey 08057.

R. H. SHUMWAY, Rockford, Illinois 61101.

STOKE'S SEEDS, INC., 86 Exchange St., Buffalo, New York 14205.

African Violets, Gesneriads, Gloxinias

    ALBERT BUELL, Eastford, Connecticut.

    FOREST MILL AFRICAN VIOLET SEED, 4125 E. 35th St., Indianapolis, Indiana.

    GEORGE W. PARK SEED CO., INC., Greenwood, South Carolina 29547.

    MICHAEL KARTUZ, 95 Chestnut St., Wilmington, Massachusetts.

    W. ATLEE BURPEE CO., Philadelphia, Pennsylvania.

Azalea and Rhododendron

    KNAPHILL NURSERY LTD., Lower Knaphill, Woking, Surrey, England.

Cacti, Other Succulents and Exotics

    CACTIFLOR, Box 787, Belen, New Mexico.

    HUMMEL'S EXOTIC GARDENS, 3926 Park Drive, Carlsbad, California.

    JOHNSON CACTUS GARDENS, Paramount, California.

    GEORGE W. PARK SEED CO., INC., Greenwood, South Carolina 29547.

    W. ATLEE BURPEE CO., Philadelphia, Pennsylvania.

    THOMPSON AND MORGAN, LTD., Ipswich, England.

Evergreen Seeds

    GIRARD NURSERY, Geneva, Ohio.

Wildflower Seeds

    ALASKA TRAILS, Star Route, Wasilla, Alaska 99687.

    CLYDE ROBIN, Castro Valley, California 94546.

    LESLIE'S WILD FLOWER NURSERY, 30 Summer St., Methuen, Massachusetts 01844.

Agricultural Colleges

Agricultural Experiment Stations

(From U.S.D.A. Agriculture Handbook No. 116. Workers in Subjects Pertaining to Agriculture in Land-Grant Colleges and Experiment Stations, May 1962.)

State	*Name*	*City*
ALABAMA	School of Agriculture, Auburn University	Auburn
	Agricultural Experiment Station	Auburn
	Alabama Agricultural and Mechanical College	Normal
ALASKA	Department of Agriculture, University of Alaska	College
	Agricultural Experiment Station	Palmer
ARIZONA	College of Agriculture, University of Arizona	Tucson
	Agricultural Experiment Station	Tucson
ARKANSAS	College of Agriculture, University of Arkansas	Fayetteville
	Agricultural Experiment Station	Fayetteville
CALIFORNIA	College of Agriculture, University of California	Berkeley
	Agricultural Experiment Station	Berkeley
	Agricultural Experiment Station	Davis
	Agricultural Experiment Station	Los Angeles
	Agricultural Experiment Station	Riverside
COLORADO	College of Agriculture, Colorado State University	Fort Collins
	Agricultural Experiment Station	Fort Collins
CONNECTICUT	College of Agriculture, University of Connecticut	Storrs
	Storrs Agricultural Experiment Station	Storrs
	The Connecticut Agricultural Experiment Station	New Haven
DELAWARE	School of Agriculture, University of Delaware	Newark
	Agricultural Experiment Station	Newark
	Delaware State College	Dover
FLORIDA	College of Agriculture, University of Florida	Gainesville
	Agricultural Experiment Station	Gainesville
	School of Agriculture, Florida Agricultural and Mechanical University	Tallahassee
GEORGIA	College of Agriculture, University of Georgia	Athens
	Georgia Coastal Plain Experiment Station	Tifton
	Georgia Agricultural Experiment Station	Griffon
	The Fort Valley State College	Fort Valley
HAWAII	College of Tropical Agriculture, University of Hawaii	Honolulu
	Agricultural Experiment Station	Honolulu

IDAHO	College of Agriculture, University of Idaho	Moscow
	Agricultural Experiment Station	Moscow
ILLINOIS	College of Agriculture, University of Illinois	Urbana
	Agricultural Experiment Station	Urbana
INDIANA	School of Agriculture, Purdue University	Lafayette
	Agricultural Experiment Station	Lafayette
IOWA	College of Agriculture, Iowa State University of Science and Technology	Ames
	Agricultural Experiment Station	Ames
KANSAS	Kansas State University of Agriculture and Applied Science	Manhattan
	Agricultural Experiment Station	Manhattan
KENTUCKY	College of Agriculture, University of Kentucky	Lexington
	Agricultural Experiment Station	Lexington
	Kentucky State College	Frankfort
LOUISIANA	Louisiana State University and Agricultural and Mechanical College, University Station	Baton Rouge
	Agricultural Experiment Station, University Station	Baton Rouge
	Southern University and Agricultural and Mechanical College Southern Branch Post Office	Baton Rouge
MAINE	College of Agriculture, University of Maine	Orono
	Agricultural Experiment Station University of Maine	Orono
MARYLAND	College of Agriculture, University of Maryland	College Park
	Agricultural Experiment Station	College Park
	Maryland State College, University of Maryland	Princess Anne
MASSACHUSETTS	College of Agriculture, University of Massachusetts	Amherst
	Agricultural Experiment Station	Amherst
MICHIGAN	Michigan State University of Agriculture and Applied Science	East Lansing
	Agricultural Experiment Station	East Lansing
MINNESOTA	Institute of Agriculture, University of Minnesota, St. Paul Campus	St. Paul
	Agricultural Experiment Station St. Paul Campus	St. Paul
MISSISSIPPI	School of Agriculture and Forestry, Mississippi State University of Applied Arts and Sciences	State College
	Agricultural Experiment Station	State College
	School of Agriculture, Alcorn Agricultural and Mechanical College	Lorman

MISSOURI	College of Agriculture, University of Missouri	Columbia
	Agricultural Experiment Station	Columbia
	Lincoln University	Jefferson City
MONTANA	Montana State College	Bozeman
	Agricultural Experiment Station	Bozeman
NEBRASKA	College of Agriculture, University of Nebraska	Lincoln
	Agricultural Experiment Station	Lincoln
NEVADA	Max C. Fleischmann College of Agriculture, University of Nevada	Reno
	Agricultural Experiment Station	Reno
NEW HAMPSHIRE	College of Agriculture, University of New Hampshire	Durham
	Agricultural Experiment Station	Durham
NEW JERSEY	State College of Agriculture and Mechanic Arts, State University	New Brunswick
	Agricultural Experiment Station of Rutgers	New Brunswick
NEW MEXICO	College of Agriculture, New Mexico State University	University Park
	Agricultural Experiment Station	University Park
NEW YORK	New York State College of Agriculture, Cornell University	Ithaca
	Agricultural Experiment Station	Ithaca
	New York State Agricultural Experiment Station	Geneva
NORTH CAROLINA	North Carolina State College of Agriculture and Engineering, University of North Carolina	Raleigh
	Agricultural Experiment Station	Raleigh
	The Agricultural and Technical College of North Carolina	Greensboro
NORTH DAKOTA	College of Agriculture, North Dakota State University of Agriculture and Applied Science	Fargo
	State University Station	
	Agricultural Experiment Station	Fargo
OHIO	College of Agriculture, Ohio State University	Columbus
	Ohio Agricultural Experiment Station	Wooster
OKLAHOMA	Oklahoma State University of Agriculture and Applied Science	Stillwater
	Agricultural Experiment Station	Stillwater
	Langston University	Langston
OREGON	School of Agriculture, Oregon State University	Corvallis
	Agricultural Experiment Station	Corvallis
PENNSYLVANIA	College of Agriculture, Pennsylvania State University	University Park
	Agricultural Experiment Station	University Park

PUERTO RICO	College of Agriculture, University of Puerto Rico	Rio Piedras
	Agricultural Experiment Station	Rio Piedras
RHODE ISLAND	College of Agriculture, University of Rhode Island	Kingston
	Agricultural Experiment Station	Kingston
SOUTH CAROLINA	Clemson Agricultural College of South Carolina, School of Agriculture	Clemson
	Agricultural Experiment Station	Clemson
	South Carolina State College	Orangeburg
SOUTH DAKOTA	South Dakota State College of Agriculture and Mechanic Arts	College Station
	Agricultural Experiment Station	College Station
TENNESSEE	College of Agriculture, University of Tennessee	Knoxville
	Agricultural Experiment Station	Knoxville
	Martin Branch, University of Tennessee	Martin
	Tennessee Agricultural and Industrial State University	Nashville
TEXAS	Agricultural and Mechanical College of Texas	College Station
	Prairie View A. and M. College	Prairie View
	Agricultural Experiment Station	College Station
UTAH	Utah State University of Agriculture and Applied Science	Logan
	Agricultural Experiment Station	Logan
VERMONT	College of Agriculture, University of Vermont	Burlington
	Agricultural Experiment Station	Burlington
VIRGINIA	School of Agriculture, Virginia Polytechnic Institute	Blacksburg
	Agricultural Experiment Station	Blacksburg
	Virginia Truck Experiment Station	Norfolk
WASHINGTON	College of Agriculture, Washington State University, Institute of Agricultural Sciences	Pullman
	Agricultural Experiment Station	Pullman
WEST VIRGINIA	College of Agriculture, West Virginia University	Morgantown
	Agricultural Experiment Station	Morgantown
WISCONSIN	College of Agriculture, University of Wyoming	Madison
	Agricultural Experiment Station	Madison
WYOMING	College of Agriculture, University of Wyoming	Laramie
	Agricultural Experiment Station	Laramie

Index

(A number in *italics* indicates a page on which an illustration appears.)

80 FLOWER SEEDLINGS
for quick recognition

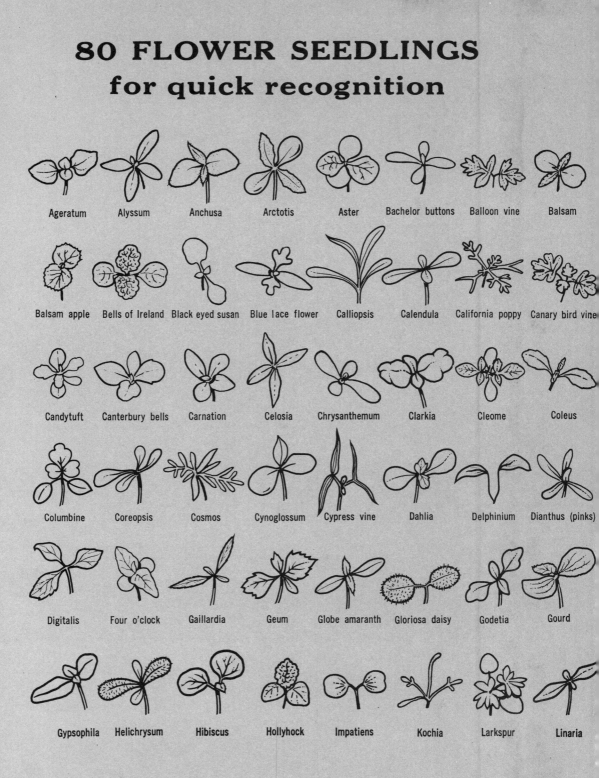

Ageratum	Alyssum	Anchusa	Arctotis	Aster	Bachelor buttons	Balloon vine	Balsam
Balsam apple	Bells of Ireland	Black eyed susan	Blue lace flower	Calliopsis	Calendula	California poppy	Canary bird vine
Candytuft	Canterbury bells	Carnation	Celosia	Chrysanthemum	Clarkia	Cleome	Coleus
Columbine	Coreopsis	Cosmos	Cynoglossum	Cypress vine	Dahlia	Delphinium	Dianthus (pinks)
Digitalis	Four o'clock	Gaillardia	Geum	Globe amaranth	Gloriosa daisy	Godetia	Gourd
Gypsophila	Helichrysum	Hibiscus	Hollyhock	Impatiens	Kochia	Larkspur	Linaria

Northrup, King & Co.